C-1130   CAREER EXAMINATION SERIES

This is your
PASSBOOK for...

Auto Shop Supervisor

Test Preparation Study Guide
Questions & Answers

COPYRIGHT NOTICE

This book is SOLELY intended for, is sold ONLY to, and its use is RESTRICTED to individual, bona fide applicants or candidates who qualify by virtue of having seriously filed applications for appropriate license, certificate, professional and/or promotional advancement, higher school matriculation, scholarship, or other legitimate requirements of education and/or governmental authorities.

This book is NOT intended for use, class instruction, tutoring, training, duplication, copying, reprinting, excerption, or adaptation, etc., by:

1) Other publishers
2) Proprietors and/or Instructors of "Coaching" and/or Preparatory Courses
3) Personnel and/or Training Divisions of commercial, industrial, and governmental organizations
4) Schools, colleges, or universities and/or their departments and staffs, including teachers and other personnel
5) Testing Agencies or Bureaus
6) Study groups which seek by the purchase of a single volume to copy and/or duplicate and/or adapt this material for use by the group as a whole without having purchased individual volumes for each of the members of the group
7) Et al.

Such persons would be in violation of appropriate Federal and State statutes.

PROVISION OF LICENSING AGREEMENTS – Recognized educational, commercial, industrial, and governmental institutions and organizations, and others legitimately engaged in educational pursuits, including training, testing, and measurement activities, may address request for a licensing agreement to the copyright owners, who will determine whether, and under what conditions, including fees and charges, the materials in this book may be used them. In other words, a licensing facility exists for the legitimate use of the material in this book on other than an individual basis. However, it is asseverated and affirmed here that the material in this book CANNOT be used without the receipt of the express permission of such a licensing agreement from the Publishers. Inquiries re licensing should be addressed to the company, attention rights and permissions department.

All rights reserved, including the right of reproduction in whole or in part, in any form or by any means, electronic or mechanical, including photocopying, recording, or by any information storage and retrieval system, without permission in writing from the Publisher.

Copyright © 2025 by
National Learning Corporation

212 Michael Drive, Syosset, NY 11791
(516) 921-8888 • www.passbooks.com
E-mail: info@passbooks.com

PASSBOOK® SERIES

THE *PASSBOOK® SERIES* has been created to prepare applicants and candidates for the ultimate academic battlefield – the examination room.

At some time in our lives, each and every one of us may be required to take an examination – for validation, matriculation, admission, qualification, registration, certification, or licensure.

Based on the assumption that every applicant or candidate has met the basic formal educational standards, has taken the required number of courses, and read the necessary texts, the *PASSBOOK® SERIES* furnishes the one special preparation which may assure passing with confidence, instead of failing with insecurity. Examination questions – together with answers – are furnished as the basic vehicle for study so that the mysteries of the examination and its compounding difficulties may be eliminated or diminished by a sure method.

This book is meant to help you pass your examination provided that you qualify and are serious in your objective.

The entire field is reviewed through the huge store of content information which is succinctly presented through a provocative and challenging approach – the question-and-answer method.

A climate of success is established by furnishing the correct answers at the end of each test.

You soon learn to recognize types of questions, forms of questions, and patterns of questioning. You may even begin to anticipate expected outcomes.

You perceive that many questions are repeated or adapted so that you can gain acute insights, which may enable you to score many sure points.

You learn how to confront new questions, or types of questions, and to attack them confidently and work out the correct answers.

You note objectives and emphases, and recognize pitfalls and dangers, so that you may make positive educational adjustments.

Moreover, you are kept fully informed in relation to new concepts, methods, practices, and directions in the field.

You discover that you are actually taking the examination all the time: you are preparing for the examination by "taking" an examination, not by reading extraneous and/or supererogatory textbooks.

In short, this PASSBOOK®, used directedly, should be an important factor in helping you to pass your test.

AUTO SHOP SUPERVISOR

DUTIES:
Supervises skilled and semi-skilled workers in the maintenance and repair of automotive equipment; performs related duties as required.

SUBJECT OF EXAMINATION:
A written test designed to evaluate knowledge, skills and/or abilities in the following areas:
1. Maintenance and repair of motor vehicles;
2. Operation, maintenance, and repair of automotive, truck, and heavy highway maintenance equipment;
3. Tools and test equipment used in the maintenance of automotive equipment;
4. Maintenance and repair of mechanically and electronically controlled internal combustion engines;
5. Scheduling work and equipment; and
6. Supervision.

HOW TO TAKE A TEST

I. YOU MUST PASS AN EXAMINATION

A. WHAT EVERY CANDIDATE SHOULD KNOW

Examination applicants often ask us for help in preparing for the written test. What can I study in advance? What kinds of questions will be asked? How will the test be given? How will the papers be graded?

As an applicant for a civil service examination, you may be wondering about some of these things. Our purpose here is to suggest effective methods of advance study and to describe civil service examinations.

Your chances for success on this examination can be increased if you know how to prepare. Those "pre-examination jitters" can be reduced if you know what to expect. You can even experience an adventure in good citizenship if you know why civil service exams are given.

B. WHY ARE CIVIL SERVICE EXAMINATIONS GIVEN?

Civil service examinations are important to you in two ways. As a citizen, you want public jobs filled by employees who know how to do their work. As a job seeker, you want a fair chance to compete for that job on an equal footing with other candidates. The best-known means of accomplishing this two-fold goal is the competitive examination.

Exams are widely publicized throughout the nation. They may be administered for jobs in federal, state, city, municipal, town or village governments or agencies.

Any citizen may apply, with some limitations, such as the age or residence of applicants. Your experience and education may be reviewed to see whether you meet the requirements for the particular examination. When these requirements exist, they are reasonable and applied consistently to all applicants. Thus, a competitive examination may cause you some uneasiness now, but it is your privilege and safeguard.

C. HOW ARE CIVIL SERVICE EXAMS DEVELOPED?

Examinations are carefully written by trained technicians who are specialists in the field known as "psychological measurement," in consultation with recognized authorities in the field of work that the test will cover. These experts recommend the subject matter areas or skills to be tested; only those knowledges or skills important to your success on the job are included. The most reliable books and source materials available are used as references. Together, the experts and technicians judge the difficulty level of the questions.

Test technicians know how to phrase questions so that the problem is clearly stated. Their ethics do not permit "trick" or "catch" questions. Questions may have been tried out on sample groups, or subjected to statistical analysis, to determine their usefulness.

Written tests are often used in combination with performance tests, ratings of training and experience, and oral interviews. All of these measures combine to form the best-known means of finding the right person for the right job.

II. HOW TO PASS THE WRITTEN TEST

A. NATURE OF THE EXAMINATION

To prepare intelligently for civil service examinations, you should know how they differ from school examinations you have taken. In school you were assigned certain definite pages to read or subjects to cover. The examination questions were quite detailed and usually emphasized memory. Civil service exams, on the other hand, try to discover your present ability to perform the duties of a position, plus your potentiality to learn these duties. In other words, a civil service exam attempts to predict how successful you will be. Questions cover such a broad area that they cannot be as minute and detailed as school exam questions.

In the public service similar kinds of work, or positions, are grouped together in one "class." This process is known as *position-classification*. All the positions in a class are paid according to the salary range for that class. One class title covers all of these positions, and they are all tested by the same examination.

B. FOUR BASIC STEPS

1) Study the announcement

How, then, can you know what subjects to study? Our best answer is: "Learn as much as possible about the class of positions for which you've applied." The exam will test the knowledge, skills and abilities needed to do the work.

Your most valuable source of information about the position you want is the official exam announcement. This announcement lists the training and experience qualifications. Check these standards and apply only if you come reasonably close to meeting them.

The brief description of the position in the examination announcement offers some clues to the subjects which will be tested. Think about the job itself. Review the duties in your mind. Can you perform them, or are there some in which you are rusty? Fill in the blank spots in your preparation.

Many jurisdictions preview the written test in the exam announcement by including a section called "Knowledge and Abilities Required," "Scope of the Examination," or some similar heading. Here you will find out specifically what fields will be tested.

2) Review your own background

Once you learn in general what the position is all about, and what you need to know to do the work, ask yourself which subjects you already know fairly well and which need improvement. You may wonder whether to concentrate on improving your strong areas or on building some background in your fields of weakness. When the announcement has specified "some knowledge" or "considerable knowledge," or has used adjectives like "beginning principles of..." or "advanced ... methods," you can get a clue as to the number and difficulty of questions to be asked in any given field. More questions, and hence broader coverage, would be included for those subjects which are more important in the work. Now weigh your strengths and weaknesses against the job requirements and prepare accordingly.

3) Determine the level of the position

Another way to tell how intensively you should prepare is to understand the level of the job for which you are applying. Is it the entering level? In other words, is this the position in which beginners in a field of work are hired? Or is it an intermediate or advanced level? Sometimes this is indicated by such words as "Junior" or "Senior" in the class title. Other jurisdictions use Roman numerals to designate the level – Clerk I, Clerk II, for example. The word "Supervisor" sometimes appears in the title. If the level is not indicated by the title, check the description of duties. Will you be working under very close supervision, or will you have responsibility for independent decisions in this work?

4) Choose appropriate study materials

Now that you know the subjects to be examined and the relative amount of each subject to be covered, you can choose suitable study materials. For beginning level jobs, or even advanced ones, if you have a pronounced weakness in some aspect of your training, read a modern, standard textbook in that field. Be sure it is up to date and has general coverage. Such books are normally available at your library, and the librarian will be glad to help you locate one. For entry-level positions, questions of appropriate difficulty are chosen – neither highly advanced questions, nor those too simple. Such questions require careful thought but not advanced training.

If the position for which you are applying is technical or advanced, you will read more advanced, specialized material. If you are already familiar with the basic principles of your field, elementary textbooks would waste your time. Concentrate on advanced textbooks and technical periodicals. Think through the concepts and review difficult problems in your field.

These are all general sources. You can get more ideas on your own initiative, following these leads. For example, training manuals and publications of the government agency which employs workers in your field can be useful, particularly for technical and professional positions. A letter or visit to the government department involved may result in more specific study suggestions, and certainly will provide you with a more definite idea of the exact nature of the position you are seeking.

III. KINDS OF TESTS

Tests are used for purposes other than measuring knowledge and ability to perform specified duties. For some positions, it is equally important to test ability to make adjustments to new situations or to profit from training. In others, basic mental abilities not dependent on information are essential. Questions which test these things may not appear as pertinent to the duties of the position as those which test for knowledge and information. Yet they are often highly important parts of a fair examination. For very general questions, it is almost impossible to help you direct your study efforts. What we can do is to point out some of the more common of these general abilities needed in public service positions and describe some typical questions.

1) General information

Broad, general information has been found useful for predicting job success in some kinds of work. This is tested in a variety of ways, from vocabulary lists to questions about current events. Basic background in some field of work, such as sociology or economics, may be sampled in a group of questions. Often these are principles which have become familiar to most persons through exposure rather than through formal training. It is difficult to advise you how to study for these questions; being alert to the world around you is our best suggestion.

2) Verbal ability

An example of an ability needed in many positions is verbal or language ability. Verbal ability is, in brief, the ability to use and understand words. Vocabulary and grammar tests are typical measures of this ability. Reading comprehension or paragraph interpretation questions are common in many kinds of civil service tests. You are given a paragraph of written material and asked to find its central meaning.

3) Numerical ability

Number skills can be tested by the familiar arithmetic problem, by checking paired lists of numbers to see which are alike and which are different, or by interpreting charts and graphs. In the latter test, a graph may be printed in the test booklet which you are asked to use as the basis for answering questions.

4) Observation

A popular test for law-enforcement positions is the observation test. A picture is shown to you for several minutes, then taken away. Questions about the picture test your ability to observe both details and larger elements.

5) Following directions

In many positions in the public service, the employee must be able to carry out written instructions dependably and accurately. You may be given a chart with several columns, each column listing a variety of information. The questions require you to carry out directions involving the information given in the chart.

6) Skills and aptitudes

Performance tests effectively measure some manual skills and aptitudes. When the skill is one in which you are trained, such as typing or shorthand, you can practice. These tests are often very much like those given in business school or high school courses. For many of the other skills and aptitudes, however, no short-time preparation can be made. Skills and abilities natural to you or that you have developed throughout your lifetime are being tested.

Many of the general questions just described provide all the data needed to answer the questions and ask you to use your reasoning ability to find the answers. Your best preparation for these tests, as well as for tests of facts and ideas, is to be at your physical and mental best. You, no doubt, have your own methods of getting into an exam-taking mood and keeping "in shape." The next section lists some ideas on this subject.

IV. KINDS OF QUESTIONS

Only rarely is the "essay" question, which you answer in narrative form, used in civil service tests. Civil service tests are usually of the short-answer type. Full instructions for answering these questions will be given to you at the examination. But in case this is your first experience with short-answer questions and separate answer sheets, here is what you need to know:

1) Multiple-choice Questions

Most popular of the short-answer questions is the "multiple choice" or "best answer" question. It can be used, for example, to test for factual knowledge, ability to solve problems or judgment in meeting situations found at work.

A multiple-choice question is normally one of three types—
- It can begin with an incomplete statement followed by several possible endings. You are to find the one ending which *best* completes the statement, although some of the others may not be entirely wrong.
- It can also be a complete statement in the form of a question which is answered by choosing one of the statements listed.

- It can be in the form of a problem – again you select the best answer.

Here is an example of a multiple-choice question with a discussion which should give you some clues as to the method for choosing the right answer:

When an employee has a complaint about his assignment, the action which will *best* help him overcome his difficulty is to
- A. discuss his difficulty with his coworkers
- B. take the problem to the head of the organization
- C. take the problem to the person who gave him the assignment
- D. say nothing to anyone about his complaint

In answering this question, you should study each of the choices to find which is best. Consider choice "A" – Certainly an employee may discuss his complaint with fellow employees, but no change or improvement can result, and the complaint remains unresolved. Choice "B" is a poor choice since the head of the organization probably does not know what assignment you have been given, and taking your problem to him is known as "going over the head" of the supervisor. The supervisor, or person who made the assignment, is the person who can clarify it or correct any injustice. Choice "C" is, therefore, correct. To say nothing, as in choice "D," is unwise. Supervisors have and interest in knowing the problems employees are facing, and the employee is seeking a solution to his problem.

2) True/False Questions

The "true/false" or "right/wrong" form of question is sometimes used. Here a complete statement is given. Your job is to decide whether the statement is right or wrong.

SAMPLE: A roaming cell-phone call to a nearby city costs less than a non-roaming call to a distant city.

This statement is wrong, or false, since roaming calls are more expensive.

This is not a complete list of all possible question forms, although most of the others are variations of these common types. You will always get complete directions for answering questions. Be sure you understand *how* to mark your answers – ask questions until you do.

V. RECORDING YOUR ANSWERS

Computer terminals are used more and more today for many different kinds of exams.
For an examination with very few applicants, you may be told to record your answers in the test booklet itself. Separate answer sheets are much more common. If this separate answer sheet is to be scored by machine – and this is often the case – it is highly important that you mark your answers correctly in order to get credit.

An electronic scoring machine is often used in civil service offices because of the speed with which papers can be scored. Machine-scored answer sheets must be marked with a pencil, which will be given to you. This pencil has a high graphite content which responds to the electronic scoring machine. As a matter of fact, stray dots may register as answers, so do not let your pencil rest on the answer sheet while you are pondering the correct answer. Also, if your pencil lead breaks or is otherwise defective, ask for another.

Since the answer sheet will be dropped in a slot in the scoring machine, be careful not to bend the corners or get the paper crumpled.

The answer sheet normally has five vertical columns of numbers, with 30 numbers to a column. These numbers correspond to the question numbers in your test booklet. After each number, going across the page are four or five pairs of dotted lines. These short dotted lines have small letters or numbers above them. The first two pairs may also have a "T" or "F" above the letters. This indicates that the first two pairs only are to be used if the questions are of the true-false type. If the questions are multiple choice, disregard the "T" and "F" and pay attention only to the small letters or numbers.

Answer your questions in the manner of the sample that follows:

32. The largest city in the United States is
    A. Washington, D.C.
    B. New York City
    C. Chicago
    D. Detroit
    E. San Francisco

1) Choose the answer you think is best. (New York City is the largest, so "B" is correct.)
2) Find the row of dotted lines numbered the same as the question you are answering. (Find row number 32)
3) Find the pair of dotted lines corresponding to the answer. (Find the pair of lines under the mark "B.")
4) Make a solid black mark between the dotted lines.

VI. BEFORE THE TEST

Common sense will help you find procedures to follow to get ready for an examination. Too many of us, however, overlook these sensible measures. Indeed, nervousness and fatigue have been found to be the most serious reasons why applicants fail to do their best on civil service tests. Here is a list of reminders:

- Begin your preparation early – Don't wait until the last minute to go scurrying around for books and materials or to find out what the position is all about.
- Prepare continuously – An hour a night for a week is better than an all-night cram session. This has been definitely established. What is more, a night a week for a month will return better dividends than crowding your study into a shorter period of time.
- Locate the place of the exam – You have been sent a notice telling you when and where to report for the examination. If the location is in a different town or otherwise unfamiliar to you, it would be well to inquire the best route and learn something about the building.
- Relax the night before the test – Allow your mind to rest. Do not study at all that night. Plan some mild recreation or diversion; then go to bed early and get a good night's sleep.
- Get up early enough to make a leisurely trip to the place for the test – This way unforeseen events, traffic snarls, unfamiliar buildings, etc. will not upset you.
- Dress comfortably – A written test is not a fashion show. You will be known by number and not by name, so wear something comfortable.

- Leave excess paraphernalia at home – Shopping bags and odd bundles will get in your way. You need bring only the items mentioned in the official notice you received; usually everything you need is provided. Do not bring reference books to the exam. They will only confuse those last minutes and be taken away from you when in the test room.
- Arrive somewhat ahead of time – If because of transportation schedules you must get there very early, bring a newspaper or magazine to take your mind off yourself while waiting.
- Locate the examination room – When you have found the proper room, you will be directed to the seat or part of the room where you will sit. Sometimes you are given a sheet of instructions to read while you are waiting. Do not fill out any forms until you are told to do so; just read them and be prepared.
- Relax and prepare to listen to the instructions
- If you have any physical problem that may keep you from doing your best, be sure to tell the test administrator. If you are sick or in poor health, you really cannot do your best on the exam. You can come back and take the test some other time.

VII. AT THE TEST

The day of the test is here and you have the test booklet in your hand. The temptation to get going is very strong. Caution! There is more to success than knowing the right answers. You must know how to identify your papers and understand variations in the type of short-answer question used in this particular examination. Follow these suggestions for maximum results from your efforts:

1) Cooperate with the monitor
The test administrator has a duty to create a situation in which you can be as much at ease as possible. He will give instructions, tell you when to begin, check to see that you are marking your answer sheet correctly, and so on. He is not there to guard you, although he will see that your competitors do not take unfair advantage. He wants to help you do your best.

2) Listen to all instructions
Don't jump the gun! Wait until you understand all directions. In most civil service tests you get more time than you need to answer the questions. So don't be in a hurry. Read each word of instructions until you clearly understand the meaning. Study the examples, listen to all announcements and follow directions. Ask questions if you do not understand what to do.

3) Identify your papers
Civil service exams are usually identified by number only. You will be assigned a number; you must not put your name on your test papers. Be sure to copy your number correctly. Since more than one exam may be given, copy your exact examination title.

4) Plan your time
Unless you are told that a test is a "speed" or "rate of work" test, speed itself is usually not important. Time enough to answer all the questions will be provided, but this does not mean that you have all day. An overall time limit has been set. Divide the total time (in minutes) by the number of questions to determine the approximate time you have for each question.

5) Do not linger over difficult questions

If you come across a difficult question, mark it with a paper clip (useful to have along) and come back to it when you have been through the booklet. One caution if you do this – be sure to skip a number on your answer sheet as well. Check often to be sure that you have not lost your place and that you are marking in the row numbered the same as the question you are answering.

6) Read the questions

Be sure you know what the question asks! Many capable people are unsuccessful because they failed to *read* the questions correctly.

7) Answer all questions

Unless you have been instructed that a penalty will be deducted for incorrect answers, it is better to guess than to omit a question.

8) Speed tests

It is often better NOT to guess on speed tests. It has been found that on timed tests people are tempted to spend the last few seconds before time is called in marking answers at random – without even reading them – in the hope of picking up a few extra points. To discourage this practice, the instructions may warn you that your score will be "corrected" for guessing. That is, a penalty will be applied. The incorrect answers will be deducted from the correct ones, or some other penalty formula will be used.

9) Review your answers

If you finish before time is called, go back to the questions you guessed or omitted to give them further thought. Review other answers if you have time.

10) Return your test materials

If you are ready to leave before others have finished or time is called, take ALL your materials to the monitor and leave quietly. Never take any test material with you. The monitor can discover whose papers are not complete, and taking a test booklet may be grounds for disqualification.

VIII. EXAMINATION TECHNIQUES

1) Read the general instructions carefully. These are usually printed on the first page of the exam booklet. As a rule, these instructions refer to the timing of the examination; the fact that you should not start work until the signal and must stop work at a signal, etc. If there are any *special* instructions, such as a choice of questions to be answered, make sure that you note this instruction carefully.

2) When you are ready to start work on the examination, that is as soon as the signal has been given, read the instructions to each question booklet, underline any key words or phrases, such as *least, best, outline, describe* and the like. In this way you will tend to answer as requested rather than discover on reviewing your paper that you *listed without describing*, that you selected the *worst* choice rather than the *best* choice, etc.

3) If the examination is of the objective or multiple-choice type – that is, each question will also give a series of possible answers: A, B, C or D, and you are called upon to select the best answer and write the letter next to that answer on your answer paper – it is advisable to start answering each question in turn. There may be anywhere from 50 to 100 such questions in the three or four hours allotted and you can see how much time would be taken if you read through all the questions before beginning to answer any. Furthermore, if you come across a question or group of questions which you know would be difficult to answer, it would undoubtedly affect your handling of all the other questions.

4) If the examination is of the essay type and contains but a few questions, it is a moot point as to whether you should read all the questions before starting to answer any one. Of course, if you are given a choice – say five out of seven and the like – then it is essential to read all the questions so you can eliminate the two that are most difficult. If, however, you are asked to answer all the questions, there may be danger in trying to answer the easiest one first because you may find that you will spend too much time on it. The best technique is to answer the first question, then proceed to the second, etc.

5) Time your answers. Before the exam begins, write down the time it started, then add the time allowed for the examination and write down the time it must be completed, then divide the time available somewhat as follows:
    - If 3-1/2 hours are allowed, that would be 210 minutes. If you have 80 objective-type questions, that would be an average of 2-1/2 minutes per question. Allow yourself no more than 2 minutes per question, or a total of 160 minutes, which will permit about 50 minutes to review.
    - If for the time allotment of 210 minutes there are 7 essay questions to answer, that would average about 30 minutes a question. Give yourself only 25 minutes per question so that you have about 35 minutes to review.

6) The most important instruction is to *read each question* and make sure you know what is wanted. The second most important instruction is to *time yourself properly* so that you answer every question. The third most important instruction is to *answer every question*. Guess if you have to but include something for each question. Remember that you will receive no credit for a blank and will probably receive some credit if you write something in answer to an essay question. If you guess a letter – say "B" for a multiple-choice question – you may have guessed right. If you leave a blank as an answer to a multiple-choice question, the examiners may respect your feelings but it will not add a point to your score. Some exams may penalize you for wrong answers, so in such cases *only*, you may not want to guess unless you have some basis for your answer.

7) Suggestions
    a. Objective-type questions
        1. Examine the question booklet for proper sequence of pages and questions
        2. Read all instructions carefully
        3. Skip any question which seems too difficult; return to it after all other questions have been answered
        4. Apportion your time properly; do not spend too much time on any single question or group of questions

5. Note and underline key words – *all, most, fewest, least, best, worst, same, opposite*, etc.
6. Pay particular attention to negatives
7. Note unusual option, e.g., unduly long, short, complex, different or similar in content to the body of the question
8. Observe the use of "hedging" words – *probably, may, most likely*, etc.
9. Make sure that your answer is put next to the same number as the question
10. Do not second-guess unless you have good reason to believe the second answer is definitely more correct
11. Cross out original answer if you decide another answer is more accurate; do not erase until you are ready to hand your paper in
12. Answer all questions; guess unless instructed otherwise
13. Leave time for review

  b. Essay questions
1. Read each question carefully
2. Determine exactly what is wanted. Underline key words or phrases.
3. Decide on outline or paragraph answer
4. Include many different points and elements unless asked to develop any one or two points or elements
5. Show impartiality by giving pros and cons unless directed to select one side only
6. Make and write down any assumptions you find necessary to answer the questions
7. Watch your English, grammar, punctuation and choice of words
8. Time your answers; don't crowd material

8) Answering the essay question

Most essay questions can be answered by framing the specific response around several key words or ideas. Here are a few such key words or ideas:

M's: manpower, materials, methods, money, management
P's: purpose, program, policy, plan, procedure, practice, problems, pitfalls, personnel, public relations

  a. Six basic steps in handling problems:
1. Preliminary plan and background development
2. Collect information, data and facts
3. Analyze and interpret information, data and facts
4. Analyze and develop solutions as well as make recommendations
5. Prepare report and sell recommendations
6. Install recommendations and follow up effectiveness

  b. Pitfalls to avoid
1. *Taking things for granted* – A statement of the situation does not necessarily imply that each of the elements is necessarily true; for example, a complaint may be invalid and biased so that all that can be taken for granted is that a complaint has been registered

2. *Considering only one side of a situation* – Wherever possible, indicate several alternatives and then point out the reasons you selected the best one
3. *Failing to indicate follow up* – Whenever your answer indicates action on your part, make certain that you will take proper follow-up action to see how successful your recommendations, procedures or actions turn out to be
4. *Taking too long in answering any single question* – Remember to time your answers properly

IX. AFTER THE TEST

Scoring procedures differ in detail among civil service jurisdictions although the general principles are the same. Whether the papers are hand-scored or graded by machine we have described, they are nearly always graded by number. That is, the person who marks the paper knows only the number – never the name – of the applicant. Not until all the papers have been graded will they be matched with names. If other tests, such as training and experience or oral interview ratings have been given, scores will be combined. Different parts of the examination usually have different weights. For example, the written test might count 60 percent of the final grade, and a rating of training and experience 40 percent. In many jurisdictions, veterans will have a certain number of points added to their grades.

After the final grade has been determined, the names are placed in grade order and an eligible list is established. There are various methods for resolving ties between those who get the same final grade – probably the most common is to place first the name of the person whose application was received first. Job offers are made from the eligible list in the order the names appear on it. You will be notified of your grade and your rank as soon as all these computations have been made. This will be done as rapidly as possible.

People who are found to meet the requirements in the announcement are called "eligibles." Their names are put on a list of eligible candidates. An eligible's chances of getting a job depend on how high he stands on this list and how fast agencies are filling jobs from the list.

When a job is to be filled from a list of eligibles, the agency asks for the names of people on the list of eligibles for that job. When the civil service commission receives this request, it sends to the agency the names of the three people highest on this list. Or, if the job to be filled has specialized requirements, the office sends the agency the names of the top three persons who meet these requirements from the general list.

The appointing officer makes a choice from among the three people whose names were sent to him. If the selected person accepts the appointment, the names of the others are put back on the list to be considered for future openings.

That is the rule in hiring from all kinds of eligible lists, whether they are for typist, carpenter, chemist, or something else. For every vacancy, the appointing officer has his choice of any one of the top three eligibles on the list. This explains why the person whose name is on top of the list sometimes does not get an appointment when some of the persons lower on the list do. If the appointing officer chooses the second or third eligible, the No. 1 eligible does not get a job at once, but stays on the list until he is appointed or the list is terminated.

X. HOW TO PASS THE INTERVIEW TEST

The examination for which you applied requires an oral interview test. You have already taken the written test and you are now being called for the interview test – the final part of the formal examination.

You may think that it is not possible to prepare for an interview test and that there are no procedures to follow during an interview. Our purpose is to point out some things you can do in advance that will help you and some good rules to follow and pitfalls to avoid while you are being interviewed.

What is an interview supposed to test?

The written examination is designed to test the technical knowledge and competence of the candidate; the oral is designed to evaluate intangible qualities, not readily measured otherwise, and to establish a list showing the relative fitness of each candidate – as measured against his competitors – for the position sought. Scoring is not on the basis of "right" and "wrong," but on a sliding scale of values ranging from "not passable" to "outstanding." As a matter of fact, it is possible to achieve a relatively low score without a single "incorrect" answer because of evident weakness in the qualities being measured.

Occasionally, an examination may consist entirely of an oral test – either an individual or a group oral. In such cases, information is sought concerning the technical knowledges and abilities of the candidate, since there has been no written examination for this purpose. More commonly, however, an oral test is used to supplement a written examination.

Who conducts interviews?

The composition of oral boards varies among different jurisdictions. In nearly all, a representative of the personnel department serves as chairman. One of the members of the board may be a representative of the department in which the candidate would work. In some cases, "outside experts" are used, and, frequently, a businessman or some other representative of the general public is asked to serve. Labor and management or other special groups may be represented. The aim is to secure the services of experts in the appropriate field.

However the board is composed, it is a good idea (and not at all improper or unethical) to ascertain in advance of the interview who the members are and what groups they represent. When you are introduced to them, you will have some idea of their backgrounds and interests, and at least you will not stutter and stammer over their names.

What should be done before the interview?

While knowledge about the board members is useful and takes some of the surprise element out of the interview, there is other preparation which is more substantive. It *is* possible to prepare for an oral interview – in several ways:

1) Keep a copy of your application and review it carefully before the interview

This may be the only document before the oral board, and the starting point of the interview. Know what education and experience you have listed there, and the sequence and dates of all of it. Sometimes the board will ask you to review the highlights of your experience for them; you should not have to hem and haw doing it.

2) Study the class specification and the examination announcement

Usually, the oral board has one or both of these to guide them. The qualities, characteristics or knowledges required by the position sought are stated in these documents. They offer valuable clues as to the nature of the oral interview. For example, if the job involves supervisory responsibilities, the announcement will usually indicate that knowledge of modern supervisory methods and the qualifications of the candidate as a supervisor will be tested. If so, you can expect such questions, frequently in the form of a hypothetical situation which you are expected to solve. NEVER go into an oral without knowledge of the duties and responsibilities of the job you seek.

3) Think through each qualification required

Try to visualize the kind of questions you would ask if you were a board member. How well could you answer them? Try especially to appraise your own knowledge and background in each area, *measured against the job sought*, and identify any areas in which you are weak. Be critical and realistic – do not flatter yourself.

4) Do some general reading in areas in which you feel you may be weak

For example, if the job involves supervision and your past experience has NOT, some general reading in supervisory methods and practices, particularly in the field of human relations, might be useful. Do NOT study agency procedures or detailed manuals. The oral board will be testing your understanding and capacity, not your memory.

5) Get a good night's sleep and watch your general health and mental attitude

You will want a clear head at the interview. Take care of a cold or any other minor ailment, and of course, no hangovers.

What should be done on the day of the interview?

Now comes the day of the interview itself. Give yourself plenty of time to get there. Plan to arrive somewhat ahead of the scheduled time, particularly if your appointment is in the fore part of the day. If a previous candidate fails to appear, the board might be ready for you a bit early. By early afternoon an oral board is almost invariably behind schedule if there are many candidates, and you may have to wait. Take along a book or magazine to read, or your application to review, but leave any extraneous material in the waiting room when you go in for your interview. In any event, relax and compose yourself.

The matter of dress is important. The board is forming impressions about you – from your experience, your manners, your attitude, and your appearance. Give your personal appearance careful attention. Dress your best, but not your flashiest. Choose conservative, appropriate clothing, and be sure it is immaculate. This is a business interview, and your appearance should indicate that you regard it as such. Besides, being well groomed and properly dressed will help boost your confidence.

Sooner or later, someone will call your name and escort you into the interview room. *This is it.* From here on you are on your own. It is too late for any more preparation. But remember, you asked for this opportunity to prove your fitness, and you are here because your request was granted.

What happens when you go in?

The usual sequence of events will be as follows: The clerk (who is often the board stenographer) will introduce you to the chairman of the oral board, who will introduce you to the other members of the board. Acknowledge the introductions before you sit down. Do not be surprised if you find a microphone facing you or a stenotypist sitting by. Oral interviews are usually recorded in the event of an appeal or other review.

Usually the chairman of the board will open the interview by reviewing the highlights of your education and work experience from your application – primarily for the benefit of the other members of the board, as well as to get the material into the record. Do not interrupt or comment unless there is an error or significant misinterpretation; if that is the case, do not hesitate. But do not quibble about insignificant matters. Also, he will usually ask you some question about your education, experience or your present job – partly to get you to start talking and to establish the interviewing "rapport." He may start the actual questioning, or turn it over to one of the other members. Frequently, each member undertakes the questioning on a particular area, one in which he is perhaps most competent, so you can expect each member to participate in the examination. Because time is limited, you may also expect some rather abrupt switches in the direction the questioning takes, so do not be upset by it. Normally, a board member will not pursue a single line of questioning unless he discovers a particular strength or weakness.

After each member has participated, the chairman will usually ask whether any member has any further questions, then will ask you if you have anything you wish to add. Unless you are expecting this question, it may floor you. Worse, it may start you off on an extended, extemporaneous speech. The board is not usually seeking more information. The question is principally to offer you a last opportunity to present further qualifications or to indicate that you have nothing to add. So, if you feel that a significant qualification or characteristic has been overlooked, it is proper to point it out in a sentence or so. Do not compliment the board on the thoroughness of their examination – they have been sketchy, and you know it. If you wish, merely say, "No thank you, I have nothing further to add." This is a point where you can "talk yourself out" of a good impression or fail to present an important bit of information. Remember, *you close the interview yourself*.

The chairman will then say, "That is all, Mr. _____, thank you." Do not be startled; the interview is over, and quicker than you think. Thank him, gather your belongings and take your leave. Save your sigh of relief for the other side of the door.

How to put your best foot forward

Throughout this entire process, you may feel that the board individually and collectively is trying to pierce your defenses, seek out your hidden weaknesses and embarrass and confuse you. Actually, this is not true. They are obliged to make an appraisal of your qualifications for the job you are seeking, and they want to see you in your best light. Remember, they must interview all candidates and a non-cooperative candidate may become a failure in spite of their best efforts to bring out his qualifications. Here are 15 suggestions that will help you:

1) Be natural – Keep your attitude confident, not cocky

If you are not confident that you can do the job, do not expect the board to be. Do not apologize for your weaknesses, try to bring out your strong points. The board is interested in a positive, not negative, presentation. Cockiness will antagonize any board member and make him wonder if you are covering up a weakness by a false show of strength.

2) Get comfortable, but don't lounge or sprawl

Sit erectly but not stiffly. A careless posture may lead the board to conclude that you are careless in other things, or at least that you are not impressed by the importance of the occasion. Either conclusion is natural, even if incorrect. Do not fuss with your clothing, a pencil or an ashtray. Your hands may occasionally be useful to emphasize a point; do not let them become a point of distraction.

3) Do not wisecrack or make small talk

This is a serious situation, and your attitude should show that you consider it as such. Further, the time of the board is limited – they do not want to waste it, and neither should you.

4) Do not exaggerate your experience or abilities
   In the first place, from information in the application or other interviews and sources, the board may know more about you than you think. Secondly, you probably will not get away with it. An experienced board is rather adept at spotting such a situation, so do not take the chance.

5) If you know a board member, do not make a point of it, yet do not hide it
   Certainly you are not fooling him, and probably not the other members of the board. Do not try to take advantage of your acquaintanceship – it will probably do you little good.

6) Do not dominate the interview
   Let the board do that. They will give you the clues – do not assume that you have to do all the talking. Realize that the board has a number of questions to ask you, and do not try to take up all the interview time by showing off your extensive knowledge of the answer to the first one.

7) Be attentive
   You only have 20 minutes or so, and you should keep your attention at its sharpest throughout. When a member is addressing a problem or question to you, give him your undivided attention. Address your reply principally to him, but do not exclude the other board members.

8) Do not interrupt
   A board member may be stating a problem for you to analyze. He will ask you a question when the time comes. Let him state the problem, and wait for the question.

9) Make sure you understand the question
   Do not try to answer until you are sure what the question is. If it is not clear, restate it in your own words or ask the board member to clarify it for you. However, do not haggle about minor elements.

10) Reply promptly but not hastily
   A common entry on oral board rating sheets is "candidate responded readily," or "candidate hesitated in replies." Respond as promptly and quickly as you can, but do not jump to a hasty, ill-considered answer.

11) Do not be peremptory in your answers
   A brief answer is proper – but do not fire your answer back. That is a losing game from your point of view. The board member can probably ask questions much faster than you can answer them.

12) Do not try to create the answer you think the board member wants
   He is interested in what kind of mind you have and how it works – not in playing games. Furthermore, he can usually spot this practice and will actually grade you down on it.

13) Do not switch sides in your reply merely to agree with a board member
   Frequently, a member will take a contrary position merely to draw you out and to see if you are willing and able to defend your point of view. Do not start a debate, yet do not surrender a good position. If a position is worth taking, it is worth defending.

14) Do not be afraid to admit an error in judgment if you are shown to be wrong

The board knows that you are forced to reply without any opportunity for careful consideration. Your answer may be demonstrably wrong. If so, admit it and get on with the interview.

15) Do not dwell at length on your present job

The opening question may relate to your present assignment. Answer the question but do not go into an extended discussion. You are being examined for a *new* job, not your present one. As a matter of fact, try to phrase ALL your answers in terms of the job for which you are being examined.

Basis of Rating

Probably you will forget most of these "do's" and "don'ts" when you walk into the oral interview room. Even remembering them all will not ensure you a passing grade. Perhaps you did not have the qualifications in the first place. But remembering them will help you to put your best foot forward, without treading on the toes of the board members.

Rumor and popular opinion to the contrary notwithstanding, an oral board wants you to make the best appearance possible. They know you are under pressure – but they also want to see how you respond to it as a guide to what your reaction would be under the pressures of the job you seek. They will be influenced by the degree of poise you display, the personal traits you show and the manner in which you respond.

ABOUT THIS BOOK

This book contains tests divided into Examination Sections. Go through each test, answering every question in the margin. We have also attached a sample answer sheet at the back of the book that can be removed and used. At the end of each test look at the answer key and check your answers. On the ones you got wrong, look at the right answer choice and learn. Do not fill in the answers first. Do not memorize the questions and answers, but understand the answer and principles involved. On your test, the questions will likely be different from the samples. Questions are changed and new ones added. If you understand these past questions you should have success with any changes that arise. Tests may consist of several types of questions. We have additional books on each subject should more study be advisable or necessary for you. Finally, the more you study, the better prepared you will be. This book is intended to be the last thing you study before you walk into the examination room. Prior study of relevant texts is also recommended. NLC publishes some of these in our Fundamental Series. Knowledge and good sense are important factors in passing your exam. Good luck also helps. So now study this Passbook, absorb the material contained within and take that knowledge into the examination. Then do your best to pass that exam.

EXAMINATION SECTION

EXAMINATION SECTION
TEST 1

DIRECTIONS: Each question or incomplete statement is followed by several suggested answers or completions. Select the one that BEST answers the question or completes the statement. *PRINT THE LETTER OF THE CORRECT ANSWER IN THE SPACE AT THE RIGHT.*

1. Of the following, the one that is a grease fitting is a _____ fitting.

    A. Morse
    B. Brown and Sharpe
    C. Zerk
    D. caliper

2. In an automobile equipped with an ammeter, the ammeter is used to

    A. indicate current flow
    B. regulate current flow
    C. act as a circuit breaker
    D. measure engine r.p.m.

3. The ignition points in the distributor of a gasoline engine are opened by means of a

    A. spring
    B. vacuum
    C. cam with lobes
    D. gear

4. MOST automobile engines that use gasoline as fuel operate as _____ engines.

    A. single cycle
    B. single stroke, single cycle
    C. two-stroke, two-cycle
    D. four-stroke, two-cycle

5. For a shop manager, the MOST important reason that equipment which is used infrequently should be considered for disposal is that

    A. such equipment may cause higher management to think that your shop is not busy
    B. the time required for its maintenance could be better used elsewhere
    C. the men may resent having to work on such equipment
    D. such equipment usually has a higher breakdown rate in operation

6. The PRIMARY function of the thermostat in the cooling system of an automobile engine is to

    A. control the operating temperature of the engine
    B. keep the operating temperature of the engine as low as possible
    C. provide the proper amount of heat for the heater
    D. retain engine heat when the engine gets hot

7. The PRIMARY purpose of the condenser in the ignition circuit of a gasoline engine is to

    A. boost the ignition voltage
    B. rectify the ignition voltage
    C. adjust the coil voltage
    D. reduce arcing at the distributor breaker points

1

8. The PRIMARY purpose of the differential in the rear drive train of an automotive vehicle is to allow each of the rear wheels to

   A. rotate at different speeds
   B. go in reverse
   C. rotate with maximum torque
   D. absorb road shocks

9. When an automobile engine does not start on a damp day, the trouble is MOST likely in the _____ system.

   A. ignition   B. cooling
   C. fuel   D. lubricating

10. The battery of an automobile is prevented from discharging back through the alternator by the blocking action of the

    A. commutator   B. diodes
    C. brushes   D. slip rings

11. The master cylinder in an automobile is actuated by the

    A. steering column B. brake pedal
    C. clutch plate   D. cam shaft

Questions 12-17.

DIRECTIONS: Questions 12 through 17 are to be answered SOLELY on the basis of the following passage.

The basic hand-operated hoisting device is the tackle or purchase, consisting of a line called a fall, reeved through one or more blocks.

To hoist a load of given size, you must set up a rig with a safe working load equal to or in excess of the load to be hoisted. In order to do this, you must be able to calculate the safe working load of a single part of line of given size; the safe working load of a given purchase which contains a line of given size; and the minimum size of hooks or shackles which you must use in a given type of purchase to hoist a given load. You must also be able to calculate the thrust which a given load will exert on a gin pole or a set of shears inclined at a given angle; the safe working load which a spar of a given size, used as a gin pole or as one of a set of shears, will sustain; and the stress which a given load will set up in the back guy of a gin pole, or in the back guy of a set of shears, inclined at a given angle.

12. The above passage refers to the lifting of loads by means of

    A. erected scaffolds   B. manual rigging devices
    C. power-driven equipment   D. conveyor belts

13. It can be concluded from the above passage that a set of shears serves to

    A. absorb the force and stress of the working load
    B. operate the tackle
    C. contain the working load
    D. compute the safe working load

14. According to the above passage, a spar can be used for a

    A. back guy   B. block   C. fall   D. gin pole

15. According to the above passage, the rule that a user of hand-operated tackle MUST follow is to make sure that the safe working load is AT LEAST

    A. equal to the weight of the given load
    B. twice the combined weight of the block and falls
    C. one-half the weight of the given load
    D. twice the weight of the given load

16. According to the above passage, the two parts that make up a tackle are

    A. back guys and gin poles
    B. blocks and falls
    C. rigs and shears
    D. spars and shackle

17. According to the above passage, in order to determine whether it is safe to hoist a particular load, you MUST

    A. use the maximum size hooks
    B. time the speed to bring a given load to a desired place
    C. calculate the forces exerted on various types of rigs
    D. repeatedly lift and lower various loads

18. If you do not understand the operation of some special tool which is used in your work, your BEST procedure would be to

    A. study up on its operation at home
    B. ask a maintainer to explain its operation
    C. ask another helper to explain its operation
    D. bother nobody and expect to pick up a little more knowledge each time you use the tool

19. For winter servicing of a gasoline engine, it is BEST to use an oil that

    A. has a low SAE number
    B. has a high SAE number
    C. has a very heavy consistency
    D. contains few additive detergents

20. If a wheel has turned through an angle of 180°, then it has made _____ revolution(s).

    A. 1/4   B. 1/2   C. 1/8   D. 18

21. The crankshaft in a gasoline engine is PRIMARILY used to

    A. change reciprocating motion to rotary motion
    B. operate the valve lifters
    C. supply power to each cylinder
    D. function as a flywheel

22. Assume that a mechanic is using a powder-actuated tool and the cartridge misfires. According to recommended safe practices regarding a misfired cartridge, the FIRST course of action the mechanic should take is to

    A. place the misfired cartridge carefully into a metal container filled with water
    B. carefully reload the tool with the misfired cartridge and try it again
    C. immediately bury the misfired cartridge at least two feet in the ground
    D. remove the wadding from the misfired cartridge and empty the powder into a pail of sand

23. The purpose of the ignition coil in a gasoline engine is PRIMARILY to

    A. smooth the voltage
    B. raise the voltage
    C. raise the current
    D. smooth the current

24. Vapor lock in a vehicle with a gasoline engine is caused by excessive heat. To prevent vapor lock, it may be necessary to relocate

    A. the ignition system
    B. the cooling system
    C. the starter motor
    D. a part of the fuel line

25. To accurately measure the small gap between relay contacts, it is BEST to use a(n)

    A. depth gauge
    B. *GO-NO GO* gauge
    C. feeler gauge
    D. inside caliper

KEY (CORRECT ANSWERS)

1.	C	11.	B
2.	A	12.	B
3.	C	13.	A
4.	D	14.	D
5.	B	15.	A
6.	A	16.	B
7.	D	17.	C
8.	A	18.	B
9.	A	19.	A
10.	B	20.	B

21. A
22. A
23. B
24. D
25. C

TEST 2

DIRECTIONS: Each question or incomplete statement is followed by several suggested answers or completions. Select the one that BEST answers the question or completes the statement. *PRINT THE LETTER OF THE CORRECT ANSWER IN THE SPACE AT THE RIGHT.*

1. Of the following, the MOST important reason for having a vehicle preventive maintenance and history card is

    A. for use in making vehicle assignments
    B. to check whether the drivers are completing their assignments
    C. for use as a control device in scheduling maintenance
    D. as a means for projecting future maintenance expenses

    1._____

2. In his efforts to maintain standards of performance, a shop manager uses a system of close supervision to detect or catch errors.
In OPPOSITE method of accomplishing the same objective is to employ a program which

    A. instills in each employee a pride of workmanship to do the job correctly the first time
    B. groups each job according to the importance to the overall objectives of the program
    C. makes the control of quality the responsibility of an inspector
    D. emphasizes that there is a *one* best way for an employee to do a specific job

    2._____

3. Assume that after taking over a repair shop, a shop manager feels that he is taking too much time maintaining records.
He should

    A. temporarily assign this job to one of his senior repair crew chiefs
    B. get together with his supervisor to determine if all these records are needed
    C. stop keeping those records which he believes are unnecessary
    D. spend a few additional hours each day until his records are current

    3._____

4. In order to apply performance standards to employees engaged in repair shop activities, a shop manager must FIRST

    A. allow workers to decide for themselves the way to do the job
    B. determine what is acceptable as satisfactory work
    C. separate the more difficult tasks from the simpler tasks
    D. stick to an established work schedule

    4._____

5. The term *preventative maintenance* is used to identify a plan whereby

    A. equipment is serviced according to a regular schedule
    B. equipment is serviced as soon as it fails
    C. equipment is replaced as soon as it becomes obsolete
    D. all equipment is replaced periodically

    5._____

6. The ratio of air to gasoline in an automobile engine is controlled by the
   A. gas filter
   B. fuel pump
   C. fuel injector
   D. intake manifold

7. *Energizer* is another name given to the
   A. automobile battery
   B. fluorescent fixture ballast
   C. battery charger
   D. generator shunt field

8. Wearshoes may be found on
   A. circuit breakers
   B. automobile brake systems
   C. snow plows
   D. door sills

9. An oscilloscope is an instrument used in
   A. measuring noise levels
   B. displaying waveforms of electrical signals
   C. indicating the concentrations of pollutants in air
   D. photographing high-speed events

10. Assume that a brake pedal of a truck goes to the floorboard when depressed. The one of the following that could cause this condition is
    A. a leak in the hydraulic lines
    B. a clogged hydraulic line
    C. scored drums
    D. glazed linings

11. The universal joints of an automobile are located on the
    A. suspension springs
    B. steering linkages
    C. wheel cylinders
    D. drive shaft

12. The MAIN purpose of a flexible coupling is to connect two shafts which are
    A. of different diameters
    B. of different shapes
    C. not in exact alignment
    D. of different material

13. When using a standard measuring micrometer, starting with a zero reading, one complete counterclockwise revolution of the sleeve will give a reading of _____ inch.
    A. .001   B. .010   C. .025   D. .250

14. If a nut is to be tightened to an exact specified value of inch-lbs., the wrench to use is a _____ wrench.
    A. spanner   B. box   C. lock-jaw   D. torque

15. Common permanent type anti-freezes for automobile cooling systems are MAINLY
    A. alcohol
    B. methanol
    C. ethylene glycol
    D. trichloroethylene

16. The function of the fuel injector on a gasoline engine is to

    A. mix the air and gasoline properly
    B. filter the fuel
    C. filter the air to engine
    D. pump the gasoline into the cylinder

17. If a car owner complains that the battery in his car is constantly running dry, the item that should be checked FIRST is the

    A. fan belt
    B. generator
    C. voltage regulator
    D. relay

18. On MOST modern automobiles, foot brake pressure is transmitted to the brake drums by

    A. air pressure
    B. mechanical linkage
    C. hydraulic fluid
    D. electromagnetic force

19. Assume that the engine of a car remains cold even though it is run for a period of time. The part that is MOST likely at fault is the

    A. heat bypass valve
    B. thermostat
    C. heater control
    D. choke

20. A rectifier changes

    A. DC to AC
    B. AC to DC
    C. single-phase power to three-phase power
    D. battery power to three-phase power

21. Continuity in a de-energized electrical circuit may be checked with a(n)

    A. voltmeter
    B. ohmmeter
    C. neon tester
    D. rheostat

22. Of the following crankcase oils, the one that should be used in sub-zero weather is SAE

    A. 10W   B. 20W   C. 20   D. 30

23. Caster in an automobile is an adjustment in the

    A. ignition system
    B. drive-shaft
    C. rear differential
    D. front suspension

24. If the spark plugs in an engine run too hot, the result is MOST likely that

    A. oil and carbon compounds will accumulate on the insulators
    B. the electrodes will wear rapidly
    C. the timing will be retarded
    D. the ignition coil may become damaged

25. A low reading on the oil pressure gauge of a gasoline engine may mean that the   25.____
  A. engine bearings are too tight
  B. crankcase oil level is too low
  C. transmission oil level is too low
  D. transmission oil needs changing

KEY (CORRECT ANSWERS)

1.	C	11.	D
2.	A	12.	C
3.	B	13.	C
4.	B	14.	D
5.	A	15.	C
6.	C	16.	A
7.	A	17.	C
8.	C	18.	C
9.	B	19.	B
10.	A	20.	B

21. B
22. A
23. D
24. B
25. B

TEST 3

DIRECTIONS: Each question or incomplete statement is followed by several suggested answers or completions. Select the one that BEST answers the question or completes the statement. *PRINT THE LETTER OF THE CORRECT ANSWER IN THE SPACE AT THE RIGHT.*

1. To remove a slotted collar having internal threads from a shaft, the BEST of the following wrenches to use is a(n) _____ wrench.

    A. Allen   B. Stillson   C. socket   D. spanner

2. When using a heavy jack placed on the ground to raise a heavy load, it is important to place a sturdy, flat board under the jack PRIMARILY in order to

    A. facilitate placing the jack under the load
    B. reduce the jacking effort
    C. prevent the jack from slipping out from under the load
    D. decrease the jacking height

3. The pulley wheels of a block and tackle are commonly called

    A. stocks   B. swivels   C. sheaves   D. guides

4. If the diameter of a machined part must be 1.035 $\pm$ 0.003", then it is ACCEPTABLE if it measures

    A. 1.031"   B. 1.032"   C. 1.039"   D. 1.335"

5. The type of threads for ordinary screws are USUALLY the _____ type.

    A. square   B. buttress   C. V   D. Acme

6. Of the following actions a repair shop manager can take to determine if the vehicles used in his shop are being utilized properly, the one which will give him the LEAST meaningful information is

    A. conducting an analysis of vehicle assignments
    B. reviewing the number of miles travelled by each vehicle with and without loads
    C. recording the unloaded weights of each vehicle
    D. comparing the amount of time vehicles are parked at job sites with the time required to travel to and from job sites

7. For a shop manager, the MOST important reason that equipment which is used infrequently should be considered for disposal is that

    A. the time required for its maintenance could be better used elsewhere
    B. such equipment may cause higher management to think that your shop is not busy
    C. the men may resent having to work on such equipment
    D. such equipment usually has a higher breakdown rate in operation

8. In an automotive gasoline engine, the camshaft is used PRIMARILY to

   A. drive the transmission
   B. operate the valve lifters
   C. change the reciprocating motion of the pistons to rotary motion
   D. operate the choke mechanism

9. A magnetic motor starter is to be controlled with momentary start-stop pushbuttons at two locations.
   The number of control wires required, respectively, in the conduit between the controller and the first station and in the conduit between the two stations is _____ and _____.

   A. 3; 3   B. 4; 4   C. 3; 4   D. 2; 4

10. If the scale on a shop drawing is 1/2 inch to the foot, then the length of a part which measures 4 1/2 inches long on the drawing has a length of APPROXIMATELY _____ feet.

    A. 2 1/8   B. 4 1/4   C. 8 1/2   D. 10 3/4

11. It is important to use safety shoes PRIMARILY to guard the feet against

    A. tripping hazards   B. heavy falling objects
    C. shock hazards   D. mud and dirt

12. When using a wrench to tighten a bolt, it is considered bad practice to extend the handle of the wrench with a pipe for added leverage PRIMARILY because

    A. the pipe may break
    B. the bolt head may be broken off
    C. more space will be needed to turn the wrench with the pipe on it
    D. no increase in leverage is obtained in this manner

13. The liquid solution in an electrical storage battery MOST commonly is

    A. alkali   B. acid
    C. pure distilled water   D. copper sulphate

14. Manifolds on an internal combustion engine are used

    A. to mount the engine to the frame
    B. for cooling the engine
    C. in the carburetor
    D. to conduct gases into and out of the engine

15. The energy stored by a storage battery is commonly given in

    A. volts   B. amperes
    C. ampere-hours   D. kilowatts

16. Vapor lock occurs in automobile

    A. gas tanks   B. crankcases
    C. transmissions   D. carburetors

17. The instrument generally used to determine the specific gravity of a lead-acid storage battery is the   17.____

    A. ammeter   B. voltmeter
    C. ohmmeter   D. hydrometer

18. A tachometer is an instrument that is used to measure   18.____

    A. horizontal distances
    B. radial distances
    C. current in electric circuits
    D. motor speed

19. A material that is commonly used as a lining for bearings in order to reduce friction is   19.____

    A. magnesium   B. cast iron
    C. babbitt   D. carborundum

20. In a motor having sleeve bearings, bearing wear can be checked by measuring the air-gap clearance between the armature and the   20.____

    A. pole pieces   B. commutator
    C. bearing   D. brushes

21. A revolution counter applied to the end of a rotating shaft reads 100 when a stopwatch is started and 850 after 90 seconds.   21.____
    The shaft is rotating at a speed of _____ rpm.

    A. 500   B. 633   C. 750   D. 950

22. If a kink develops in a wire rope, it would be BEST to   22.____

    A. hammer out the kink with a lead hammer
    B. straighten out the kink by putting it in a vise and applying sufficient pressure
    C. discard the portion of rope containing the kink
    D. keep the rope in use and allow the kink to work itself out

23. The one of the following flat drive-belts that gives the BEST service in dry places is a(n) _____ belt.   23.____

    A. rawhide   B. oak-tanned
    C. chrome-tanned   D. semirawhide

24. The letter representing the standard V-belt section which has the lowest horsepower-per-belt rating is   24.____

    A. E   B. C   C. B   D. A

25. The criteria governing preventive maintenance of vehicles require that all of the following be done at certain intervals.   25.____
    The one which must be done MOST frequently is

    A. changing the engine oil
    B. changing the engine oil filter
    C. checking the radiator coolant level
    D. rotating the tires

26. The one of the following that should NOT be lubricated is a(n)

    A. spur gear train
    B. motor commutator
    C. roller chain drive
    D. automobile axle

27. The one of the following oils that has the LOWEST viscosity is S.A.E.

    A. 70 B. 50 C. 20 D. 10W

28. The one of the following V-belt sections which has the HIGHEST horsepower-per-belt rating is _____ section.

    A. A B. B C. C D. D

29. The one of the following transmission devices which should be oiled MOST often is the

    A. V-belt
    B. roller chain
    C. rigid coupling
    D. clutch plate

30. The one of the following statements concerning lubricating oil which is CORRECT is:

    A. SAE 10 is heavier and more viscous than SAE 30
    B. Diluting lubricating oil with gasoline increases its viscosity
    C. Oil reduces friction between moving parts
    D. In hot weather, thin oil is preferable to heavy oil

KEY (CORRECT ANSWERS)

1. D		16. D	
2. C		17. D	
3. C		18. D	
4. B		19. C	
5. C		20. A	
6. C		21. A	
7. A		22. C	
8. B		23. B	
9. C		24. D	
10. C		25. C	
11. B		26. B	
12. B		27. D	
13. B		28. D	
14. D		29. B	
15. C		30. C	

EXAMINATION SECTION
TEST 1

DIRECTIONS: Each question or incomplete statement is followed by several suggested answers or completions. Select the one that BEST answers the question or completes the statement. *PRINT THE LETTER OF THE CORRECT ANSWER IN THE SPACE AT THE RIGHT.*

1. Of the following procedures by which a foreman may train his assistant to take his place during his absence, the one most generally acceptable as the BEST is for the foreman to

    A. guide the assistant in actually carrying out all the important procedures involved in the work he will have to do
    B. have the assistant attend group meetings and ask questions
    C. explain carefully to the assistant all the procedures involved, having him practice these procedures in the actual situation when the foreman is away
    D. put the assistant in charge of the unit for a few days to let him learn by actual practice

    1.____

2. Assume that you are a foreman and you assign one of your hardest working men to do some paper work which he has never done before. Because of his inexperience, he makes many errors.
    Of the following, the MOST advisable course of action for you to take is to

    A. express your appreciation for his willingness and show him how to do the work better
    B. praise his effort but reprimand him for his performance
    C. praise his work to show appreciation of his efforts
    D. say nothing but do not assign him to that work again

    2.____

3. Assume that you are a foreman and a man under your supervision, who is very efficient, is constantly complaining about the type of work assigned to him. You have noticed that his complaints have a bad effect on the other men. Of the following, the BEST course of action for you to take in this situation is to

    A. ask the men to try to overlook his faults
    B. determine the cause of his attitude and try to make an adjustment in his work assignment
    C. secure his transfer to another shop or unit being supervised by a different foreman
    D. let the man make his own work assignments

    3.____

4. Of the following, the MOST important reason for operating within a budget is that a budget will

    A. permit a department or agency to cut down on provisional appointments
    B. control spending in advance
    C. explain the area of responsibility of a department or agency
    D. set up a good base for comparison with the previous year's activities

    4.____

5. As a foreman, you observe that one of the men under your supervision seems to be rejected by the other men of the unit and tends to stay by himself.
    Of the following, the MOST advisable course of action for you to take is to

    5.____

A. ignore the situation unless it interferes with the work of the unit
B. determine the reason and, if possible, attempt to rectify the situation
C. have the man transferred
D. inform the other men that they should change their attitude

6. The orders of a foreman are LEAST likely to be carried out properly if he

A. gives detailed orders
B. writes out his orders
C. lacks patience when giving them
D. asks for his orders to be repeated

Questions 7-8.

DIRECTIONS: Questions 7 and 8 are to be answered in accordance with the information given below.

The specifications for a crankshaft main bearing journal are as follows:
Diameter   -   2.2482" - 2.2490"
Max. out-of-round -   .0004"
Max. taper   -   .0003"/inch.

A mechanic has measured a crankshaft main bearing journal on horizontal and vertical axis, as shown in the diagram, and reported them as:

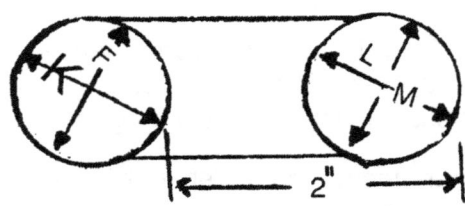

7. In accordance with the information given above, the measured journal

A. is within specifications
B. requires regrind due to excessive taper
C. requires regrind due to excessive out-of-round
D. requires regrind due to being undersize

8. In accordance with the information given above, if the mechanic reported measures of
F 2.2490"
K 2.2487"
L 2.2492"
M 2.2489"
the piece would be rejected as not meeting specifications because it is

A. undersize
B. excessively out-of-round
C. excessively tapered
D. oversize

9. The conditions of Emission Systems Warranties are usually based on regulations promulgated by the

A. American Petroleum Institute
B. Federal Clean Air Act

C. Environmental Protection Administration
D. Society of Automotive Engineers

10. After 6,000 miles of operation in approximately 6 months, it would be expected that motor vehicle warranties would cover

    A. ignition points with a loose pivot pin
    B. front wheel alignment
    C. a burned clutch disc
    D. a plugged fuel filter

11. In order to reduce harmful emissions, control of inlet air temperature to the carburetor is maintained by the _____ system.

    A. AIR   B. CCS
    C. PCV   D. Thermoactor

12. When you instruct one of your mechanics in the use of an ordinary oscilloscope for tuning an internal combustion engine, you should indicate to him that its use eliminates the need for a

    A. dwell meter   B. timing light
    C. compression tester   D. tachometer

Questions 13-16.

DIRECTIONS: Questions 13 through 16 are to be answered in accordance with the following information.

A *make* or *buy* decision must be made concerning pump shafts.
The shaft is 24 inches long and requires a cut-off, turning, and milling operation.
Material cost is $4.00/ft. Machining time and costs are as indicated:

	Initial Setup time (hrs.)	Mach. time/piece (hrs.)	Mach. rate/hr.
Cut-off	.5	.195	$ 5.00
Lathe	2.0	1.480	15.00
Mill	1.0	.500	10.00

13. With reference to the information given above, the minimum cost per piece based on producing these pump shafts in lots of 100 would be MOST NEARLY

    A. $17.40   B. $34.80   C. $36.60   D. $38.60

14. With reference to the information given above, the SMALLEST per unit cost for material and set-ups occurs in

    A. material   B. milling   C. turning   D. cut-off

15. With reference to the information given above, the GREATEST cost, per lot of 100 pieces, occurs in

    A. milling   B. material   C. turning   D. cut-off

16. With reference to the information given above, a steel supplier has quoted you a price of $750.00 for 100 pieces of stock to make the pump shafts. They would be delivered cut to length.
The amount saved per 100 shafts by purchasing from this supplier would be MOST NEARLY

   A. $50.00 B. $100.00 C. $150.00 D. $200.00

17. The State Department of Motor Vehicles excludes certain vehicles from the necessity of inspection.
Vehicles NOT excluded are

   A. front wheel drive passenger cars
   B. dump trucks equipped as snow plows
   C. police patrol cars
   D. road sweepers

18. The service brakes on a passenger car are to be inspected for issuance of a State Certificate of Inspection.
Of the following statements, the one that MOST correctly describes a procedure that must be followed or a condition that must exist before the certificate may be issued is

   A. one front and one rear brake drum must be removed
   B. the vehicle will be rejected if the pedal reserve is less than one-half of the total possible travel
   C. the master cylinder reservoir must be at least two-thirds full
   D. a brake equalization test must be performed

19. When a vehicle with a curved windshield is being inspected for issuance of a State Certificate of Inspection, it would be rejected if the windshield had

   A. cloudiness extending 1 1/2" from any edge
   B. four 3/4" diameter *stars* on any portion of the windshield
   C. a 9" crack and a 6" crack emanating from one point
   D. four 1 1/4" *stars,* one of which is located 2" from the bottom edge of the windshield

20. In connection with the boring of cylinders in an engine block, it is *desirable* that the crankshaft

   A. be in place and the main bearing caps be torqued to specifications
   B. be removed but the main bearing caps be replaced and torqued to specifications
   C. be in place and the main bearing caps be up hand tight
   D. and the main bearing caps be removed

21. Upon applying the brake after a failure in the primary (front brake) section of a dual master cylinder system, it would be noted that for the same stopping action as before the failure there would be

   A. increased pedal travel with increased pedal pressure
   B. increased pedal travel with no increase in pedal pressure
   C. no increase in pedal pressure or pedal travel
   D. increased pedal pressure with no increase in pedal travel

Questions 22-24.

DIRECTIONS: Questions 22 through 24, inclusive, are to be answered in accordance with the following paragraph.

You have been instructed to expedite the fabrication of three special sand spreader trucks using chassis that are available in the shop. All three trucks must be completed by November 1. Based on workload and available hours, the foreman of the body shop indicates that he could manufacture one complete sand spreader body per month, with one additional week required for mounting and securing each body to the available chassis. No work could begin on the body until the engines and hydraulic components, which would have to be purchased, were available for use. The Purchasing Department has promised the delivery of engines and hydraulic components three months after the order is placed. (Assume that all months have four weeks; and the same crew is doing the assembling and manufacturing.)

22. With reference to the above paragraph, the LATEST date that the engines and associated hydraulic components could be requisitioned in order to meet the specified deadline would be MOST NEARLY the end of the _____ week in _____.

    A. second; March
    B. first; April
    C. first; May
    D. first; June

22.____

23. With reference to the above paragraph, the date of completion of the first sand spreader truck, assuming that the Purchasing Department placed the order at the beginning of the second week in February and ultimate delivery of the engines and components was delayed by a month, would be MOST NEARLY the end of the _____ week in _____.

    A. second; June
    B. fourth; June
    C. second; July
    D. fourth; July

23.____

24. With reference to the above paragraph, the date of completion of the last sand spreader truck, assuming that the Purchasing Department placed the order at the beginning of the second week in February and actual delivery of the engines and components was made two weeks early, would be MOST NEARLY the end of the _____ week in _____.

    A. second; August
    B. first; September
    C. third; September
    D. second; October

24.____

25. A vacuum gage connected to the intake manifold of an idling V-8 gasoline engine reads steady but low. The LEAST likely reason for this is

    A. late ignition timing
    B. late valve timing
    C. improper air-fuel mixture
    D. manifold air leaks

25.____

26. The MOST likely cause of a metallic knock coming from the engine while running under light load at 25 mph is

    A. a loose main bearing
    B. a loose piston pin
    C. a loose connecting rod bearing
    D. too early ignition timing

26.____

27. The usual procedure in making a battery capacity test is to draw a current

    A. equal to three times the ampere-hour rating for 15 seconds
    B. equal to the ampere-hour rating for 15 seconds
    C. equal to twice the ampere-hour rating for one minute
    D. adjusted to drop the battery voltage to two-thirds of its rated voltage in 15 seconds

28. A rectangularly shaped truck repair facility is 180 feet wide and 260 feet long. A 10-foot space is provided along each wall for benches and equipment. A 60-foot wide area in the middle of the floor is to remain clear for its entire 260-foot length. The entrance to the shop is at one end of this open area.
    Assuming that each truck occupies a working space 25 feet long and 12 feet wide, the maximum number of trucks that could be parked perpendicularly to the 260-foot walls (assuming no obstructions) would be MOST NEARLY

    A. 40   B. 60   C. 80   D. 120

29. If no spark is seen at the screwdriver tip when checking a distributor by shorting the movable point to ground while the primary system is energized and the ignition points are open, the MOST NEARLY correct statement that can be made is that

    A. this is normal in a properly operating ignition system
    B. the secondary circuit is open
    C. the condenser is shorted
    D. the points are defective

30. Ignition timing is MOST properly set

    A. with the vacuum advance line connected to the distributor
    B. prior to adjusting the point dwell
    C. with the engine running at a minimum speed of 1500 RPM
    D. after adjusting the point dwell

31. The vibration damper on an auto engine is fastened to the

    A. camshaft   B. flywheel
    C. crankshaft   D. driveshaft

32. Most small gas engines use a _____ ignition system.

    A. magneto   B. transistorized
    C. battery   D. induction

33. Carburetor icing occurs MOST often

    A. on humid, hot days
    B. when an engine is overheated
    C. on cool, damp days
    D. when an engine is run for long periods at idle speed

34. The function of the float in a carburetor is to

    A. close the needle valve
    B. control flow of gas into pump circuit
    C. operate choke circuit when engine is cold
    D. bleed off gasoline from primary tubes

35. To improve stability when cornering, manufacturers add a device to cars called a 35.____

   A. control arm
   B. stabilizer bar
   C. constant velocity joint
   D. Pitman arm

36. Adjustment of the tie rods on a car will affect 36.____

   A. camber
   B. king pin inclination
   C. caster
   D. toe-in

37. A restriction in the exhaust system is indicated on a vacuum gauge by a 37.____

   A. steady needle
   B. low reading
   C. gradual decrease in reading
   D. fast fluctuating needle

38. Disc brakes on a car have a distinct advantage over conventional drum brakes in that they 38.____

   A. fade less when hot
   B. are cheaper to manufacture
   C. are easier to service
   D. require less pedal pressure to apply

39. In a diesel engine, the fuel is ignited by the 39.____

   A. spark plug
   B. injector plug
   C. heat of compression
   D. magneto

40. Engine timing is generally set by using a 40.____

   A. torque wrench
   B. dividing head
   C. strobe light
   D. centrifugal mechanism

41. If an engine is operated for long periods of time at part throttle opening, the 41.____

   A. spark plugs will become covered with carbon
   B. carburetor will become clogged
   C. fuel filter will accumulate more water
   D. points will blacken

42. Leaking intake valve guides will cause 42.____

   A. excessive oil consumption
   B. overheating
   C. valves to act sluggishly
   D. valve seats to burn

43. Flooding of a carburetor is generally caused by 43.____

   A. loose bolts holding carburetor to manifold
   B. air leaks in float bowl
   C. loose jets in carburetor body
   D. stuck float needle valve

44. On many cars, the fuel pump is combined with the

   A. vacuum pump
   B. power steering pump
   C. generator
   D. power brake booster

45. Carbon fouling of a spark plug is an indication of

   A. excessive oil burning
   B. too rich a mixture
   C. poor grade of gasoline
   D. plug misfiring

46. If tests show that generator output is excessive even after the F terminal has been disconnected, the trouble may be traced to

   A. the regulator
   B. the generator
   C. poor ground
   D. discharged battery

47. An automobile alternator converts alternating current to direct current by means of

   A. silicon diodes
   B. a current regulator
   C. a solenoid coil
   D. improper choke operation

48. Hard starting is very often caused by

   A. a faulty condenser
   B. poor grade of gasoline
   C. improper grade of oil
   D. improper choke operation

49. A car with a history of *burned points* would PROBABLY indicate

   A. improper gap setting
   B. improper condenser
   C. too high a setting of the voltage regulator
   D. incorrect dwell angle

50. When it is necessary to recondition brake drums, the MAXIMUM allowable amount of oversize is _____".

   A. .025   B. .030   C. .040   D. .060

KEY (CORRECT ANSWERS)

1. A	11. B	21. A	31. C	41. A
2. A	12. A	22. B	32. A	42. A
3. B	13. C	23. C	33. C	43. D
4. B	14. D	24. A	34. A	44. A
5. B	15. C	25. C	35. B	45. B
6. C	16. C	26. C	36. D	46. B
7. A	17. A	27. A	37. C	47. A
8. D	18. D	28. C	38. A	48. D
9. B	19. D	29. C	39. C	49. C
10. A	20. B	30. D	40. C	50. D

TEST 2

DIRECTIONS: Each question or incomplete statement is followed by several suggested answers or completions. Select the one that BEST answers the question or completes the statement. *PRINT THE LETTER OF THE CORRECT ANSWER IN THE SPACE AT THE RIGHT.*

1. When starting a vehicle equipped with an alternator, the current from the battery generally flows to the alternator   1.____

   A. commutator
   B. stator windings
   C. rotor windings
   D. rectifier

2. Assume that in a repair job it becomes necessary to expand the piston skirt so that the piston-to-cylinder clearance becomes one-half of that normally required.   2.____
   Of the following methods of expanding piston skirts, the one which is BEST used to obtain the above results is

   A. pressure and heat
   B. knurling
   C. peening
   D. spring expanders

3. The statement that is MOST NEARLY correct concerning vapor lock in an operating engine is that   3.____

   A. the more volatile the fuel the greater the tendency for it to vapor lock
   B. the tendency to vapor lock is decreased by hard driving
   C. the tendency to vapor lock is decreased when driving at high altitude
   D. minor defects in engine cooling contributes greatly to vapor lock

4. Of the following statements concerning cylindrical and centerless grinders, the one which is MOST NEARLY correct is: 4.____

   A. The *through-feed* method of work handling is applicable to the cylindrical grinder
   B. Less metal needs to be removed to produce a round piece of work on a centerless grinder
   C. Internal grinding of cylindrical objects cannot be done on a centerless grinder
   D. To grind a piece of work of different diameters in a centerless grinder, the work piece must be fed on one side and ejected on the other side

5. Many cars are equipped with a device that varies the spark angle with manifold vacuum. When the manifold vacuum suddenly increases, it is likely that the angle of spark   5.____

   A. advances
   B. remains the same as before
   C. decreases
   D. is retarded

6. Assume that engine tightening specifications for the cylinder head bolts on a late model Chevrolet is 95 ft.lbs. If the wrench available has an effective leverage of 15", the force necessary to satisfactorily tighten the bolts is MOST NEARLY _____ lbs.   6.____

   A. 6.3   B. 47.0   C. 75.0   D. 118.8

21

7. In connection with power brakes on an operating vehicle, the statement MOST NEARLY correct is:
   A. Air-suspended units are under vacuum pressure until the brakes are applied
   B. Vacuum-suspended units are balanced with atmospheric pressure until the brakes are applied
   C. Vacuum-suspended units are unbalanced by means of the engine vacuum when the pedal is depressed
   D. Air-suspended units are unbalanced by means of the engine vacuum when the pedal is depressed

8. In reboring a diesel cylinder block bore to receive a new 4.631"-.001" O.D. liner, the MAXIMUM allowable block bore should generally be
   A. 4.626"   B. 4.627"   C. 4.632"   D. 4.634"

9. A common rail system of fuel injection is BEST described as a system using a
   A. single pump for compressing the fuel, plus a metering element for each cylinder
   B. single pump for metering and compressing the fuel, plus a dividing device for supplying the fuel to the various cylinders
   C. separate metering and compressing pump for each cylinder of the engine
   D. single pump for compressing the fuel, plus a transfer pump to meter the fuel for each cylinder

10. Assume that a storage floor area of 300 square feet can safely support 120 lbs. per sq.ft. The MAXIMUM number of 50-gallon oil drums that can be stored on this floor is MOST NEARLY (assume one gallon of water weighs 8.3 lbs. and the specific gravity of oil is .85)
    A. 210   B. 105   C. 87   D. 75

11. A Brinell number of 450 corresponds MOST NEARLY to a Rockwell C number of
    A. 52   B. 48   C. 40   D. 35

12. The one of the following which causes the front wheels of a car to right themselves after a turn is the
    A. toe-in   B. camber
    C. side thrust   D. caster

13. The process used to produce only a superficially hard wear-resisting surface on a machined part is generally called
    A. nitriding   B. tempering
    C. flame hardening D. cyaniding

14. When a gasoline engine is idling with no external load, it usually demands a rich mixture or charge.
    The MOST probable reason for this is that
    A. when the intake valve opens, a higher pressure exists in the cylinder than in the intake manifold
    B. when the throttle is near the closed position, the pressure at the end of the exhaust stroke is always below atmospheric

C. when the throttle is near the closed position, the pressure in the intake manifold is above atmospheric
D. inert exhaust gas increases the explosive mixture or charge

15. Cam ground pistons are used PRIMARILY because

   A. they can be used in badly worn engines without reboring the cylinders
   B. their use increases the compression ratio
   C. their use aids in the lubrication of the cylinder walls
   D. they eliminate piston slap in engine warm-up and permit expansion

16. After a D.C. generator has been repaired and installed in a passenger car, it must be polarized.
   If the generator field is externally grounded, the BEST procedure to follow in polarizing the generator is to

   A. just touch with a jumper between terminals marked *Gen* and *Bat* of the voltage regulator
   B. disconnect the field wire from the regulator and touch this wire to the regulator *Bat* terminal
   C. disconnect the field wire from the regulator and touch this wire to the *Gen* terminal
   D. just touch with a jumper between terminals marked *Gen* and *Field* of the voltage regulator

17. The outside surfaces of aluminum alloy pistons are usually made highly resistant to wear by means of which one of the following methods?

   A. Induction hardening   B. Anodizing
   C. Normalizing   D. Spheroidizing

18. The temperature of the burning air-fuel mixture in an internal combustion gasoline engine is MOST NEARLY _____ °F.

   A. 1000   B. 1500   C. 2500   D. 4500

19. Assume that after removing the cylinder head of an engine, a wet, oily condition is noticed on the block between two adjacent cylinders.
   This is PROBABLY caused by

   A. a ruptured pump diaphragm
   B. a scored cylinder wall
   C. worn valve guides
   D. a blown cylinder head gasket

20. Assume that the valve timing diagram of a Cadillac engine shows the intake valve opened for a period of 290°.
   The distance that this 290° represents on the circumference of an 18" flywheel is MOST NEARLY

   A. 28.5"   B. 37.5"   C. 45.5"   D. 52.5"

21. Assume that a job order calls for an AISI-3115 or a S.A.E.-3120 steel to be used in the fabrication of an automotive component.
This material is MOST likely a _____ steel.

    A. silicon-manganese
    B. nickel-chromium
    C. chromium
    D. manganese

22. A pinging sound in an engine is most likely to occur on open throttle at low or moderate engine speed.
This pinging is further increased by which one of the following conditions?

    A. Use of high octane fuel
    B. Heavy carbon deposits in cylinder
    C. Low atmospheric temperature
    D. Intake manifold heater valve in the *off* position when engine is warm

23. A key factor in lathe development today has been the introduction of new cutting tool materials. Of the following, the LATEST material in lathe cutting tools is

    A. stellite
    B. cemented-carbide
    C. cast alloys
    D. ceramics

24. A regulator used to control the output of an alternator usually consists of a number of parts.
The one of the following which is NOT a part of this type of regulator is the

    A. load relay
    B. current limiter
    C. voltage regulator
    D. reverse-current relay

25. Shoulder wear on both sides of treads of a rubber tire is PROBABLY caused by

    A. overinflation
    B. cornering
    C. underinflation
    D. incorrect toe-in or toe-out

26. Of the following types of alloy bearings, the one that requires a bearing wall of substantial thickness if it is NOT bonded to a steel back is

    A. aluminum
    B. copper
    C. cadmium
    D. tin-base babbit

27. When a particular piston of a gasoline engine is in a *rock* position, it may CORRECTLY be said that the

    A. crankshaft can move about 25° without causing the valves to open or close
    B. piston has reached the bottom of its stroke
    C. crankshaft cannot move without causing the piston to move
    D. crankshaft can move about 15° without causing the piston to move up or down

28. A grinding wheel marked C14-N12-S20 would be used MOST effectively for grinding

    A. cast iron
    B. a milling cutter
    C. SAE 1330 steel
    D. SAE 1090 steel

29. To test for leaks around the intake manifold of an idling engine, the mechanic would MOST likely use   29.____

    A. soap bubbles
    B. talc powder
    C. oil
    D. heavy grease

30. When assembling a gear-type oil pump, used on passenger cars, the end clearance on the inside of the pump must be MOST NEARLY   30.____

    A. .001"   B. .003"   C. .006"   D. .010"

31. Of the following descriptions of engine noises, the one that is USUALLY associated with the valve mechanism is a   31.____

    A. light rap or clattering with a light load at approximately 25 MPH
    B. click, snap or sharp rattle on acceleration
    C. sharp, metallic, double-knock with the engine idling
    D. clicking sound occurring at regular intervals

32. Assume when using a vacuum gauge to troubleshoot an engine which does not have overlapping valve timing,
    it is noticed that the needle on the vacuum gauge drifts slowly back and forth. This generally indicates   32.____

    A. poor air-fuel mixture
    B. an air leak in the intake manifold
    C. late valve timing
    D. a blown cylinder head gasket

33. Assume that a rectangular concrete shop floor, 100 feet x 125 feet, is to be painted with two coats of paint.
    If the paint covers 450 square feet per gallon on the first coat and 900 square feet per gallon on the second coat, the total number of gallons of paint required to do the above job is MOST NEARLY   33.____

    A. 30   B. 36   C. 42   D. 48

34. Assume a 1/2" hole is drilled 1 1/2" off-center on a 4" diameter circular disc.
    If a shaft is keyed through the 1/2" hole and the disc is used as a cam, the lift of the cam will be   34.____

    A. 2 3/4"   B. 3"   C. 3 1/4"   D. 3 1/2"

35. In a diesel engine, good combustion is BEST obtained when the diesel fuel is burned in the presence of MOST NEARLY _____ excess air.   35.____

    A. no
    B. 10%
    C. 60 to 70%
    D. 100 to 150%

36. For most passenger cars used by the various departments, the crankshaft end play in a reassembled engine should be MOST NEARLY   36.____

    A. .001"   B. .005"   C. .010"   D. .015"

37. Assume that a Ford Transistorized Ignition System uses a 2 mfd condenser in the amplifier assembly.
    The function of this condenser is to

    A. discharge its current directly into the secondary high voltage circuit
    B. prevent metal build-up on the distributor points similar to the conventional ignition system
    C. absorb high inductive energy during initial distributor point opening
    D. discharge energy into the primary coil at the same moment as the battery current s the primary coil

38. Assume that a 12 spline shape is to be cut on a shaft in a milling machine.
    If the shaft diameter is 1 5/8", the index plate circle to use is MOST NEARLY

    A. 20   B. 19   C. 17   D. 15

39. A light spring expander is used in conjunction with piston rings to increase the wall pressure in slightly worn or tapered cylinders.
    This expander is USUALLY located _____ ring.

    A. below the scraper   B. above the compression
    C. behind the scraper   D. behind the compression

40. Assume that the breakdown cost of a particular motor job is as follows:
    Parts $160.00
    Labor   75.00
    Overhead   30.00
    The percentage of the total cost for labor is MOST NEARLY

    A. 20%   B. 25%   C. 28%   D. 32%

41. Setting the spark plug gap opening closer than normally required would PROBABLY result in _____ idling and _____ in top engine speed.

    A. smoother; increase   B. rougher; decrease
    C. smoother; decrease   D. rougher; increase

42. If air should be trapped within the fuel pump of a solid injection diesel engine, it is likely that

    A. no fuel would be delivered
    B. the pump discharge pressure will increase
    C. the charge of the fuel to the engine will be lean
    D. a mixture of fuel and air would be delivered

43.

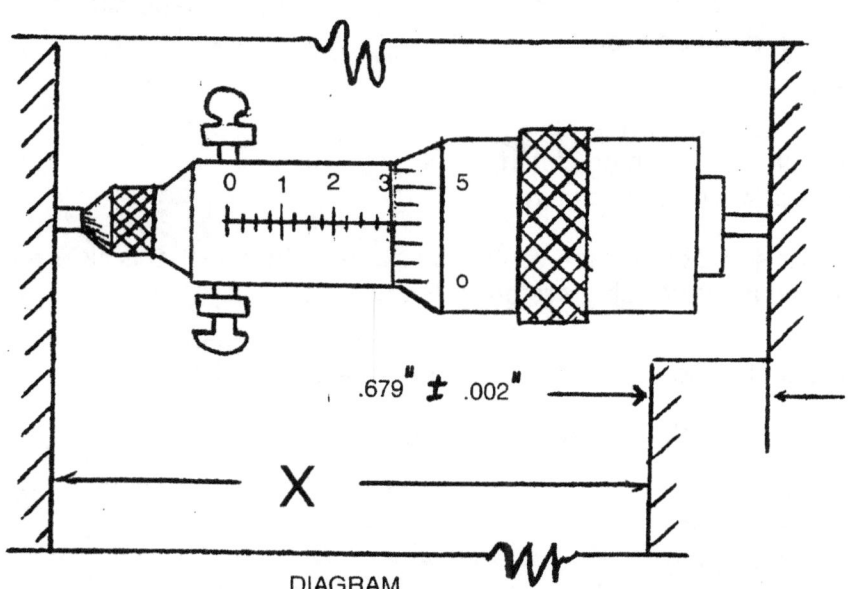

DIAGRAM

With the thimble at the zero setting, the overall length (of the above diagram) of the inside type micrometer measures exactly 2.500".
When the micrometer is opened as shown above, the MINIMUM distance for X is MOST NEARLY

A. 1.819"   B. 1.852"   C. 2.122"   D. 2.149"

44. During a three-minute battery test of a 12V battery, if the cell voltages are uneven by more than 0.1V or 0.15V, the mechanic should

    A. test total battery voltage with charger still operating on fast charge
    B. test electrolyte specific gravity and charge battery
    C. replace the battery
    D. add electrolyte, charge the battery slowly, and re-test

45. The piston ring end clearance of a ring installed in the top groove of a piston for a 3 1/4" cylinder bore is MOST NEARLY

A. 0.004"   B. 0.007"   C. 0.009"   D. 0.013"

46. The gas pressure in the hose of the acetylene line supplying an ordinary oxy-acetylene welding torch, when the torch is in operation, should be kept between _____ psi.

A. 1-15   B. 30-45   C. 50-75   D. 75-100

47. Water sludge in engine crankcase oil is MOST usually caused by

    A. using a low viscosity oil
    B. condensation in the crankcase
    C. mixing different brands of motor oil
    D. using a high viscosity oil

48. In a typical Chrysler Torque Flite three-speed transmission, the band-clutch applications for drive position -2nd speed are

    A. front and rear clutches
    B. front clutch and kickdown band
    C. front clutch and overrunning clutch
    D. kickdown and overrunning clutch

49. Of the following parts of a crankcase ventilation system, the one that is NOT a part of the positive-type crankcase ventilating system is the

    A. intake breather
    B. road draft tube
    C. manifold suction tube
    D. metering valve

50. A *cylinder balance test* is NOT usually used to locate

    A. worn piston rings
    B. a leaky intake manifold
    C. a defective spark plug
    D. a valve not opening properly due to a worm cam shaft

KEY (CORRECT ANSWERS)

1. C	11. B	21. B	31. D	41. D
2. B	12. A	22. B	32. A	42. A
3. A	13. D	23. D	33. C	43. C
4. B	14. A	24. D	34. B	44. C
5. A	15. D	25. C	35. C	45. D
6. C	16. A	26. A	36. B	46. A
7. D	17. B	27. C	37. C	47. B
8. C	18. D	28. A	38. D	48. B
9. A	19. D	29. C	39. C	49. B
10. B	20. C	30. B	40. C	50. A

EXAMINATION SECTION
TEST 1

DIRECTIONS: Each question or incomplete statement is followed by several suggested answers or completions. Select the one that BEST answers the question or completes the statement. *PRINT THE LETTER OF THE CORRECT ANSWER IN THE SPACE AT THE RIGHT.*

1. All of the following are probable causes of an engine's failure to start EXCEPT
   A. cylinders not wired in proper order
   B. poor coolant circulation
   C. resistance unit burned out
   D. defective condenser

   1.____

2. In an *expert* system for offboard computer diagnosis, which stage of knowledge acquisition in developing problem-solving rules occurs FIRST?
   A. Implementation		B. Identification
   C. Formalization		D. Conceptualization

   2.____

3. Some suspension units consist of tandem axles joined by a single cross support that also acts as a vertical pivot for the entire unit.
   These units are known as
   A. axials	B. field frames	C. bogies	D. helicals

   3.____

4. In automotive electronics, the fractional duration that ignition points are closed is known as
   A. slip	B. gain	C. dwell	D. delay

   4.____

5. A brake system's warning lights may be tested by
   A. testing the bulbs with an ohmmeter
   B. depressing the brake pedal and opening a wheel cylinder bleeder screw
   C. jumping the wires at the brake distributor switch assembly
   D. testing the system with an ammeter

   5.____

6. Of the following procedures performed prior to grinding a valve seat, which should be performed FIRST?
   A. Reaming	B. Adjusting	C. Cleaning	D. Replacement

   6.____

7. What type of clutch is responsible for controlling a car's air conditioning compressor?
   A. Centrifugal		B. Free-wheeling
   C. Magnetic		D. Mechanical

   7.____

8. Which of the following is a DISADVANTAGE associated with onboard computer diagnostic systems? 8.____
   A. Inability to incorporate self-diagnosis
   B. Limited number of systems available for diagnosis
   C. Cannot be manually activated
   D. Inability to detect intermittent failures

9. Which parts in a motor or generator contact the rotating armature commutator or rings? 9.____
   A. Cams   B. Brushes   C. Rod caps   D. Bushings

10. What is the MAIN advantage associated with the use of offboard computer diagnostic systems? 10.____
    A. Decreased task load
    B. Continuous testing intervals
    C. Can be manually activated by the driver
    D. Capable of simultaneous multiple diagnoses

11. An EGO sensor used in a microprocessor-based control/diagnostic system 11.____
    A. is perfectly linear
    B. is unaffected by temperature
    C. has two different output levels, depending on the fuel mixture
    D. is unaffected by engine exhaust levels

12. To what drive train component is the ring gear in the differential bolted? 12.____
    A. Drive pinion   B. Axle shaft
    C. Differential case   D. Carrier

13. What is transmitted by the slip rings on an automotive alternator? 13.____
    A. Alternating current to the field coils
    B. Alternating current from the stator windings
    C. Direct current from the field coils
    D. Direct current to the alternator output terminals

14. Which of the following is a PROBABLE cause of an engine's missing at low speed? 14.____
    A. Poor compression   B. Leaky head gasket
    C. Carbon deposits in cylinders   D. Loose flywheel

15. In order for an onboard computer diagnostic system to detect a failure in the cars electronic system, the failure must be 15.____
    A. associated with engine performance
    B. intermittent
    C. symptomatic
    D. nonreversible

16. What is the term for the part of a shaft which rotates in a bearing? 16.____
    A. Lunette   B. Journal   C. Jackshaft   D. Kingpin

17. What is the USUAL steering gear reduction for passenger vehicles? _____-to-1. 17.____
    A. 2 B. 4 C. 8 D. 12

18. What is indicated by a low reading from 5 to 10 on an engine vacuum test? 18.____
    A. Broken piston ring   B. Weak cylinders
    C. Late valve timing   D. Valve sticking

19. Which of the following is NOT a component of the automotive power train? 19.____
    A. Steering gear   B. Clutch
    C. Transmission   D. Differential

20. Which instrument is NORMALLY used to check the condition of a resistance spark plug? 20.____
    A. Voltmeter   B. Ohmmeter   C. Ammeter   D. Potentiometer

21. Which device is used to measure the resistance of a circuit or electrical machine? 21.____
    A. Ohmmeter   B. Voltmeter   C. Resistor   D. Ammeter

22. What reading will appear on an infrared meter which indicates a failure of the catalytic converter? _____ HC/ _____ CO 22.____
    A. Low; high   B. Low; low   C. High; low   D. High; high

23. In automatic transmissions, the servo 23.____
    A. operates the shifter valves
    B. applies the clutch
    C. applies the bands
    D. controls the output from the variable vane pump

24. If an onboard diagnostic system's fault code indicates that the O_2 sensor is not ready, all of the following are possible causes EXCEPT 24.____
    A. O_2 sensor is not functioning correctly
    B. defective connections or leads
    C. lack of O_2 contacting sensor
    D. control unit is not processing O_2 signal

25. The mechanical compressor in a car's air conditioning system is driven by 25.____
    A. an electric motor   B. the axles
    C. the propeller shaft   D. the crankshaft

KEY (CORRECT ANSWERS)

1.	B	11.	C
2.	B	12.	C
3.	C	13.	C
4.	C	14.	A
5.	B	15.	D
6.	C	16.	B
7.	C	17.	B
8.	D	18.	C
9.	B	19.	A
10.	A	20.	B

21. A
22. C
23. C
24. C
25. D

TEST 2

DIRECTIONS: Each question or incomplete statement is followed by several suggested answers or completions. Select the one that BEST answers the question or completes the statement. *PRINT THE LETTER OF THE CORRECT ANSWER IN THE SPACE AT THE RIGHT.*

1. When installing disc brake linings, a hammer should be used to 1.____
   A. tighten the shoe retainer B. seat the pads in the calipers
   C. shape the pads D. remove the linings

2. What engine component is lubricated by the oil squirt hole in the connecting rod? 2.____
   A. Connecting rod bearing B. Crankshaft
   C. Cylinder wall D. Piston pin

3. Which of the following is a PROBABLE cause of backfiring through a carburetor? 3.____
   A. Short circuit in switch B. Water in gasoline
   C. Overheating D. Sticky thermostat

4. What is the GREATEST danger associated with hydraulic braking systems? 4.____
   A. Uneven braking B. Defective metering valve
   C. Loss of brake fluid D. Dirty or clogged wheel cylinder

5. Under what conditions must an engine be operated during a cylinder balance test? 5.____
   A. With the spark plugs firing, one at a time, at 1500 rpm
   B. With all plugs shorted but two which fire at non-simultaneous equal intervals
   C. At idle speed, with all plugs shorted but two which fire at non-simultaneous equal intervals
   D. At idle speed, with the spark plugs shorted, one at a time

6. Which of the following is a requisite property of brake fluid? 6.____
   A. Has detergents for keeping hoses unobstructed
   B. High wetting characteristics
   C. High viscosity
   D. High boiling point and low freezing point

7. What is measured by the mass airflow sensor in a microprocessor-based control/diagnostic system? The 7.____
   A. rate at which air is flowing into an engine
   B. composition of a given mass of air
   C. rate at which exhaust is flowing out of an engine
   D. density of atmospheric air

8. What is placed at the joint of a steel frame in order to strengthen the joint? 8.____
   A. Wobble plate B. Gusset plate
   C. Jackshaft D. Lint pin

9. What is indicated if a combustion meter reading is 10% higher with the air cleaner in place than when the air cleaner has been removed?
   A. Clogged injectors
   B. Dirty air cleaner
   C. Clogged vent
   D. Normal operation

10. Which of the following is a PROBABLE cause of an engine failing to stop?
    A. Lack of pressure on gasoline tank
    B. Disconnected magneto ground
    C. High altitude
    D. Spark plug gaps too wide

11. Automotive sensors used in computer-operated diagnostic or control systems typically see changes in each of the following EXCEPT
    A. electrical signals
    B. temperature
    C. position
    D. pressure

12. What type of feeler gauge should be used to set the gap on a new set of spark plugs?
    A. Flat   B. Ramp-type   C. Wire   D. Round

13. Intake and exhaust manifolds are built with their walls contacting each other in order to
    A. reduce atomization
    B. pre-heat the fuel mixture
    C. facilitate valve action
    D. conserve space

14. Fuel tank vapors stored in the charcoal canister
    A. are released to the atmosphere through a bleed valve
    B. are released to the atmosphere through a port in the canister
    C. are cycled back into the fuel tank
    D. become part of the fuel mixture when the engine is started

15. The information handled by a computerized engine control system flows from
    A. computer to sensor to display
    B. actuator to display to computer
    C. sensor to computer to actuator
    D. sensor to display to computer

16. In a car with manual transmission, spring pressure clamps the friction disc between the pressure plate and the _____ when the clutch is engaged.
    A. sun gear
    B. reaction plate
    C. flywheel
    D. differential

17. If the insulation material used with a crimp connector on electric wiring is coded red, what range of gauges is considered typical?
    A. 10-12   B. 12-18   C. 14-16   D. 18-22

18. An air conditioning system's expansion valve controls the
    A. pressure of refrigerant in the compressor
    B. temperature of refrigerant in the condenser
    C. amount of refrigerant in the evaporator
    D. temperature of air in the car's interior

19. Each of the following is a probable cause of engine overheating EXCEPT
    A. slipping fan belt
    B. frozen radiator
    C. improper valve timing
    D. short circuit in distributor rotor

20. When using a short finder to trace a short circuit, which of the following steps should be performed LAST?
    A. Turn on all switches in a series with the circuit being tested
    B. Move the short finder meter along circuit wiring
    C. Remove the blown fuse while leaving the battery connected
    D. Connect the pulse unit of short finder across the fuse terminals

21. If a light load test is performed on a battery and the battery shows less than 1.95 volts in all cells, then the battery
    A. is overly discharged
    B. should be replaced
    C. needs charging
    D. is in good condition

22. A *thermistor* is a
    A. newly-developed type of transistor
    B. device for regulating engine temperature
    C. temperature control system operated by a car passenger
    D. semiconductor temperature sensor

23. An *expert* system for offboard computer diagnosis differs from other computerized diagnostic systems because it is capable of
    A. carrying out several diagnostic operations at once
    B. recommending repair procedures
    C. determining the causes of problems without manual assistance
    D. sensing faults in a circuitry that is not related to engine performance

24. In which type of engine are all valve contained in the cylinder block?
    A. V-type   B. Two-stroke   C. F-head   D. L-head

25. The function of a MAP sensor in a microprocessor-based control/diagnostic system is to
    A. sense anomalous changes in a vehicle's traveling direction
    B. measure changes in mean atmospheric pressure
    C. measure manifold absolute pressure
    D. measure fluctuations in manifold air flow

KEY (CORRECT ANSWERS)

1. C
2. C
3. D
4. C
5. B

6. D
7. A
8. B
9. B
10. B

11. A
12. C
13. B
14. D
15. C

16. C
17. D
18. C
19. C
20. B

21. A
22. D
23. B
24. D
25. C

___

TEST 3

DIRECTIONS: Each question or incomplete statement is followed by several suggested answers or completions. Select the one that BEST answers the question or completes the statement. *PRINT THE LETTER OF THE CORRECT ANSWER IN THE SPACE AT THE RIGHT.*

1. What is indicated by a sudden periodic drop of 1 or 2 points during a vacuum test on a car's engine?   1.____
   A. Spark plug failure
   B. Damaged distributor cap
   C. Coil failure
   D. Low oil pressure

2. A stud axle is articulated to an axle-beam or steering head by means of a   2.____
   A. journal   B. kingpin   C. gusset plate   D. poppet

3. Which of the following should be checked FIRST when examining a front suspension?   3.____
   A. Kingpins
   B. Steering connections
   C. Bumper and frame level
   D. Suspension arm pivots

4. Which of the following procedures involving a combustion efficiency tester will detect manifold leaks?   4.____
   A. Accelerating the engine to fast speed and checking for meter deflection
   B. Pumping the accelerator and checking for instant response in the combustion meter
   C. Applying a kerosene/oil mixture to the flange and manifold gaskets and checking for meter deflection
   D. Placing the engine on full choke and checking for meter deflection

5. If a car's battery is always fully charged, which of the following should be checked?   5.____
   A. Short circuiting in alternator
   B. Output amperage of the alternator
   C. volt regulator output
   D. Volt regulator points

6. Which of the following are companion cylinders in a car's V-8 engine?   6.____
   A. 1 and 8   B. 2 and 8   C. 3 and 4   D. 2 and 7

7. Which of the following is a PROBABLE cause of firing in a car's muffler?   7.____
   A. Too rich a fuel mixture
   B. Carbon deposits in cylinder
   C. Improperly adjusted valve tappets
   D. Water in gasoline

8. What is the MAJOR benefit associated with the use of *expert* offboard computer diagnostic systems?   8.____
   A. High task load capability
   B. Continuous testing intervals
   C. Consistent application of problem-solving strategies
   D. Simultaneous multiple-system capability

9. Which type of valve is used to sense how fast a vehicle is traveling?
   A. Throttle   B. Governor   C. Manual   D. Modulator

10. A two-unit alternator is composed of a
    A. voltage limiter and current limiter
    B. current limiter and reverse current relay
    C. voltage limiter and field relay
    D. current limiter and field relay

11. Which type of gears are used for the forward speeds of fully synchronized standard transmissions?
    A. Helical
    B. Double helical
    C. Hypoid
    D. Spur

12. When checking a circuit for voltage drop, which of the following steps should be performed FIRST?
    A. Select the voltmeter range just above the battery circuit
    B. Connect the positive lead of the voltmeter to the end of the wire closest to the battery
    C. Connect the negative lead of the voltmeter to the end of the wire farthest from the battery
    D. Switch on the circuit

13. Each of the following is a probable cause of engine knocking EXCEPT
    A. compression too low
    B. loose piston
    C. spark too far advanced
    D. engine overheated

14. In what portion of an *expert* system for offboard computer diagnosis are logical operation performed?
    A. Domain
    B. Inference engine
    C. Knowledge base
    D. Interface

15. In the propeller shaft of an automotive transmission, a universal joint allows variation in the
    A. speed of rotation
    B. angle of drive
    C. length of the shaft
    D. direction of rotation

16. Which of the following is a POSSIBLE use for an engine analyzer?
    A. Setting the choke
    B. Measuring intake fuel flow rate
    C. Setting ignition points
    D. Measuring fuel mixture

17. What is the term for the smaller of two mating or meshing gears?
    A. Linch   B. Master   C. Pinion   D. Pilot

18. Conditioned air in an automotive air conditioning system is cooled as it passes through the
    A. condenser   B. evaporator   C. compressor   D. receiver

19. In order to determine the correct valve timing of an engine, the opening and closing of the valves should be measured in reference to the
    A. cylinder compression ratio
    B. fuel mixing jets
    C. distributor setting
    D. piston position

    19.____

20. In modern engines using computer-based control systems, diagnosis is performed
    A. with an engine analyzer
    B. with a timing light only
    C. with a timing light and voltmeter
    D. in the digital control system

    20.____

21. What is the MOST probable cause of a car drifting from side to side on a level road?
    A. Bent steering arm
    B. Tight shock absorber
    C. Loose steering connections
    D. Bent axle

    21.____

22. Which device, as part of a special type of pump, drives plunger back and forth as it rotates, producing the pumping action?
    A. Trunnion
    B. Torus
    C. Camber link
    D. Wobble plate

    22.____

23. In a microprocessor-based control/diagnostic system, a typical engine crankshaft angular position sensor is MOST effectively located on the
    A. camshaft
    B. crankshaft
    C. compressor pulley
    D. flywheel

    23.____

24. Which type of gauge will allow a mechanic to MOST accurately set the proper electrode gap on a spark plug?
    A. Flat feeler
    B. Round wire feeler
    C. Square wire feeler
    D. Dial

    24.____

25. What type of logical rule bases are programmed into MOST expert diagnostic systems?
    A. Either/or
    B. Set/subset
    C. If/then
    D. Inductive

    25.____

KEY (CORRECT ANSWERS)

1. A
2. B
3. C
4. C
5. C

6. B
7. A
8. C
9. B
10. C

11. A
12. B
13. A
14. B
15. B

16. C
17. C
18. B
19. D
20. D

21. C
22. D
23. B
24. B
25. C

EXAMINATION SECTION
TEST 1

DIRECTIONS: Each question or incomplete statement is followed by several suggested answers or completions. Select the one that BEST answers the question or completes the statement. *PRINT THE LETTER OF THE CORRECT ANSWER IN THE SPACE AT THE RIGHT.*

1. A mechanic who discovers that the friction-disc facing of a dry clutch is saturated with oil should
    A. use a heavier oil
    B. wash the facing in solvent
    C. replace the facing
    D. increase clutch spring pressure

    1.____

2. Which of the following steps, performed prior to the removal of a transmission oil cooler, should occur FIRST?
    A. Removal of transmission case
    B. Removal of valve body assembly
    C. Checking transmission fluid level
    D. Draining radiator

    2.____

3. An alternator voltage regulator controls alternator output by
    A. grounding the negative diodes
    B. grounding the stator windings
    C. controlling the voltage output at the B terminal
    D. controlling the current feed to the rotor

    3.____

4. Which clutch part is located between the engine flywheel and the pressure plate?
    A. Release lever
    B. Fork
    C. Friction disc
    D. Adjusting screw

    4.____

5. In a digital microcomputer used for the control or diagnosis of automotive engine, some device is needed to convert the computer's output data into a form readable by people.
   The component which serve this function are known as
    A. data buses
    B. microprocessors
    C. peripherals
    D. accumulators

    5.____

6. What is being adjusted when a mechanic pulls the entire control arm toward the frame?
    A. Caster
    B. Camber
    C. Tracking
    D. Kingpin inclination

    6.____

7. Which of the following is a characteristic that could NOT typically be identified by a onboard computer diagnostic system?
    A. Faulty EGR circuits
    B. The cause of a short circuit
    C. Low ECT input
    D. Lean fuel mixture

    7.____

8. In an automatic transmission, the oil filter is USUALLY secured by means of   8._____
   A. screws or a clip   B. the oil pan
   C. a bracket assembly   D. a spring

9. In a microprocessor-based control/diagnostic system, which type of actuator   9._____
   recirculates exhaust gas to the intake charge?
   A. Fuel metering   B. Ignition   C. EGR   D. EGO

10. Which of the following is a PROBABLE cause of an engine's missing at high   10._____
    speed?
    A. Carbon deposits in cylinder   B. Scored cylinder
    C. Short circuit in distributor rotor   D. Weak valve spring

11. Which of the following operations is performed by a sensor in a microprocessor-   11._____
    based control/diagnostic system?
    A. Sending signals to the driver
    B. Selecting the transmission gear ratio
    C. Measuring variables in physical qualities
    D. Serving as an output device

12. When a hydraulic brake pedal is released quickly, the initial makeup fluid is   12._____
    supplied to the master cylinder's pressure chamber through the
    A. piston bleeder holes   B. compensating port
    C. check valve   D. port holes

13. Which part of a transaxle drives the output shafts?   13._____
    A. Ring gear assembly   B. Pinion gears
    C. Side gears   D. Chain

14. Which of the following problems would be MOST difficult to solve with an   14._____
    onboard computer diagnostic system?
    A. Air pump switching valve failure
    B. Imbalanced injectors
    C. Fuel pump circuit fault
    D. Defective electronic spark timing circuit

15. What is the MOST likely cause of a buzzing noise in the automatic transmission?   15._____
    A. Vacuum leakage   B. Malfunctioning front pump
    C. Bent pilot shaft   D. Worn clutch plates

16. What is the function of an actuator in a microprocessor-based control/diagnostic   16._____
    system?
    A. Indicates results of a measurement
    B. Creates a response to an electrical signal
    C. Serves as an input device
    D. Provides a mathematical model for an engine

17. The constant flow method of fuel injection places its burden on each of the following components EXCEPT
    A. an engine-driven injection pump equipped with plungers
    B. injector nozzles
    C. metering valve
    D. bypass unit

18. Which device is used specifically to regulate current by means of variable resistance?
    A. Capacitor   B. Rheostat   C. Ohmmeter   D. Volute

19. Which type of spring is used in a spring-loaded disc clutch?
    A. Cantilever   B. Volute   C. Helical   D. Diaphragm

20. When the engine is running, power steering fluid travels from
    A. control valve to reservoir to pump
    B. pump to control valve to reservoir
    C. reservoir to pump to control valve
    D. reservoir to control valve to pump

21. Piezoresistivity is
    A. a resistance property of insulators
    B. a property of certain semiconductors in which resistivity varies with strain
    C. the ratio of resistivity in a semiconductor to the property being measured by a sensor
    D. a type of metal bonding pad

22. Which of the following would be a PROBABLE cause of engine stoppage?
    A. Fuel pump breakdown   B. Disconnected magneto ground
    C. High altitude   D. Blown cylinder-head gasket

23. If the insulation material used with a crimp connector on electric wiring is coded yellow, what range of gauges is considered typical?
    A. 10-12   B. 12-18   C. 14-16   D. 18-22

24. What is the MOST common firing order of an in-line 6-cylinder engine?
    A. 1-6-2-5-3-4   B. 1-3-6-4-2-5   C. 1-2-5-6-3-4   D. 1-5-3-6-2-4

25. The pressure sensor of most fuel injection systems is located
    A. in the injection chamber
    B. at the nozzle port
    C. within the pump housing
    D. beneath the floor, at the side of the engine compartment

KEY (CORRECT ANSWERS)

1. C
2. D
3. C
4. C
5. C

6. B
7. B
8. A
9. C
10. D

11. C
12. D
13. C
14. A
15. B

16. B
17. A
18. B
19. A
20. B

21. C
22. A
23. A
24. D
25. D

TEST 2

DIRECTIONS: Each question or incomplete statement is followed by several suggested answers or completions. Select the one that BEST answers the question or completes the statement. *PRINT THE LETTER OF THE CORRECT ANSWER IN THE SPACE AT THE RIGHT.*

1. What is the term for a spring-loaded ball that engages a notch? 1.____
   A. Roller bearing B. Poppet C. Venturi D. Lunette

2. What changes alternating current to direct current in the alternator? 2.____
   A. Field relay
   B. Stator windings
   C. Rotor slip rings
   D. Diodes

3. If a mechanic is using an expert diagnostic system and encounters no rules in the conflict set, what should be done? 3.____
   A. Use highest-priority rules for predicted condition
   B. Stop the procedure
   C. Use the rule that most commonly appears under similar conditions
   D. Switch to a different database

4. With which drive train component does a transmission's reverse idler gear ALWAYS mesh? 4.____
   A. Clutch plate
   B. Second gear
   C. Countershaft reverse gear
   D. Main shaft reverse gear

5. Which of the following is the MOST probable cause for a noise that is present in the rear end only when a car goes around curves? 5.____
   A. Loose universal joint
   B. Trouble in the differential case assembly
   C. Trouble in the drive-pinion assembly
   D. Dry wheel bearing

6. In a microprocessor-based control/diagnostic system, which type of sensor is basically a resistor with a movable contact? 6.____
   A. Crankshaft position
   B. Throttle angle
   C. EGO
   D. Knock

7. What is being indicated by bubbles in an air conditioning sight gauge if the unit has been running for several minutes? 7.____
   A. Low refrigerant
   B. Low compressor pressure
   C. System leakage
   D. Normal operation

8. When checking connecting rods for alignment, the angle the rod aligner mandrel makes with the face plate should be _____ degrees, depending on the type of jig used. 8.____
   A. 10 or 20 B. 45 or 90 C. 90 or 180 D. 180 or 320

9. Which type of fuel injection system typically sprays fuel into each intake port on the manifold side of the intake valve?
   A. Direct
   B. Port
   C. Sequential
   D. Single-point

10. The purpose of a suction throttling valve used in an automotive air conditioning system is to
   A. prevent freezing in the evaporator
   B. control compressor cycles
   C. control the metering of the expansion valve
   D. maintain low condenser pressure

11. In a microprocessor-based control/diagnostic system, which type of actuator consists of a spray nozzle and a solenoid-operated plunger?
   A. Thermostat
   B. Ignition
   C. EGO
   D. Fuel injector

12. Which component of a band and servo assembly is DIRECTLY affected by hydraulic pressure?
   A. Anchor
   B. Band
   C. Servo piston
   D. Stem

13. If an ammeter shows a small fluctuating reading and a spark test reveals no spark, what is the MOST likely source of the trouble?
   A. Primary circuit
   B. Secondary circuit
   C. Battery
   D. Ignition switch

14. All of the following are characteristics of a top-feed fuel injector, as opposed to a bottom-feed EXCEPT
   A. uses incoming air for cooling purposes
   B. higher cost
   C. greater pressure requirements
   D. heavier mass

15. All of the following are probable causes of an engine's lacking power EXCEPT
   A. too rich a fuel mixture
   B. lack of coolant
   C. high altitude
   D. leaky manifold gaskets

16. Which device should be used to check for runout or wobble on a disc brake that has been lathe-mounted?
   A. Timing light
   B. Electric meter
   C. Dial indicator
   D. Torque wrench

17. A(n) _____ is the term for a wire or wires that form a common path to and from the various components a microcomputer uses for the diagnosis or control of an automotive engine.
   A. analog
   B. runner
   C. bus
   D. port

18. The notch on the head of a piston should be facing the _____ during the installation of a piston assembly.
    A. minor thrust side
    B. major thrust side
    C. rear of the engine
    D. front of the engine

19. The requisite knowledge and expertise used in an expert diagnostic system's programming is acquired from a person known as the
    A. domain expert
    B. user
    C. inference engine
    D. knowledge engineer

20. All of the following are probable causes of an engine's missing at all speeds EXCEPT
    A. valve tappets adjusted too closely
    B. dirty plug
    C. loose piston
    D. leak in intake manifold

21. The function of a MAP sensor in a microprocessor-based control/diagnostic system is to measure
    A. anomalous changes in a vehicle's traveling direction
    B. changes in mean atmospheric pressure
    C. manifold absolute pressure
    D. fluctuations in manifold air flow

22. What procedure is recommended upon discovering that brake fluid is contaminated?
    A. Bleed the hydraulic system
    B. Flush the system with alcohol, and then adding clean fluid
    C. Add a detergent oil to the system
    D. Replace the fluid, along with all hydraulic rubber cups and seals

23. Which of the following could be indicated by a vibrating reading on a vacuum gauge that appears only at high engine speeds?
    A. Pitted distributor points
    B. Incorrect ignition timing
    C. Blow-by
    D. Weak valve springs

24. In a microprocessor-based control/diagnostic system, which type of sensor uses magnetostrictive techniques?
    A. Knock
    B. Throttle angle
    C. EGO
    D. MAP

25. The amount that the steering knuckle pivots are angled away from a true vertical is known as
    A. camber
    B. phase
    C. tilt
    D. caster

KEY (CORRECT ANSWERS)

1.	B	11.	D
2.	D	12.	C
3.	B	13.	B
4.	C	14.	A
5.	C	15.	D
6.	B	16.	C
7.	A	17.	C
8.	C	18.	D
9.	B	19.	D
10.	A	20.	C

21. C
22. D
23. D
24. A
25. D

TEST 3

DIRECTIONS: Each question or incomplete statement is followed by several suggested answers or completions. Select the one that BEST answers the question or completes the statement. *PRINT THE LETTER OF THE CORRECT ANSWER IN THE SPACE AT THE RIGHT.*

1. All of the following are components of a positive crankcase ventilating system EXCEPT the 1.____
   A. manifold suction tube
   B. metering valve
   C. road draft tube
   D. intake breather

2. The MAXIMUM voltage for sensor and actuator circuits used in onboard diagnostic systems is 2.____
   A. 3   B. 5   C. 10   D. 15

3. Which of the following is a PROBABLE result of adjusting valves with too little clearance? 3.____
   A. Delayed timing
   B. Burning oil
   C. Lower fuel economy
   D. Overheated valves

4. In a fuel metering actuator that is used in a microprocessor-based control/diagnostic system, *duty cycle* refers too the ratio of fuel 4.____
   A. *off* time to fuel *on* time
   B. *on* time to fuel *off* time
   C. *on* time to fuel *on* time plus fuel *off* time
   D. *off* time to fuel *off* time pus fuel *on* time

5. In a synchromesh transmission, gears are engaged by a _____ in order to prevent gear clashing. 5.____
   A. slip joint or spline
   B. friction and dog clutch
   C. planetary unit
   D. dog clutch

6. An EGO sensor is a 6.____
   A. device for measuring the oxygen concentration in automotive engine exhaust
   B. spark plug advance mechanism
   C. device for measuring crankshaft acceleration
   D. device for measuring the concentrations of various exhaust gases

7. What type of expander must be used under an oil ring? 7.____
   A. Step joint
   B. Diagonal joint
   C. Rigid
   D. Vented

8. Which of the following procedures is included in the performance of a compression test on a car engine? 8.____
   A. Perform entire test while engine is cold
   B. Test one cylinder at a time, with the corresponding plug temporarily removed

C. Crank for no more than two compression strokes
D. Block open throttle and choke

9. Air enters most Bosch electronic fuel injection systems through the   9.____
   A. oil bath cleaner   B. injector choke
   C. compressor line   D. injector manifold

10. The idler arm is attached to the _____ in a typical steering mechanism   10.____
    A. center link   B. tie rod   C. pitman arm   D. spindle

11. In a microprocessor-based control/diagnostic system, which type of crankshaft   11.____
    position sensor uses a disk having several holes?
    A. Optical   B. Ignition timing
    C. Hall-effect   D. Magnetic reluctance

12. In a mechanical fuel pump, pressure is maintained by means of   12.____
    A. a spring under the diaphragm   B. a motor
    C. a needle valve   D. rotating vanes

13. If a third pump is used in a fuel injection system, it is mounted   13.____
    A. on the fuel tank pump pickup tube
    B. in the line between the pickup tube and the pressure pump
    C. in the line between the pressure pump and fuel metering assembly
    D. at the fuel metering assembly

14. Which part of a cooling system thermostat opens and closes system valves?   14.____
    A. Pressure valve   B. Vacuum valve
    C. Bellows   D. Seater

15. What is the term for the front portion of a vehicle body or cab which partially   15.____
    encloses the dash panel and forms the windshield frame?
    A. Cowl   B. Hull   C. Head   D. Mask

16. How many digits make up a fault code used in a typical onboard computer   16.____
    diagnostic system?
    A. 1   B. 2   C. 3   D. 4

17. Which of the following should be checked FIRST when all brakes are dragging?   17.____
    A. Brake fluid level   B. Master cylinder compensating port
    C. Wheel cylinders   D. Brake pedal free travel

18. Which type of sensor measure is NOT capable of measuring the amount of   18.____
    air flowing through a fuel injection system?
    A. Speed-density   B. Plate
    C. Differential   D. Mass airflow

19. Which type of engine contains valves both in the head and the cylinder block?   19.____
    A. V-type   B. Two-stroke   C. F-head   D. L-head

20. Toe-in adjustments made by turning the adjusting sleeves on the tie rods in equal amounts in opposite directions are done to
    A. keep the wheels in balance
    B. keep the steering wheel centered
    C. avoid over-adjustment
    D. prevent excessive steering wheel play

21. Which of the following is NOT a possible cause of an overly lean fuel mixture that appears during a no-load carburetor mixture test?
    A. Plugged metering jets
    B. Stuck float
    C. Bad metering rod adjustment
    D. Manifold air leak

22. Which of the following is NOT a component of a pressure regulator used in fuel injection systems?
    A. Spring   B. Manifold   C. Diaphragm   D. Valve

23. During installation of the transmission, _____ can be used to turn the drive plate in order to connect it with the converter.
    A. the transmission unit
    B. the cranking motor
    C. the output shaft
    D. a wrench

24. Which type of bearing is NOT used on automotive drive axles?
    A. Sleeve   B. Roller   C. Taper   D. Ball

25. What is the term for the action or process of producing voltage by the relative motion of a magnetic field and a conductor?
    A. Induction
    B. Resistance
    C. Condensation
    D. Conduction

KEY (CORRECT ANSWERS)

1.	C		11.	A
2.	B		12.	A
3.	D		13.	D
4.	C		14.	C
5.	B		15.	A
6.	A		16.	B
7.	B		17.	D
8.	D		18.	C
9.	A		19.	C
10.	A		20.	B

21. C
22. B
23. B
24. A
25. A

EXAMINATION SECTION
TEST 1

DIRECTIONS: Each question or incomplete statement is followed by several suggested answers or completions. Select the one that BEST answers the question or completes the statement. *PRINT THE LETTER OF THE CORRECT ANSWER IN THE SPACE AT THE RIGHT.*

1. All of the following are probable sources of drivability problems EXCEPT the 1.____
   A. battery system
   B. engine condition
   C. ignition system
   D. fuel delivery system

2. Bending the _____ is the BEST way to adjust the ignition point contact. 2.____
   A. movable point arm
   B. breaker plate
   C. stationary point bracket
   D. pivot post

3. If an ignition system's breaker points are pitted, what should a mechanic check FIRST? 3.____
   A. Distributor condenser
   B. Distributor cap
   C. Circuit breaker
   D. Coil

4. Which cooling system component should be checked if a car's air conditioning blower operates properly but system output is still inadequate? 4.____
   A. Receiver-drier
   B. Evaporator core
   C. Temperature control
   D. Condenser

5. Excessive wear of brake linings will MOST likely cause 5.____
   A. stiff pedal
   B. drum scoring
   C. sticky wheel
   D. drag on brakes

6. The PCV valve is connected between the 6.____
   A. transmission and clutch
   B. injector and fuel pump
   C. exhaust pipe and intake manifold
   D. crankcase and intake manifold

7. What device is MOST effective for checking fuel pump performance? 7.____
   A. Vacuum switch
   B. Micrometer
   C. Voltmeter
   D. Stethoscope prod

8. For what purpose are the points of a conventional ignition system adjusted to increase the point gap? To 8.____
   A. advance the ignition timing
   B. increase the dwell angle
   C. decrease the dwell angle with no change in timing
   D. slow the ignition timing

9. Which of the following is NOT a type of temperature sensor used in microprocessor-based control/diagnostic systems?
   A. Wire-wound resistor
   B. Potentiometer
   C. Semiconductor resistor
   D. Thermistor

10. The various relationships and fundamental data associated with the use of an expert diagnostic system are known as the
    A. domain
    B. inference engine
    C. knowledge base
    D. interface

11. Which type of electric starting motor is often used because of its high starting torque?
    A. Compound-wound
    B. Shunt-wound
    C. Series-wound
    D. Capacitor

12. The auto system that is LEAST likely to cause engine operating problems is the _____ system.
    A. starting
    B. charging
    C. ignition
    D. fuel injection

13. Which device is capable of measuring volts, ohms, and amperes in solid-state electronic equipment?
    A. Digital multimeter
    B. Analog multimeter
    C. Jumper wires
    D. Continuity tester

14. Which of the following is a PROBABLE cause of backfiring in an intake manifold?
    A. Broken connecting rod
    B. Incorrect valve timing
    C. Sticky choke valve
    D. A lean cold-engine fuel mixture

15. An EGO sensor that is used in a microprocessor-based control/diagnostic system should NOT be used for control at a temperature less than _____ ºC.
    A. 0
    B. 100
    C. 200
    D. 300

16. What is the PROBABLE result of setting a spark plug gap more closely than normal?
    A. Smoother idling
    B. Hard starting
    C. Easier starting
    D. Rougher idling

17. Adjusting the _____ will help the steering of a car return to a straight position after cornering.
    A. toe-in
    B. toe-out
    C. caster
    D. camber

18. What is the basic work register in microcomputers that is used for automotive engine control an diagnostics?
    A. Status register
    B. Condition code register
    C. Brancher
    D. Accumulator

19. A car lacks power and a popping sound can be heard. 19.____
    What is the MOST likely cause?
    A. Shorted spark plug
    B. Uneven fuel supply
    C. Pitted breaker points
    D. Bad distributor timing

20. What is the term for the reinforcing ridge around a tire opening where it fits 20.____
    the wheel rim?
    A. Piping
    B. Binder
    C. Ram
    D. Bead

21. When checking a circuit for voltage drop, which of the following steps 21.____
    should be performed LAST?
    A. Select the voltmeter range just above the battery circuit
    B. Connect the positive lead of the voltmeter to the end of the wire closest to the battery
    C. Connect the negative lead of the voltmeter to the end of the wire farthest from the battery
    D. Switch on the circuit

22. If a battery frequently needs recharging, all of the following are probable 22.____
    causes EXCEPT
    A. poorly sized alternator drive pulley
    B. cell leakage
    C. poorly grounded voltage regulator
    D. sulfated battery

23. The diagnosis of intermittent failures in computer-based engine control systems 23.____
    is
    A. readily found using standard service bay equipment
    B. accomplished by displaying fault codes to the driver at the time of the failure
    C. sometimes accomplished by means of warning lamps on the dash display
    D. routinely accomplished with the onboard diagnostic capability of the control system

24. Before disassembling an air-release parking brake, it is necessary to FIRST 24.____
    A. remove the diaphragm clamp
    B. remove the quick release valve
    C. compress the apply spring
    D. fill the air reservoir

25. What is the MOST probable result of incorrect camber on car wheels? 25.____
    A. Abnormal tire wear along one side of the tread
    B. Damaged shocks
    C. Front-end shimmy
    D. Pulling to the side while braking

KEY (CORRECT ANSWERS)

1.	A		11.	C
2.	C		12.	D
3.	A		13.	A
4.	C		14.	D
5.	B		15.	D
6.	D		16.	D
7.	D		17.	B
8.	A		18.	D
9.	B		19.	B
10.	C		20.	D

21.	D
22.	B
23.	C
24.	C
25.	A

TEST 2

DIRECTIONS: Each question or incomplete statement is followed by several suggested answers or completions. Select the one that BEST answers the question or completes the statement. *PRINT THE LETTER OF THE CORRECT ANSWER IN THE SPACE AT THE RIGHT.*

1. The fuel pump in MOST fuel injection systems operates when the engine has oil pressure, and when the cranking speed is above _____ rpm.
    A. 50-75 B. 150-200 C. 500-1000 D. 1000-2000

    1.____

2. What is indicated by an occasional 3-4 inch drop in a vacuum gauge test?
    A. Slowed timing
    B. Carburetor failure
    C. Valve sticking
    D. Incorrectly gapped plugs

    2.____

3. All of the following are types of compressors used in automotive air conditioning systems EXCEPT
    A. 90-degree V
    B. 2-cylinder in-line
    C. axial
    D. hermetically sealed

    3.____

4. How much free action does a mechanic typically allow in the brake pedal?
    A. None B. 1/8 inch C. 1/4 inch D. 1/2 inch

    4.____

5. Tire wear that is concentrated on both sides of the tread is USUALLY the result of
    A. toe-out
    B. improper balance
    C. over-inflation
    D. under-inflation

    5.____

6. Temperature sensors that are a part of microprocessor-based electronic control/diagnostic systems use a type of semiconductor to measure temperature.
    The resistance of this semiconductor
    A. is always 100,000 ohms
    B. varies in direct proportion to temperature
    C. varies in inverse proportion to temperature
    D. varies in direct proportion to engine speed

    6.____

7. Using a test lamp across the breaker points, and with the ignition switch on, a mechanic will rotate the _____ to obtain the correct timing.
    A. distributor housing until the light goes out
    B. distributor housing until the light goes on
    C. engine until the light goes out
    D. engine until the light goes on

    7.____

8. In constant-flow fuel injection systems, pressure and circulation are provided by a(n)
    A. injection pump
    B. hydraulic line
    C. engine-driven rotary pump
    D. bellows

    8.____

9. Which of the following could NOT be determined by using an armature growler to test a starting motor armature?
   A. Insulation condition
   B. Location of short circuits
   C. Amount of resistance
   D. Commutator condition

10. What is measured by the crankcase angular position sensor in a microprocessor-based control/diagnostic system? The
    A. oil pressure angle
    B. angle between a line drawn through a crankshaft axis, a mark on the flywheel, and a reference line
    C. angle between the connecting rods and the crankshaft
    D. pitch angle of the crankshaft

11. If the insulation material used with a crimp conector on electric wiring is coded blue, what range of gauges is considered typical?
    A. 10-12   B. 12-18   C. 14-16   D. 18-22

12. Which type of pump is used ONLY as a supply pump in some fuel injection systems?
    A. Rotary   B. Diaphragm   C. Turbine   D. Roller

13. In what part of a car's air conditioning system does the refrigerant lose heat?
    A. Receiver   B. Compressor   C. Condenser   D. Evaporator

14. When disc brake pads are retracted so as not to make contact with the rotor surface, the amount of retraction
    A. is limited by the metering valve
    B. must be a minimum of 1/16 inch
    C. is affected by the piston return springs
    D. is affected by the piston seals

15. What is the term for the high curved portion of a cam that produce maximum valve lift?
    A. Peak
    B. Nose circle
    C. Flank circle
    D. Radial circle

16. The current from a battery generally flows to the alternator _____ when a vehicle is started?
    A. rectifier
    B. rotor winding
    C. stator windings
    D. commutator

17. If the cam dwell angle of a distributor is less than the specified minimum, it is LIKELY that the
    A. rubbing block will wear down
    B. distributor contact points will become pitted
    C. ignition coil output will increase at high engine speeds
    D. ignition timing will be off

18. The ignition quality of diesel fuel is measured against an index known as the   18._____
    A. lean parameter   B. cetane rating
    C. atomization ratio   D. vortex flow chart

19. During timing operations on a six-cylinder engine, a timing light should be connected to spark plug number   19._____
    A. 6   B. 4   C. 2   D. 1

20. In a microprocessor-based control/diagnostic system, which type of actuator serves to lower NO emissions?   20._____
    A. Ignition   B. Fuel metering
    C. EGR   D. EGO

21. What is indicated by a faintly vibrating needle during an engine vacuum test?   21._____
    A. Weak cylinders
    B. Leaking valves
    C. Obstruction in the exhaust system
    D. A broken piston ring

22. Which of the following components is NOT carried by a car's wheel knuckle assembly?   22._____
    A. Disc brake caliper mounting   B. Rotor
    C. Steering arm   D. Drum backing plate

23. If a mechanic hears a squealing noise during operation after the installation of an automatic transmission, what is the MOST likely source of the trouble?   23._____
    A. Rear bearing
    B. Regulator body mating surfaces
    C. Speedometer pinion
    D. Front pump drive sleeve or pump pinion

24. How should a mechanic decrease ignition point dwell?   24._____
    A. Rotate distributor body in the direction opposite the distributor shaft rotation
    B. Install weaker springs in the advance unit
    C. Increase the point gap
    D. Decrease the point gap

25. Before charging a battery, the battery ground cable should be disconnected at the battery.   25._____
    This is done in order to protect the
    A. alternator regulator   B. alternator diodes
    C. ignition coil   D. ignition module

4 (#2)
KEY (CORRECT ANSWERS)

1.	B		11.	C
2.	C		12.	C
3.	D		13.	C
4.	C		14.	D
5.	D		15.	B
6.	C		16.	B
7.	B		17.	D
8.	C		18.	B
9.	C		19.	D
10.	B		20.	C

21. A
22. B
23. D
24. A
25. B

TEST 3

DIRECTIONS: Each question or incomplete statement is followed by several suggested answers or completions. Select the one that BEST answers the question or completes the statement. *PRINT THE LETTER OF THE CORRECT ANSWER IN THE SPACE AT THE RIGHT.*

1. Against what part of a bearing do rollers or balls move? 1.____
   A. Sleeve   B. Spread   C. Knuckle   D. Race

2. All of the following are desirable characteristics of an EGO sensor used in a microprocessor-based electronic control/diagnostic system EXCEPT 2.____
   A. variable voltages with respect to exhaust temperature
   B. rapid switching of output voltage in response to exhaust gas oxygen changes
   C. abrupt change in voltage at the optimal combustion ratio
   D. large difference in sensor output voltage between rich and lean mixture conditions

3. A _____ joint is used to allow changes in the length of a propeller shaft. 3.____
   A. slip   B. shaft   C. universal   D. idler

4. Which of the following should be adjusted LAST in performing a tune-up on a car with a carburetor? 4.____
   A. Drive belts   B. Manifold heat control valve
   C. Carburetor   D. EGR valve

5. What device operates the plungers in a fuel injection pump? 5.____
   A. Pump camshaft   B. Belt
   C. Engine camshaft   D. Drive chain

6. Ignition of the combustion charge before the spark has formed across the plug electrodes is known as 6.____
   A. cold firing   B. knocking
   C. backfiring   D. preignition

7. Gear-train end play can be adjusted by 7.____
   A. changing the snap ring
   B. removing the clutch plates and installing retainer ring
   C. changing the selective thrust washer
   D. installing different pinion carriers

8. Unlike a conventional spark plug, a resistor plug will 8.____
   A. require higher voltage to function
   B. lengthen the capacitive part of the spark
   C. shrink the inductive part of the spark
   D. have an auxiliary air gap

9. Which measuring device is used MAINLY to check for voltage in a circuit while power is connected to the circuit?
   A. Digital multimeter
   B. Jumper wires
   C. Test lights
   D. Short finder

10. The flexible link that allows a suspension spring's length to change as it flexes is the
    A. shackle   B. strut   C. flange   D. trailing arm

11. What type of electrical connectors are generally used with component that are occasionally disconnected?
    A. Crimp   B. Bullet   C. Butt   D. Snap-splice

12. Which of the following device is NOT appropriate for checking the distributor automatic advance operations?
    A. Tachometer
    B. Voltmeter
    C. Vacuum pump
    D. Timing light

13. Engine bearings are commonly made from each of the following materials EXCEPT
    A. babbit
    B. case-hardened steel
    C. aluminum
    D. copper-lead mix

14. What should be used with bolts or screws on bearing surface designed to retain end thrust?
    A. Toggles
    B. Plain washers
    C. Thrust washers
    D. Lock washers

15. An automotive technician's basic measurement tool is the
    A. dial gauge
    B. feeler gauge
    C. telescopic gauge
    D. micrometer

16. What is used to attach a thrust plate to an engine block?
    A. Sheet metal screws
    B. Cap screws
    C. Wire spring clips
    D. Stamped metal clips

17. In an *expert* system for offboard computer diagnosis, which stage of knowledge acquisition in developing problem-solving rules occurs LAST?
    A. Implementation
    B. Identification
    C. Formalization
    D. Conceptualization

18. All of the following are possible causes of incorrect steering axis inclination and toe-out figures EXCEPT
    A. worn tires
    B. bent suspension
    C. worn ball joint
    D. worn steering parts

19. In a magnetic circuit, reluctance is a quality that is analogous to the _____ of an electrical circuit. 19.____
    A. capacitance
    B. voltage
    C. amperage
    D. resistance

20. Which device is used MAINLY to check for both open and short circuits? 20.____
    A. Short finder
    B. Jumper wires
    C. Test light
    D. Continuity tester

21. Which type of spring is MOST commonly used in automotive suspension systems? 21.____
    A. Torsion bar
    B. Coil spring
    C. Multiple-leaf spring
    D. Monoleaf spring

22. At the most basic level, the special type of language used to form microcomputer instructions, such as the ones used in automotive controls and diagnostics, is known as 22.____
    A. digital coding
    B. assembly language
    C. branch language
    D. fault coding

23. Most automotive camshafts are made from 23.____
    A. hardened alloy cast-iron
    B. steel'
    C. sintered iron
    D. tempered aluminum alloy

24. What progressively increasing quality should be indicated by a combustion tester as an engine accelerates from idle to cruising speeds? 24.____
    A. Higher rate of combustion
    B. Higher fuel-air ratio
    C. Lower thermal efficiency
    D. Leaner fuel mixture

25. What sizing process conforms metal to size by applying pressure? 25.____
    A. Stamping
    C. Burnishing
    C. Canting
    D. Beading

KEY (CORRECT ANSWERS)

1. D
2. A
3. A
4. C
5. A

6. D
7. C
8. C
9. C
10. A

11. B
12. B
13. B
14. C
15. D

16. B
17. A
18. A
19. D
20. D

21. B
22. B
23. A
24. D
25. B

EXAMINATION SECTION
TEST 1

DIRECTIONS: Each question or incomplete statement is followed by several suggested answers or completions. Select the one that BEST answers the question or completes the statement. *PRINT THE LETTER OF THE CORRECT ANSWER IN THE SPACE AT THE RIGHT.*

1. Of the following, the ACCEPTED method reconditioning a connected rod big end bore is to
   A. use a press to return the rod cap's diameter to standard size
   B. hone the bore to the next standard bearing oversize
   C. remove an amount of stock equal to the oversize from the split on the cap and then hone to standard size
   D. remove equal amounts of stock from both the cap and the rod at the split and then hone to standard size

1.____

2. After a cylinder that has a 3,000 inch bore has been honed, it is found to be tapered .003 inch. The removed aluminum piston is to be reused.
The piston should be
   A. cleaned and reinstalled
   B. knurled to increase the diameter of the entire skirt by .003 inch
   C. knurled at the top of the skirt to 3.001 inches and at the bottom of the skirt to 3.000 inches
   D. knurled at the top of the skirt to 3.000 inches and at the bottom of the skirt to 3.001 inches

2.____

3. Of the following, the PROPER sequence of operations in reconditioning valve seats for replacement valves that have oversize stems is to
   A. clean guide, ream guide, grind seat, and narrow seat
   B. clean guide, grind seat, ream guide, and narrow seat
   C. clean guide, narrow seat, grind seat, and ream guide
   D. grind seat, narrow seat, clean guide, and ream guide

3.____

4. An engine cylinder measures 3.520 inches at the bottom of the bore and 3.529 inches near the top. The factory bore measured .500 inches. New pistons to be installed after boring should GENERALLY be _____ inch oversize.
   A. .010   B. .020   C. .030   D. .050

4.____

5. An engine vacuum gauge used to measure intake-manifold pressure reads in
   A. pounds per square inch   B. inches of mercury
   C. pounds per square foot   D. ounces per inch

5.____

6. A hydrometer is being used to determine the specific gravity of a lead-acid storage battery which is at a temperature of 120 degrees Fahrenheit. The hydrometer gives a reading of 1.230.
The true specific gravity of the electrolyte at that temperature is MOST NEARLY
   A. 1.198   B. 1.205   C. 1.230   D. 1,246

7. The micrometer reading shown in the figure at the right is
   A. .525"
   B. .555"
   C. .562"
   D. .568"

8. In connection with the inspection and the turning or the grinding of brake drums on passenger cars, the BEST practice is to
   A. weld a cracked brake drum
   B. turn or grind the brake drum if it is out of round by more than .060 inches
   C. turn or grind the drums in pairs so that both front drums are the same diameter and both back drums are the same diameter
   D. increase the standard drum diameter to a maximum of 0.12 inches by turning or grinding

9. Of the following, the BEST tool to use to undercut mica on the commutator of a starting motor is a
   A. round nose chisel   B. hacksaw blade
   C. flat chisel   D. hand reamer

10. In a properly adjusted gasoline-powered automotive engine, the MAXIMUM percentage of the energy in the gasoline that can be transferred by the engine to the driving wheels of an automobile is MOST NEARLY
    A. 20%   B. 40%   C. 60%   D 80%

11. The lever length of a torque wrench is 24 inches.
    If a force of 50 pounds is properly applied at the handle when torquing a nut, the applied torque, in foot-pounds, is
    A. 50   B. 100   C. 400   D. 1200

12. While a fuel pump discharge pressure test is being performed, it is found that the pressure drops rapidly when the engine is stopped.
    This indicates a
    A. leaking pump-outlet valve   B. leaking suction hose
    C. leaking pump-diaphragm   D. normal condition

13. Of the following, the size of copper conductor which has the GREATEST current-carrying capacity is _____ AWG.
    A. 12   B. 8   C. 0   D. 000

14. Of the following, the statement pertaining to soldering which is MOST correct is:
    A. 60/40 solder would best be used for automotive-body repair
    B. Acid flux should not be used on copper parts such as radiators
    C. Main flux should be used on electrical connections
    D. The strength of the joint is not dependent on the joint thickness

15. When a car axle ring gear and pinion is being adjusted, the ring gear is moved toward the pinion
    This movement will change the tooth contact toward the _____ of the ring gear.
    A. toe   B. heel   C. dedendum   D. addendum

16. An automotive hydraulic brake system has a 1 inch diameter master cylinder and a 1.2 inch diameter wheel cylinder.
    The force applied by the wheel cylinder piston will be MOST NEARL _____ the force applied to the master cylinder piston.
    A. equal to   B. 1.44 times   C. 1.20 times   D. 0.833 times

17. Of the following, the statement regarding the rebuilding of hydraulic brake master cylinder which is MOST correct is that
    A. a light coat of grease should be applied to the parts during assembly to prevent rusting
    B. very light scratches in the bore can be polished out with emery cloth
    C. the parts must be cleaned in denatured alcohol
    D. deep scratches and pitting can be removed by honing to permit cylinder reuse

18. An automobile is standing still with the engine running and the clutch disengaged.
    Of the following, the part of the clutch assembly that is stationary is the
    A. flywheel   B. clutch cover
    C. pressure plate   D. clutch disk

19. Of the following liquids, the BEST one to use for cleaning automotive cylinders after they have been honed is
    A. hot, soapy water   B. gasoline
    C. turpentine   D. kerosene

20. In an in-line gasoline-powered automotive engine, the manifold heat-control valve is mounted to the
    A. intake manifold   B. cylinder head
    C. exhaust manifold   D. crankcase

KEY (CORRECT ANSWERS)

1.	D	11.	B
2.	C	12.	A
3.	A	13.	D
4.	C	14.	C
5.	B	15.	A
6.	D	16.	B
7.	C	17.	C
8.	C	18.	D
9.	B	19.	A
10.	A	20.	C

TEST 2

DIRECTIONS: Each question or incomplete statement is followed by several suggested answers or completions. Select the one that BEST answers the question or completes the statement. *PRINT THE LETTER OF THE CORRECT ANSWER IN THE SPACE AT THE RIGHT.*

1. When a ring ridge is removed from a cylinder, the BEST practice is to 1.____
   A. pull the piston from the cylinder before removing the ridge
   B. cut slightly below the level of the ridge into the cylinder
   C. blend the ridge area into the cylinder proper after removing the ridge
   D. leave a slight undercut in the cylinder wall after removing the ridge

2. The cleaning of ball and roller bearings is MOST effectively and safely 2.____
   accomplished by first wiping of surplus grease and oil and then
   A. soaking them in kerosene
   B. soaking them in gasoline
   C. soaking them in carbon-tetrachloride
   D. spinning them by using air pressure

3. The overheating of an engine would NOT likely be caused by 3.____
   A. a stuck manifold heat-control valve
   B. advanced ignition timing
   C. a lean carburetor mixture
   D a leaking cylinder-head gasket

4. The excitation of the field of an automotive alternator is provided by current 4.____
   from the
   A. stator   B. rotor   C. diode   D. battery

5. A clicking or tapping noise which persists after the engine has warmed up is 5.____
   USUALLY
   A. loose fan belts   B. loose main bearings
   C. defective valve lifters   D. worn piston pins

6. Compression piston rings for gasoline-powered engines are MOST generally 6.____
   made from
   A. copper   B. high-quality cast iron
   C. aluminum   D. tempered steel

7. A vehicle has the coil spring mounted between the frame and the lower 7.____
   suspension arm.
   The front end ball joints on this vehicle may be checked by
   A. jacking up the lower suspension arm
   B. jacking up the frame
   C. blocking the upper suspension arm and jacking the frame
   D. jacking between the suspension arms

8. The capacity of a conventional automobile ignition system condenser is MOST NEARLY
   A. 0.02 microfarads
   B. 0.2 microfarads
   C. 0.2 farads
   D. 2.0 farads

9. Of the following, the BEST sequence of operations to follow when removing grease and scale from carburetor and fuel pump parts would be
   A. degreasing soak, alkaline soak, water rinse, acid dip, hot water rise
   B. acid dip, degreasing soak, alkaline rinse, water rinse
   C. acid dip, water rinse, alkaline dip, water rinse, degreasing soak, water rinse
   D. acid dip, water rinse, alkaline dip, degreasing soak, acid rinse, water rinse

10. A ballast-type resistor in the primary circuit of a conventional automotive ignition system will
    A. deliver constant reduced voltage to the soil
    B. be bypassed at high engine speeds
    C. increase coil primary voltage at low engine speeds
    D. decrease in resistance value as its temperature increases

11. In order to minimize the coil load when installing a coil in an automobile in which the positive terminal of the battery is grounded, the coil should be wired with its
    A. *negative* terminal connected to the distributor
    B. *positive* terminal connected to the distributor
    C. *negative* terminal connected to the ground
    D. *positive* terminal connected to the positive battery terminal through the starter switch

12. Loose connecting-rod bearings are USUALLY indicated by a
    A. light rap or clatter when the engine is running with a light load at approximately 25 mph
    B. metallic rattle when the engine is idling unevenly
    C. clicking noise when the engine is cold
    D. sharp metallic double knock when the engine is idling

13. An ignition system is not functioning properly. In order to check the system, the high tension wire from the coil is held close to a ground at the same time as the ignition points are opened and closed.
    If a good spark occurs from the high tension wire to the ground, it would indicate that the problem is NOT with the
    A. motor
    B. condenser
    C. spark plug wires
    D. distributer cap

14. When an automotive generator regulator is adjusted, a 1/4 ohm resistor is inserted in the line from the batter terminal of the regulator to the battery. This permits adjustment to be made to the
    A. current regulator
    B. circuit breaker
    C. voltage regulator
    D. field relay

15. A tire showing excessive wear on one side of the tread indicate IMPROPER 15.____
    A. caster B. camber C. toe-in D. tire pressure

16. Front wheel roller bearings should be adjusted to 16.____
    A. .001 to .003 inch end play
    B. .010 inch end play
    C. a 20-foot-pound torque on nut
    D. a mild pressure

17. In automotive air conditioning systems, the MOST commonly used refrigerant is 17.____
    A. dichlorodifluoromethane (12)
    B. carbon dioxide (CO_2)
    C. ammonia (NH_3)
    D. sulfur dioxide (SO_2)

18. In an automotive air conditioning system, the opening of the expansion valve is controlled PRIMARILY by the 18.____
    A. temperature within the vehicle
    B. evaporator temperature
    C. condenser temperature
    D. condenser pressure

19. When the front end of a vehicle with independent suspension is aligned, the front of the upper suspension arm is moved away from the center line of the vehicle. 19.____
    The adjustment will change
    A. the caster only, in the positive direction
    B. both the caster and the camber, in the positive direction
    C. both the caster and the camber, in the negative direction
    D. the caster in the positive direction and the camber in the negative direction

20. The vapor discharge valve in a diaphragm-type fuel pump normally 20.____
    A. controls pump discharge pressure
    B. is installed directly after the fuel outlet valve
    C. opens with rising fuel temperature
    D. is vented to the carburetor air cleaner to minimize pollution

KEY (CORRECT ANSWERS)

1. C	6. B	11. B	16. A
2. A	7. A	12. A	17. A
3. B	8. B	13. B	18. B
4. D	9. A	14. C	19. B
5. C	10. A	15. B	20. C

TEST 3

DIRECTIONS: Each question or incomplete statement is followed by several suggested answers or completions. Select the one that BEST answers the question or completes the statement. *PRINT THE LETTER OF THE CORRECT ANSWER IN THE SPACE AT THE RIGHT.*

1. In an automotive ignition system, the distributor dwell 1.____
   A. is governed by the ignition point gap
   B. is equal to 360 degrees divided by the number of cylinders
   C. is equal to the number of degrees of rotation that the points are open
   D. will decrease with increasing centrifugal advance

2. When an oscilloscope indicates too short a dwell in the ignition system, the MOST probable reason is that the 2.____
   A. points are set too far apart   B. points are set too close together
   C. degrees of dwell are too great   D. coil output is too high

3. An automobile with a properly operating conventional assembly has one rear wheel jacked up. The engine is running in *drive* with 20 mph indicated on the speedometer. 3.____
   The MOST correct statement concerning this situation is that the
   A. vehicle will move off the jack because it has been driven by the wheel on the ground
   B. jacked rear wheel is turning at 20 mph road speed
   C. jacked rear wheel is turning at 40 mph road speed
   D. jacked rear wheel is turning at 10 mph road speed

4. Of the following tubing materials and connections, the BEST one to use when replacing hydraulic brake lines is 4.____
   A. steel tubing with compression fittings
   B. steel tubing with double-lap flare
   C. steel tubing with single-lap flare
   D. half hard copper tubing with double-lap flare

5. In a single-type brake master cylinder, a plugged compensating port would be suspected if 5.____
   A. the brakes drag
   B. the brake pedal is very low
   C. the brakes fade
   D. excessive pedal pressure is required

6. The PRIMARY purpose of the diverter valve in an AIR (Thermactor) emission control system is to 6.____
   A. prevent exhaust gases from reaching the pump
   B. cut off the flow of air to the exhaust manifold when the manifold pressure decreases suddenly

2 (#3)

    C. provide maximum ignition advance when decelerating in order to prevent backfiring
    D. provide advance timing during prolonged idling

7. An automotive clutch throw-out bearing   7.____
    A. is mounted on the transmission input shaft
    B. is mounted on the transmission bearing retainer
    C. rotates when the clutch is engaged
    D. must be in continuous contact with the clutch release levers

8. An advantage of using a clutch that utilizes a diaphragm spring instead of coil spring is that such a clutch eliminates the need for   8.____
    A. a throw-out bearing   B. a pivot ring
    C. a throw-out fork   D. clutch release levers

9. Of the following statements concerning disc brakes, the one which is INCORRECT IS: 9.____
    A. All scoring of the disc must be ground out before the pads are replaced
    B. It is necessary to pump the brake pedal after changing the pads in order to make the brake function
    C. The piston seal automatically adjusts the pads to the disc clearance
    D. The run-out of the disc may not exceed .003"

10. Turning the carburetor idle aid adjusting screw outward will   10.____
    A. enrich the idle-air-fuel mixture
    B. lean the idle air-fuel mixture
    C. close down on the main throttle valve
    D. reduce the idle rpm

11. The function of an automotive choke vacuum break piston or diaphragm is to   11.____
    A. attempt to close the choke when the engine is accelerated
    B. apply an additional torque on the choke to assist the thermostatic spring in keeping the choke closed
    C. attempt to open the choke when the engine is accelerated
    D. act opposite to the incoming air pressure on the throat plate

12. A brake assembly has two single-ended cylinders, one on the top and one on the bottom. The opposite ends of the brake shoes are anchored to the backing plate.
This type of brake would be considered as being   12.____
    A. a duo-servo   B. self-energizing
    C. self-centering   D. a uni-servo

13. An exhaust gas analyzer operating on the principle of thermal conductivity of the exhaust gas reads 12.0/1.0. This indicates that the   13.____
    A. mixture is lean
    B. mixture is rich
    C. carburetor setting conforms to Sec. 207 of the Federal Clean Air Act
    D. mixture has 12% excess air

14. When adjusting a recirculating ball, manual type, steering gear,
    A. the worm bearing preload adjustment should be made with the steering wheel in the *straight-ahead* position
    B. the pitman shaft preload adjustment should be made with the steering wheel in the *straight-ahead* position
    C. the pitman shaft preload should be made prior to worm bearing preload adjustments
    D. both worm bearing and pitman shaft preload adjustments should be made with the steering wheel one turn from the center

15. The device used in automatic transmissions to provide the force required to engage a band clutch is called a
    A. booster   B. shifter   C. spool   D. servo

16. The function of the governor valve in an automatic transmission NORMALLY is to
    A. maintain constant pressure in the control circuits
    B. provide proportionally increasing pressure to the shift valve as road speed increases
    C. provide pressure to the shift valve at a predetermined road speed
    D. increase band pressure during heavy acceleration

17. On many automatic transmissions, the function performed by the TV linkage is carried out by use of a
    A. vacuum modulator   B. servo
    C. dashpot   D. compensator valve

18. A centrifugal vacuum type of speed governor
    A. is mounted between the carburetor and intake manifold
    B. would not govern speed if the air lines were removed or tampered
    C. would close the throttle if the air lines were removed or tampered
    D. has a speed-control adjustment which is made at the carburetor

19. In an air brake system, a limiting quick release valve is NORMALLY found in
    A. the line to the front brake chamber
    B. the line to the rear brake chamber
    C. series with the trailer protection valve
    D. the governor control

20. Air-actuated brake shoes are adjusted by
    A. adjusting the length of the chamber piston rod
    B. shifting the brake chamber along the slotted holes in the mount
    C. moving the cam on the splined shaft
    D. rotating the camshaft to move the shoe closer to the brake drum

KEY (CORRECT ANSWERS)

1. A   11. A
2. A   12. B
3. C   13. A
4. B   14. B
5. A   15. D

6. B   16. C
7. B   17. A
8. D   18. B
9. A   19. A
10. B   20. D

EXAMINATION SECTION
TEST 1

DIRECTIONS: Each question or incomplete statement is followed by several suggested answers or completions. Select the one that BEST answers the question or completes the statement. *PRINT THE LETTER OF THE CORRECT ANSWER IN THE SPACE AT THE RIGHT.*

1. When servicing a fleet of Cat D8 tractors, the PROPER method of refueling is to

    A. top off the tanks before each shift
    B. leave some room for expansion when filling at the start of each shift
    C. top off the tanks at the end of each shift
    D. use portable pumps for filling where possible

2. In order to PROPERLY install a flat metal lock, used with a cap screw, the lock should be bent

    A. in two 45-degree bends
    B. over a curved surface
    C. to catch the inside of the cap screw
    D. sharply on a flat surface of the cap screw

3. Bearings which require heat for installation should be heated in

    A. lubricating oil to 250° F
    B. diesel fuel to 300° F
    C. lubricating oil to 400° F
    D. diesel fuel to 400° F

4. A standard torque down test on a bolt, to be used with standard heat treated bolts and stud nuts in assembling Cat equipment, is _____ foot-lbs.

    A. 110 ± 115   B. 265 ± 50   C. 800 ± 400   D. 1500 ± 200

5. When assembling duo-cone floating seals in a Cat D8 tractor, the toric sealing ring SHOULD be assembled with

    A. a thumb and finger
    B. a torque wrench
    C. a 2000 PSI hydraulic press
    D. regular pliers and a screwdriver

6. When servicing the hydraulic system of a Cat D8 tractor and 8S bulldozer, the mechanic SHOULD put the control levers in the _____ position.

    A. hold   B. float   C. release   D. neutral

7. The one of the following conditions that would NOT be a possible direct cause of a Cat diesel engine in a crawler tractor overheating is

    A. low coolant level
    B. low fuel pressure
    C. corroded water pump
    D. leaking precombustion chamber gaskets

8. When a Cat D8 tractor water temperature regulator is being checked for proper opening temperature, the regulator SHOULD start to open at

   A. 120° F B. 144° F C. 152° F D. 164° F

9. In a Cat D8 tractor, the water pump is sealed with a _____ seal.

   A. duo-cone
   B. leather-faced bellows
   C. carbon-faced bellows
   D. O-ring

10. The sealed pressure overflow assembly in a Cat D8 tractor's radiator assembly has the PRIMARY purpose of

    A. maintaining a constant coolant level
    B. preventing air from entering
    C. preventing coolant from leaking out
    D. maintaining a constant pressure during tractor operation

11. The MAIN oil pump on a Cat D8 engine is driven by a

    A. gear from the timing gear train
    B. belt from the fan belt assembly
    C. gear from the flywheel
    D. series of gears from the camshaft

12. The engine oil pump on a Cat D8 tractor is located in the front section of the oil pan and can be worked on by

    A. removing the rear section of the oil pan
    B. removing the timing gear case
    C. removing the oil pan covers
    D. disassembling the bell housing

13. In the case of a Cat D8 power shift tractor transmission failure, a CRITICAL requirement before returning the tractor to operation is to install a new

    A. engine oil cooler
    B. transmission oil cooler core assembly
    C. engine filter element
    D. transmission air cleaner

14. Valve rotation is a term which refers to the

    A. removal and reassembly of all valves
    B. turn of the valves during engine operation
    C. placement of the valves in another location in the firing sequence
    D. normal tune-up procedure for the valves

15. The end gap in a newly-installed piston ring SHOULD be measured with a _____ gage.

    A. feeler B. ring C. plug D. surface

16. Pistons which have been removed from a diesel engine for repair and replacement should be replaced IF

    A. they are scored above the top compressing ring
    B. the ring grooves are carboned up
    C. they are badly scored below the compressing ring
    D. the top ring is worn

17. When adjusting the alternator for proper voltage on a newly-styled power-shift Cat D8 tractor, a mechanic SHOULD use a(n)

    A. ammeter and a pair of pliers
    B. voltmeter and a socket wrench
    C. voltmeter and a screwdriver
    D. voltage regulator and a screwdriver

18. The one of the following phrases that does NOT accurately describe the type of power-shift transmission in a 46A power-shift Cat D8 tractor is

    A. planetary drive
    B. oil actuated
    C. constant mesh
    D. hydraulically engaged

19. When checking to insure proper PSI settings on the steering clutch actuating pistons, the steering clutches of a Cat D8 tractor SHOULD be

    A. *engaged* with the engine at full throttle
    B. *disengaged* with the engine at low idle
    C. *engaged* with the engine at low idle
    D. *disengaged* with the engine at full throttle

20. The hydraulic pump on the Cat D8 tractor power-shift transmission supplies oil to the transmission

    A. only
    B. and torque converter only
    C. , torque converter, and steering clutches only
    D. , torque converter, steering clutches, and brakes

21. When the track on a Cat D8 tractor is being assembled, the pad belts should have a torqued down pressure of AT LEAST _____ PSI.

    A. 50 ±10   B. 100 ± 20   C. 150 ± 30   D. 250 ± 50

22. The seals between the pin and bushings of the Cat D8 tractor are of the _____ type.

    A. bellows
    B. O-ring
    C. duo-cone
    D. leather-faced

23. As a safety measure, before removing the master pin on the tracks of any track-type tractor, it is BEST to

    A. remove all pressure from the hydraulic track adjustor
    B. have the idler in the up position
    C. have the idler in the down position
    D. remove the duo-cone seals

24. When tracks on a Cat D8 are properly adjusted to minimize wear, the sag between the carrier-roller and idler should be no more than

    A. ¼" to ½"
    B. ½" to 1½"
    C. 1" to 1½"
    D. 1½" to 2½"

25. To change the front idler on a tractor from the low to the high position, a mechanic MUST rotate the

    A. bearing 180° only
    B. bearing and idler 180°
    C. idler 180° only
    D. shaft 180° only

26. The turbo-charger on any diesel engine performs the BASIC function of _____ air pressure.

    A. *decreasing* the intake
    B. *increasing* the intake
    C. *decreasing* the exhaust
    D. *increasing* the exhaust

27. The PRIMARY reason for removal of carbon from a turbine wheel of an automotive-type turbo-charger is to

    A. prevent hot spots
    B. prevent loss of air pressure
    C. increase manifold temperature
    D. prevent dynamic imbalance

28. If a timing gear has 120 teeth and turns at 700 RPM, the speed that a 420 tooth gear mated to it will turn at is _____ RPM.

    A. 150 B. 200 C. 500 D. 2450

29. The engine hydraulic system and transmission on a certain type of tractor use the same type oil. This oil is delivered in 55 gal. drums.
    How many drums are needed to make all three changes on ten of these tractors whose capacities are the following:
        Engine .... 58 quarts
        Transmission .... 70 quarts
        Hydraulic system .... 22 gallons

    A. 100 drums
    B. 50 drums
    C. 54 drums
    D. 10 drums

30. A new shop layout requires the following:
        1,000 sq. ft. for tool room
        3,000 sq. ft. for parts room
        10,000 sq. ft. for service bays
        5,500 sq. ft. for isles
    The building should be AT LEAST _____ yards wide and _____ yards long.

    A. 10; 70 B. 20; 70 C. 25; 70 D. 30; 70

31. After moving a track-type tractor equipped with a bulldozer into an area for servicing, the operator should ALWAYS

    A. lower the blade
    B. ground the scarifier
    C. tilt the blade forward
    D. lower the bowl

32. The diameter of the main journals on the crankshaft of a new series Cat D8 tractor is 4.259 to 4.261 inches.
    The MAXIMUM allowable main-bearing clearance should be no more than

    A. .003   B. .005   C. .007   D. .010

33. NORMAL procedure in removing the liners from a wet-type diesel engine would require the use of a

    A. puller ring and 4 lb. hammer
    B. brass puller rod and hammer
    C. manual puller
    D. hydraulic puller

34. When the crankshaft of a Cat D8 is worn sufficiently to require regrinding and standard oversized bearings are used, the shaft should be turned down to EITHER _____ undersize.

    A. .025" or .050"
    B. .010" or .020"
    C. .050" or 0.10"
    D. .001" or .002"

35. To insure MAXIMUM cable life on a crawler-drawn scraper, the mechanic should

    A. grease the cable with engine oil
    B. replace the cable when any part is worn
    C. pull out a few feet of cable when worn
    D. grease the sheave grooves with gear lub

36. PROPER procedure in filling a large earthmoving tire with air should include use of

    A. hand-held air lines
    B. steel hammers
    C. self-attaching air chucks
    D. chains and lifting hooks

37. The bearing journals on a standard six-cylinder diesel engine with a four-stroke firing cycle are spaced _____ apart.

    A. 30°   B. 60°   C. 90°   D. 120°

38. The BASIC advantage of using an alternator over a generator on an automotive diesel engine is that the alternator

    A. provides alternating current
    B. provides full voltage at idle speeds
    C. provides better starting in cold weather
    D. is easier to adjust

39. The normal SAE definition of net flywheel horsepower includes a requirement that the engine be running at rated RPM and that it be equipped with

   A. no attachments
   B. fan, generator and no water pump or radiator
   C. fan, generator, water pump and radiator
   D. fan, generator, water pump and no radiator

40. GENERALLY, a diesel engine in a tractor or loader is operated with its compression ratio _____ as that of a gasoline engine.

   A. four times as great
   B. the same
   C. twice as great
   D. five times as great

KEY (CORRECT ANSWERS)

1. C	11. A	21. D	31. A
2. D	12. C	22. C	32. C
3. A	13. B	23. A	33. D
4. D	14. B	24. C	34. A
5. A	15. A	25. B	35. C
6. A	16. A	26. B	36. C
7. B	17. C	27. D	37. B
8. D	18. C	28. B	38. B
9. C	19. B	29. D	39. C
10. D	20. D	30. D	40. C

TEST 2

DIRECTIONS: Each question or incomplete statement is followed by several suggested answers or completions. Select the one that BEST answers the question or completes the statement. *PRINT THE LETTER OF THE CORRECT ANSWER IN THE SPACE AT THE RIGHT.*

1. In a normal automotive and earthmoving application, a STANDARD commercial diesel engine ignites the fuel at

    A. 450° F   B. 900° F   C. 1450° F   D. 212° F

2. The one of the following that is NOT normally used as a starting system for automotive and earthmoving diesel engines in mobile equipment is

    A. a gasoline starting engine
    B. a direct electric starting motor
    C. air pressure
    D. a hydraulic motor

3. A four-cycle diesel engine has a firing sequence BEST described as

    A. power, scavenging, compression, stroke, and firing
    B. intake, compression, firing, power, and exhaust
    C. exhaust, compression, firing, and power
    D. exhaust, intake, firing, and power

4. When a diesel engine is equipped with a gasoline starting engine, the compression release control is opened

    A. *after* the main engine is turning over
    B. *before* the main engine is turning over
    C. *after* the starting engine is at full RPM
    D. *after* the starting engine is turning the diesel engine

5. The one of the following that is NOT a normal method used to help start a diesel engine in cold weather is

    A. dip stick heaters   B. glow plugs
    C. manifold heating   D. ethylene glycol injection

6. The BASIC reason for cam grinding a diesel engine cylinder is so that

    A. the piston rings will seat better
    B. the piston will not stick in the lines
    C. it will become more nearly round when running hot
    D. it will not be as hard to turn over when starting

7. The turbo-charger used on a GM diesel engine is BEST described as _____ driven.

    A. exhaust-gas   B. intake-gas
    C. mechanically   D. hydraulically

8. When removing an 8S hydraulic bulldozer from a Cat D8 tractor for tractor servicing, the bulldozer lift cylinders SHOULD be secured with

   A. hanger link, bolt, nut, and lockwasher
   B. master pin and link
   C. bracket and hose coupler
   D. *J* bolt clamps and pins

9. On an earthmoving machine, the hydraulic crossover valve has a function of being able to use

   A. two circuits with one valve
   B. one circuit with two valves
   C. both circuits at the same time
   D. varying pressures in the same circuit

10. When making adjustments on a clutch of a double-drum cable control mounted on a Cat D8 tractor used for pulling a scraper, a mechanic should ALWAYS

    A. disengage the clutch
    B. shut off the engine
    C. loosen the clamp nut and clutch-engaging nut lock bolt
    D. move the clutch-engaging rod one inch beyond the *clutch engaged* mark

11. The engine oil that should be used for a Cat D8 tractor using a Cat engine is

    A. superior lubricant Series 1
    B. superior lubricant Series 3
    C. standard multiviscosity Series 2
    D. standard multiviscosity Series 1

12. The engine oil that should be used for a Cummins diesel engine is

    A. superior lubricant Series 1
    B. superior lubricant Series 3
    C. standard multiviscosity Series 2
    D. standard multiviscosity Series 1

13. When the sulphur content of the diesel fuel used in a Cat diesel engine goes above 0.4%, the oil change period should be changed from _____ to _____ Service Meter Hours.

    A. 500; 300   B. 250; 125   C. 500; 100   D. 250; 100

14. In a four-stroke diesel engine, each piston fires every _____ of the crankshaft.

    A. revolution   B. 2 revolutions
    C. 4 revolutions   D. ½ revolution

15. In an automotive engine, when the alternator is functioning properly and a low charging rate is experienced, the mechanic should check the

    A. magneto   B. generator
    C. regulator   D. battery cables

16. The PROPER equipment to use in removing a sprocket from a Cat D8 tractor is a

    A. hydraulic puller
    B. chain hoist and fall
    C. socket wrench
    D. bar and rubber hammer

17. The PROPER amount of pressure for installation of a Cat D8 sprocket on its splines is _____ to _____ tons.

    A. 10; 20   B. 20; 25   C. 35; 40   D. 60; 65

18. Segmented sprocket teeth on a tractor makes it EASIER to

    A. make pin contact
    B. make bushing contact
    C. clean the tracks
    D. assemble the tracks

19. The one of the following that is NOT an OSHA requirement while working on heavy construction machinery is wearing

    A. safety glasses
    B. safety shoes
    C. a hard hat
    D. loose clothing

20. The one of the following that is the BEST way to store oily rags is

    A. in a closed metal container
    B. piled in a corner of the repair shop
    C. in a covered wooden box
    D. piled under a work bench

21. The reason for NOT going to full throttle immediately when starting a turbo-charged automotive-type diesel engine is to

    A. allow the bearings to warm up
    B. prevent the engine oil from diluting
    C. ensure bearing lubrication
    D. ensure equal heating of the turbine blades

22. A Cummins diesel engine model designated as NTA-370 is BEST described as

    A. naturally aspirated, torque adjusted, and 370 max. horsepower
    B. four valve head, turbo-charged, after cooled, and 370 max. horsepower
    C. naturally aspirated, turbo-charged, after cooled, and 370 max. horsepower
    D. 16 valve turbo-charged intercooled and 370 max. horsepower

23. Of the following phrases, the one that does NOT describe a common arrangement common in a V-type automotive diesel engine is

    A. two cam shafts
    B. two timing gear trains
    C. one crankshaft
    D. two exhaust manifolds

24. The normal oil temperature range for a Cummins diesel engine is MOST NEARLY

    A. 140 to 160° F
    B. 140 to 220° F
    C. 180 to 290° F
    D. 180 to 225° F

25. The one of the following that is NOT a safety requirement when using ether as a cold weather starting aid on a diesel engine is never

   A. spray directly into the manifold
   B. use near an open flame
   C. use with a preheater
   D. use with a flame-thrower

Questions 26-28.

DIRECTIONS: Questions 26 through 28, inclusive, are to be answered in accordance with the following paragraph.

The following is a set of instructions on engine shut-down procedure: When an engine equipped with an electric shut-down valve is used, the engine can be shut down completely by turning off the switch key on installations equipped with an electric shut-down valve, or by turning the manual shut-down valve lever. Turning off the switch key which controls the electric shut-down valve always stops the engine unless the override button on the shut-down valve has been locked in the open position. If the manual override on the electric shut-down valve is being used, turn the button full counterclockwise to stop the engine.

CAUTION: Never leave the switch key or the override button in the valve open or run position when the engine is not running. With overhead tanks, this would allow fuel to drain into the cylinder, causing hydraulic lock.

26. According to the above paragraph, it becomes apparent that if an engine does not stop when the electric shut-down valve switch key is shut off,

   A. an open manual switch is present
   B. the override button is locked in the closed position
   C. a closed manual switch is functioning
   D. the override button is locked in the open position

27. When using an engine equipped with an electric shut-down valve,

   A. no alternate method is available
   B. a manual method is not present
   C. a manual override can shut the engine down
   D. a manual override will not work

28. As a matter of caution, the switch key in the closed position or the override button in the stop position will

   A. assist in keeping fuel in the cylinders
   B. prevent fuel from flooding the cylinder cavities
   C. assist in producing hydraulic lock
   D. aid fuel dilution

29. A detroit diesel engine with the designation of 8V-53N is BEST described as an _____ with a cubic inch displacement of _____ cu. in.

   A. 8 cylinder V-type; 212
   B. 16 cylinder V-type; 424
   C. 8 cylinder N-type; 848
   D. 8 cylinder V-type; 424

30. Diesel engine fuels are rated by number from 1 to 4. The relationship between the flash point of a fuel and its number is that, as the flash point

   A. *increases*, the numbers either increase or decrease, depending on the volatility of the fuel
   B. *increases*, the numbers increase
   C. *decreases*, the numbers increase
   D. *decreases*, the numbers decrease

31. In order to locate a misfiring cylinder in a GM diesel engine, the valve cover should be removed and each cylinder checked by

   A. holding down the injector follower
   B. using a pressure gage
   C. regapping the plugs
   D. increasing the fuel to each cylinder one at a time

32. When a GM diesel engine is being serviced, the NORMAL interval for cleaning the cooling system is _____ hours or _____ miles.

   A. 200; 600
   B. 500; 15,000
   C. 1000; 30,000
   D. 1500; 60,000

33. The one of the following situations that will NOT cause the automatic electrical shutdown system on a GM engine to stop the engine is

   A. a loss of coolant
   B. a loss of oil pressure
   C. overspeeding
   D. a decrease in R.P.M.

34. A medium range thermostat for a Cummins diesel engine NORMALLY has a range of

   A. 170 to 185° F
   B. 140 to 160° F
   C. 180 to 195° F
   D. 120 to 145° F

35. When filling a diesel engine cooling system, the mix required is 80% antifreeze and 20% water. You are required to fill seven systems containing 30 gals. each.
   The number of 5 gal. cans of antifreeze that are required is MOST NEARLY

   A. 210   B. 168   C. 34   D. 26

36. When changing a *throw-away* type fuel filter element on a Cummins diesel engine, the housing should be tightened

   A. with a torque wrench
   B. with a socket wrench
   C. with a hand clamp and a screwdriver
   D. by hand

37. Hydraulic hoses are NORMALLY rated by _____ rating.

   A. cord ply
   B. stul mesh
   C. P.S.I.
   D. C.F.M.

38. The starting system of a diesel engine is actuated by two 12-volt batteries in parallel. 38.___
    The electric current produced is _____ volt _____.

    A. 12; D.C.   B. 24; D.C.   C. 12; A.C.   D. 24; A.C.

39. Fan belt checks and adjustments, using the suggested A,B,C Cummins maintenance 39.___
    manual method, are FIRST required at the _____ interval.

    A. A   B. B   C. C   D. D

40. When two 12-volt 450-ampere-hour batteries are installed in series, the system is rated 40.___
    as _____ volt-_____ amp hour.

    A. 24; 450   B. 12; 900   C. 12; 450   D. 24; 900

KEY (CORRECT ANSWERS)

1. C	11. B	21. C	31. A
2. D	12. A	22. B	32. C
3. B	13. B	23. B	33. D
4. B	14. B	24. D	34. A
5. D	15. C	25. A	35. C
6. C	16. A	26. D	36. D
7. C	17. D	27. C	37. C
8. A	18. D	28. B	38. A
9. A	19. D	29. D	39. B
10. B	20. A	30. B	40. A

WORK SCHEDULING

EXAMINATION SECTION
TEST 1

DIRECTIONS: Each question or incomplete statement is followed by several suggested answers or completions. Select the one that BEST answers the question or completes the statement. *PRINT THE LETTER OF THE CORRECT ANSWER IN THE SPACE AT THE RIGHT.*

Questions 1-6.

DIRECTIONS: Questions 1 through 6 are to be answered SOLELY on the basis of the information given in the ELEVATOR OPERATORS' WORK SCHEDULE shown below.

ELEVATOR OPERATORS' WORK SCHEDULE				
Operator	Hours of Work	A.M. Relief Period	Lunch Hour	P.M. Relief Period
Anderson	8:30-4:30	10:20-10:30	12:00-1:00	2:20-2:30
Carter	8:00-4:00	10:10-10:20	11:45-12:45	2:30-2:40
Daniels	9:00-5:00	10:20-10:30	12:30-1:30	3:15-3:25
Grand	9:30-5:30	11:30-11:40	1:00-2:00	4:05-4:15
Jones	7:45-3:45	9:45-9:55	11:30-12:30	2:05-2:15
Lewis	9:45-5:45	11:40-11:50	1:15-2:15	4:20-4:30
Nance	8:45-4:45	10:50-11:00	12:30-1:30	3:05-3:15
Perkins	8:00-4:00	10:00-10:10	12:00-1:00	2:40-2:50
Russo	7:45-3:45	9:30-9:40	11:30-12:30	2:10-2:20
Smith	9:45-5:45	11:45-11:55	1:15-2:15	4:05-4:15

1. The two operators who are on P.M. relief at the SAME time are   1._____

   A. Anderson and Daniels B. Carter and Perkins
   C. Jones and Russo D. Grand and Smith

2. Of the following, the two operators who have the SAME lunch hour are   2._____

   A. Anderson and Perkins B. Daniels and Russo
   C. Grand and Smith D. Nance and Russo

3. At 12:15, the number of operators on their lunch hour is   3._____

   A. 3 B. 4 C. 5 D. 6

4. The operator who has an A.M. relief period right after Perkins and a P.M. relief period right before Perkins is   4._____

   A. Russo B. Nance C. Daniels D. Carter

5. The number of operators who are scheduled to be working at 4:40 is   5._____

   A. 5 B. 6 C. 7 D. 8

6. According to the schedule, it is MOST correct to say that 6.____
    A. no operator has a relief period during the time that another operator has a lunch hour
    B. each operator has to wait an identical amount of time between the end of lunch and the beginning of P.M. relief period
    C. no operator has a relief period before 9:45 or after 4:00
    D. each operator is allowed a total of 1 hour and 20 minutes for lunch hour and relief periods

---

KEY (CORRECT ANSWERS)

1. D
2. A
3. C
4. D
5. A
6. D

TEST 2

DIRECTIONS: Each question or incomplete statement is followed by several suggested answers or completions. Select the one that BEST answers the question or completes the statement. *PRINT THE LETTER OF THE CORRECT ANSWER IN THE SPACE AT THE RIGHT.*

Questions 1-7.

DIRECTIONS: Questions 1 through 7 are to be answered SOLELY on the basis of the time sheet and instructions given below.

The following time sheet indicates the times that seven laundry workers arrived and left each day for the week of August 23. The times they arrived for work are shown under the heading IN, and the times they left are shown under the heading OUT. The letter (P) indicates time which was used for personal business. Time used for this purpose is charged to annual leave. Lunch time is one-half hour from noon to 12:30 P.M. and is not accounted for on this time record.

The employees on this shift are scheduled to work from 8:00 A.M. to 4:00 P.M. Lateness is charged to annual leave. Reporting after 8:00 A.M. is considered late.

	MON.		TUES.		WED.		THURS.		FRI.	
	AM IN	PM OUT	AM IN	PM OUT	AM IN	PM OUT	AM IN	PM OUT	AM IN	PM OUT
Baxter	7:50	4:01	7:49	4:07	8:00	4:07	8:20	4:00	7:42	4:03
Gardner	8:02	4:00	8:20	4:00	8:05	3:30(P)	8:00	4:03	8:00	4:07
Clements	8:00	4:04	8:03	4:01	7:59	4:00	7:54	4:06	7:59	4:00
Tompkins	7:56	4:00	Annual leave		8:00	4:07	7:59	4:00	8:00	4:01
Wagner	8:04	4:03	7:40	4:00	7:53	4:04	8:00	4:09	7:53	4:00
Patterson	8:00	2:30(P)	8:15	4:04	Sick leave		7:45	4:00	7:59	4:04
Cunningham	7:43	4:02	7:50	4:00	7:59	4:02	8:00	4:10	8:00	4:00

1. Which one of the following laundry workers did NOT have any time charged to annual leave or sick leave during the week?

    A. Gardner   B. Clements   C. Tompkins   D. Cunningham

1._____

2. On which day did ALL the laundry workers arrive on time?

    A. Monday   B. Wednesday   C. Thursday   D. Friday

2._____

3. Which of the following laundry workers used time to take care of personal business?

    A. Baxter and Clements
    C. Gardner and Patterson
    B. Patterson and Cunningham
    D. Wagner and Tompkins

3._____

4. How many laundry workers were late on Monday?

    A. 1   B. 2   C. 3   D. 4

4._____

5. Which one of the following laundry workers arrived late on three of the five days?

    A. Baxter   B. Gardner   C. Wagner   D. Patterson

5._____

6. The percentage of laundry workers reporting to work late on Tuesday is MOST NEARLY

   A. 15% B. 25% C. 45% D. 50%

7. The percentage of laundry workers that were absent for an entire day during the week is MOST NEARLY

   A. 6% B. 9% C. 15% D. 30%

KEY (CORRECT ANSWERS)

1. D
2. D
3. C
4. B
5. B
6. C
7. D

TEST 3

Questions 1-9.

DIRECTIONS: Questions 1 through 9 are to be answered SOLELY on the basis of the following information and timesheet given below.

The following is a foreman's timesheet for his crew for one week. The hours worked each day or the reason the man was off on that day are shown on the sheet. *R* means rest day. *A* means annual leave. *S* means sick leave. Where a man worked only part of a day, both the number of hours worked and the number of hours taken off are entered. The reason for absence is entered in parentheses next to the number of hours taken off.

Name	Saturday	Sunday	Monday	Tuesday	Wednesday	Thursday	Friday
Smith	R	R	7	7	7	3 4(A)	7
Jones	R	7	7	7	7	7	R
Green	R	R	7	7	S	S	S
White	R	R	7	7	A	7	7
Doe	7	7	7	7	7	R	R
Brown	R	R	A	7	7	7	7
Black	R	R	S	7	7	7	7
Reed	R	R	7	7	7	7	S
Roe	R	R	A	7	7	7	7
Lane	7	R	R	7	7	A	S

1. The caretaker who worked EXACTLY 21 hours during the week is

    A. Lane   B. Roe   C. Smith   D. White

2. The TOTAL number of hours worked by all caretakers during the week is

    A. 268   B. 276   C. 280   D. 288

3. The two days of the week on which MOST caretakers were off are

    A. Thursday and Friday
    B. Friday and Saturday
    C. Saturday and Sunday
    D. Sunday and Monday

4. The day on which three caretakers were off on sick leave is

    A. Monday   B. Friday   C. Saturday   D. Sunday

5. The two workers who took LEAST time off during the week are

    A. Doe and Reed
    B. Jones and Doe
    C. Reed and Smith
    D. Smith and Jones

6. The caretaker who worked the LEAST number of hours during the week is

    A. Brown   B. Green   C. Lane   D. Roe

7. The caretakers who did NOT work on Thursday are

    A. Doe, White, and Smith
    B. Green, Doe, and Lane
    C. Green, Doe, and Smith
    D. Green, Lane, and Smith

8. The day on which one caretaker worked ONLY 3 hours is 8.____

   A. Friday   B. Saturday   C. Thursday   D. Wednesday

9. The day on which ALL caretakers worked is 9.____

   A. Monday   B. Thursday   C. Tuesday   D. Wednesday

KEY (CORRECT ANSWERS)

1. A
2. B
3. C
4. B
5. B
6. B
7. B
8. C
9. C

TEST 4

Questions 1-6.

DIRECTIONS: Questions 1 through 6 are to be answered SOLELY on the basis of the table below which shows the initial requests made by staff for vacation. It is to be used with the RULES AND GUIDELINES to make the decisions and judgments called for in each of the questions.

VACATION REQUESTS FOR THE ONE YEAR PERIOD FROM MAY 1, YEAR X THROUGH APRIL 30, YEAR Y				
Name	Work Assignment	Date Appointed	Accumulated Annual Leave Days	Vacation Periods Requested
DeMarco	MVO	Mar. 2003	25	May 3-21; Oct. 25-Nov. 5
Moore	Dispatcher	Dec. 1997	32	May 24-June 4; July 12-16
Kingston	MVO	Apr. 2007	28	May 24-June 11; Feb. 7-25
Green	MVO	June 2006	26	June 7-18; Sept. 6-24
Robinson	MVO	July 2008	30	June 28-July 9; Nov. 15-26
Reilly	MVO	Oct. 2009	23	July 5-9; Jan. 31-Mar. 3
Stevens	MVO	Sept. 1996	31	July 5-23; Oct. 4-29
Costello	MVO	Sept. 1998	31	July 5-30; Oct. 4-22
Maloney	Dispatcher	Aug. 1992	35	July 5-Aug. 6; Nov. 1-5
Hughes	Director	Feb. 1990	38	July 26-Sept. 3
Lord	MVO	Jan. 2010	20	Aug. 9-27; Feb. 7-25
Diaz	MVO	Dec. 2009	28	Aug. 9-Sept. 10
Krimsky	MVO	May 2006	22	Oct. 18-22: Nov. 22-Dec. 10

RULES AND GUIDELINES

1. The two Dispatchers cannot be on vacation at the same time, nor can a Dispatcher be on vacation at the same time as the Director.

2. For the period June 1 through September 30, not more than three MVO's can be on vacation at the same time.

3. For the period October 1 through May 31, not more than two MVO's at a time can be on vacation.

4. In cases where the same vacation time is requested by too many employees for all of them to be given the time under the rules, the requests of those who have worked the longest will be granted.

5. No employee may take more leave days than the number of annual leave days accumulated and shown in the table.

6. All vacation periods shown in the table and described in the questions below begin on a Monday and end on a Friday.

7. Employees work a five-day week (Monday through Friday). They are off weekends and holidays with no charges to leave balances. When a holiday falls on a Saturday or Sunday, employees are given the following Monday off without charge to annual leave.

95

2 (#4)

8. Holidays:　　May 31　　　　October 25　　　　January 1
　　　　　　　　July 4　　　　　November 2　　　　February 12
　　　　　　　　September 6　　November 25　　　February 21
　　　　　　　　October 11　　　December 25　　　February 21

9. An employee shall be given any part of his initial requests that is permissible under the above rules and shall have first right to it despite any further adjustment of schedule.

---

1. Until adjustments in the vacation schedule can be made, the vacation dates that can be approved for Krimsky are

   A. Oct. 18-22; Nov. 22-Dec. 10
   B. Oct. 18-22; Nov. 29-Dec. 10
   C. Oct. 18-22 *only*
   D. Nov. 22-Dec. 10 *only*

2. Until adjustments in the vacation schedule can be made, the vacation dates that can be approved for Maloney are

   A. July 5-Aug. 6; Nov. 1-5
   B. July 5-23; Nov. 1-5
   C. July 5-9; Nov. 1-5
   D. Nov. 1-5 *only*

3. According to the table, Lord wants a vacation in August and another in February. Until adjustments in the vacation schedule can be made, he can be allowed to take _____ of the August vacation and _____ of the February vacation.

   A. all; none
   B. all; almost half
   C. almost all; almost half
   D. almost half; all

4. Costello cannot be given all the vacation he has requested because

   A. the MVO's who have more seniority than he has have requested time he wishes
   B. he does not have enough accumulated annual leave
   C. a dispatcher is applying for vacation at the same time as Costello
   D. there are five people who want vacation in July

5. According to the table, how many leave days will DeMarco be charged for his vacation from October 25 through November 5?

   A. 10　　　B. 9　　　C. 8　　　D. 7

6. How many leave days will Moore use if he uses the requested vacation allowable to him under the rules?

   A. 9　　　B. 10　　　C. 14　　　D. 15

KEY (CORRECT ANSWERS)

1. D
2. B
3. A
4. B
5. C
6. A

TEST 5

Questions 1-8.

DIRECTIONS: Questions 1 through 8 are to be answered SOLELY on the basis of Charts I, II, III, and IV. Assume that you are the supervisor of Operators R, S, T, U, V, W, and X, and it is your responsibility to schedule their lunch hours.

The charts each represent a possible scheduling of lunch hours during a lunch period from 11:30 - 2:00. An operator-hour is one hour of time spent by one operator. Each box on the chart represents one half-hour. The boxes marked L represent the time when each operator is scheduled to have her lunch hour. For example, in Chart I, next to Operator R, the boxes for 11:30 - 12:00 and 12:00 -12:30 are marked L. This means that Operator R is scheduled to have her lunch hour from 11:30 to 12:30.

I

	11:30-12:00	12:00-12:30	12:30-1:00	1:00-1:30	1:30-2:00
R	L	L			
S		L	L		
T		L	L		
U			L	L	
V			L	L	
W				L	L
X				L	L

II

	11:30-12:00	12:00-12:30	12:30-1:00	1:00-1:30	1:30-2:00
R				L	L
S			L	L	
T	L	L			
U		L	L		
V				L	L
W				L	L
X			L	L	

III

	11:30-12:00	12:00-12:30	12:30-1:00	1:00-1:30	1:30-2:00
R	L	L			
S				L	L
T	L	L			
U			L	L	
V	L	L			
W			L	L	
X			L	L	

IV

	11:30-12:00	12:00-12:30	12:30-1:00	1:00-1:30	1:30-2:00
R	L	L			
S	L	L			
T		L	L		
U			L	L	
V				L	L
W				L	L
X			L	L	

1. If, under the schedule represented in Chart II, Operator R has her lunch hour changed to 12:30-1:30, that leaves how many operator-hours of phone coverage from 1:00-2:00?

   A. 2   B. 2 1/2   C. 3   D. 4 1/2

2. If Operator S asks you whether she and Operator T may have the same lunch hour, you could accommodate her by using the schedule in Chart

   A. I   B. II   C. III   D. IV

3. From past experience you know that the part of the lunch period when the phones are busiest is from 12:30-1:30. Which chart shows the BEST phone coverage from 12:30 to 1:30?

   A. I   B. II   C. III   D. IV

4. At least three operators have the same lunch hour according to Chart(s)

   A. II and III
   B. II and IV
   C. III only
   D. IV only

98

5. Which chart would provide the POOREST phone coverage during the period 12:00-1:30, based on total number of operator-hours from 12:00 to 1:30?

   A. I B. II C. III D. IV

6. Which chart would make it possible for U, W, and X to have the same lunch hour?

   A. I B. II C. III D. IV

7. The portion of the lunch period during which the telephones are least busy is 11:30-12:30.
   Which chart is MOST likely to have been designed with that fact in mind?

   A. I B. II C. III D. IV

8. Assume that you have decided to use Chart IV to schedule your operators' lunch hours on a specific day. Operator T asks you if she can have her lunch hour changed to 1:00-2:00.
   If you grant her request, how many operators will be working during the period 12:00 to 12:30?

   A. 1 B. 2 C. 4 D. 5

KEY (CORRECT ANSWERS)

1. D
2. A
3. B
4. A
5. A
6. C
7. C
8. D

TEST 6

Questions 1-13.

DIRECTIONS: Questions 1 through 13 consist of a statement. You are to indicate whether the statement is TRUE (T) or FALSE (F). *PRINT THE LETTER OF THE CORRECT ANSWER IN THE SPACE AT THE RIGHT.* Questions 1 through 13 are to be answered SOLELY on the basis of the information given in the table below.

Name	Year Employed	Ferry Assigned	Hours of Work	Lunch Period	Days Off
Adams	1999	Hudson	7 AM - 3 PM	11-12	Fri. and Sat.
Baker	1992	Monroe	7 AM - 3 PM	11-12	Sun. and Mon.
Gunn	1995	Troy	8 AM - 4 PM	12-1	Fri. and Sat.
Hahn	1989	Erie	9 AM - 5 PM	1-2	Sat. and Sun.
King	1998	Albany	7 AM - 3 PM	11-12	Sun. and Mon.
Nash	1993	Hudson	11 AM - 7 PM	3-4	Sun. and Mon.
Olive	2003	Fulton	10 AM - 6 PM	2-3	Sat. and Sun.
Queen	2002	Albany	11 AM - 7 PM	3-4	Fri. and Sat.
Rose	1990	Troy	11 AM - 7 PM	3-4	Sun. and Mon.
Smith	1991	Monroe	10 AM - 6 PM	2-3	Fri. and Sat.

1. The chart shows that there are only five (5) ferries being used.   1.___

2. The attendant who has been working the LONGEST time is Rose.   2.___

3. The <u>Troy</u> has one more attendant assigned to it than the Erie.   3.___

4. Two (2) attendants are assigned to work from 10 P.M. to 6 A.M.   4.___

5. According to the chart, no more than one attendant was hired in any year.   5.___

6. The NEWEST employee is Olive.   6.___

7. There are as many attendants on the 7 to 3 shift as on the 11 to 7 shift.   7.___

8. MOST of the attendants have their lunch either between 12 and 1 or 2 and 3.   8.___

9. All the employees work four (4) hours before they go to lunch.   9.___

10. On the <u>Hudson</u>, Adams goes to lunch when Nash reports to work.   10.___

11. All the attendants who work on the 7 to 3 shift are off on Saturday and Sunday.   11.___

12. All the attendants have either a Saturday or Sunday as one of their days off.   12.___

13. At least two (2) attendants are assigned to each ferry.   13.___

2 (#6)

KEY (CORRECT ANSWERS)

1. F
2. F
3. T
4. F
5. T

6. T
7. T
8. F
9. T
10. T

11. F
12. T
13. F

———

EXAMINATION SECTION
TEST 1

DIRECTIONS: Each question or incomplete statement is followed by several suggested answers or completions. Select the one that BEST answers the question or completes the statement. *PRINT THE LETTER OF THE CORRECT ANSWER IN THE SPACE AT THE RIGHT.*

1. Of the following, the one MOST important quality required of a good supervisor is
   A. ambition   B. leadership   C. friendliness   D. popularity

   1.____

2. It is often said that a supervisor can delegate authority but never responsibility. This means MOST NEARLY that
   A. a supervisor must do his own work if he expects it to be done properly
   B. a supervisor can assign someone else to do his work, but in the last analysis, the supervisor himself must take the blame for any actions followed
   C. authority and responsibility are two separate things that cannot be borne by the same person
   D. it is better for a supervisor never to delegate his authority

   2.____

3. One of your men who is a habitual complainer asks you to grant him a minor privilege.
   Before granting or denying such a request, you should consider
   A. the merits of the case
   B. that it is good for group morale to grant a request of this nature
   C. the man's seniority
   D. that to deny such a request will lower your standing with the men

   3.____

4. A supervisory practice on the part of a foreman which is MOST likely to lead to confusion and inefficiency is for him to
   A. give orders verbally directly to the man assigned to the job
   B. issue orders only in writing
   C. follow up his orders after issuing them
   D. relay his orders to the men through co-workers

   4.____

5. It would be POOR supervision on a foreman's part if he
   A. asked an experienced maintainer for his opinion on the method of doing a special job
   B. make it a policy to avoid criticizing a man in front of his co-workers
   C. consulted his assistant supervisor on unusual problems
   D. allowed a cooling-off period of several days before giving one of his men a deserved reprimand

   5.____

6. Of the following behavior characteristics of a supervisor, the one that is MOST likely to lower the morale of the men he supervises is
   A. diligence
   B. favoritism
   C. punctuality
   D. thoroughness

7. Of the following, the BEST method of getting an employee who is not working up to his capacity to produce more work is to
   A. have another employee criticize his production
   B. privately criticize his production but encourage him to produce more
   C. criticize his production before his associates
   D. criticize his production and threaten to fire him

8. Of the following, the BEST thing for a supervisor to do when a subordinate has done a very good job is to
   A. tell him to take it easy
   B. praise his work
   C. reduce his workload
   D. say nothing because he may become conceited

9. Your orders to your crew are MOST likely to be followed if you
   A. explain the reasons for these orders
   B. warn that all violators will be punished
   C. promise easy assignments to those who follow these orders best
   D. say that they are for the good of the department

10. In order to be a good supervisor, you should
    A. impress upon your men that you demand perfection in their work at all times
    B. avoid being blamed for your crew's mistakes
    C. impress your superior with your ability
    D. see to it that your men get what they are entitled to

11. In giving instructions to a crew, you should
    A. speak in as loud a tone as possible
    B. speak in a coaxing, persuasive manner
    C. speak quietly, clearly, and courteously
    D. always use the word *please* when giving instructions

12. Of the following factors, the one which is LEAST important in evaluating an employee and his work is his
    A. dependability
    B. quantity of work done
    C. quality of work done
    D. education and training

13. When a District Superintendent first assumes his command, it is LEAST important for him at the beginning to observe
    A. how his equipment is designed and its adaptability
    B. how to reorganize the district for greater efficiency
    C. the capabilities of the men in the district
    D. the methods of operation being employed

14. When making an inspection of one of the buildings under your supervision, the BEST procedure to follow in making a record of the inspection is to
    A. return immediately to the office and write a report from memory
    B. write down all the important facts during or as soon as you complete the inspection
    C. fix in your mind all important facts so that you can repeat them from memory if necessary
    D. fix in your mind all important facts so that you can make out your report at the end of the day

15. Assume that your superior has directed you to make certain changes in your established procedure. After using this modified procedure on several occasions, you find that the original procedure was distinctly superior and you wish to return to it.
    You should
    A. let your superior find this out for himself
    B. simply change back to the original procedure
    C. compile definite data and information to prove your case to your superior
    D. persuade one of the more experienced workers to take this matter up with your superior

16. An inspector visited a large building under construction. He inspected the soil lines at 9 A.M., water lines at 10 A.M., fixtures at 11 A.M., and did his office work in the afternoon. He followed the same pattern daily for weeks.
    This procedure was
    A. *good*, because it was methodical and he did not miss anything
    B. *good*, because it gave equal time to all phases of the plumbing
    C. *bad*, because not enough time was devoted to fixtures
    D. *bad*, because the tradesmen knew when the inspection would occur

17. Assume that one of the foremen in a training course, which you are conducting, proposes a poor solution for a maintenance problem.
    Of the following, the BEST course of action for you to take is to
    A. accept the solution tentatively and correct it during the next class meeting
    B. point out all the defects of this proposed solution and wait until somebody thinks of a better solution
    C. try to get the class to reject this proposed solution and develop a better solution
    D. let the matter pass since somebody will present a better solution as the class work proceeds

18. As a supervisor, you should be seeking ways to improve the efficiency of shop operations by means such as changing established work procedures.
    The following are offered as possible actions that you should consider in changing established work procedures:
    I. Make changes only when your foremen agree to them
    II. Discuss changes with your supervisor before putting them into practice

III. Standardize any operation which is performed on a continuing basis
IV. Make changes quickly and quietly in order to avoid dissent
V. Secure expert guidance before instituting unfamiliar procedures
Of the following suggested answers, the one that describes the actions to be taken to change established work procedures is
   A. I, IV, V   B. II, III, V   C. III, IV, V   D. All of the above

19. A supervisor determined that a foreman, without informing his superior, delegated responsibility for checking time cards to a member of his gang. The supervisor then called the foreman into his office where he reprimanded the foreman.
This action of the supervisor in reprimanding the foreman was
   A. *proper*, because the checking of time cards is the foreman's responsibility and should not be delegated
   B. *proper*, because the foreman did not ask the supervisor for permission to delegate responsibility
   C. *improper*, because the foreman may no longer take the initiative in solving future problems
   D. *improper*, because the supervisor is interfering in a function which is not his responsibility

20. A capable supervisor should check all operations under his control.
Of the following, the LEAST important reason for doing this is to make sure that
   A. operations are being performed as scheduled
   B. he personally observes all operations at all times
   C. all the operations are still needed
   D. his manpower is being utilized efficiently

21. A supervisor makes it a practice to apply fair and firm discipline in all cases of rule infractions, including those of a minor nature.
This practice should PRIMARILY be considered
   A. *bad*, since applying discipline for minor violations is a waste of time
   B. *good*, because not applying discipline for minor infractions can lead to a more serious erosion of discipline
   C. *bad*, because employees do not like to be disciplined for minor violations of the rules
   D. *good*, because violating any rule can cause a dangerous situation to occur

22. A maintainer would PROPERLY consider it poor supervisory practice for a foreman to consult with him on
   A. which of several repair jobs should be scheduled first
   B. how to cope with personal problems at home
   C. whether the neatness of his headquarters can be improved
   D. how to express a suggestion which the maintainer plans to submit formally

23. Assume that you have determined that the work of one of your foremen and the men he supervises is consistently behind schedule. When you discuss this situation with the foreman, he tells you that his men are poor workers and then complains that he must spend all of his time checking on their work.
The following actions are offered for your consideration as possible ways of solving the problem of poor performance of the foreman and his men:
    I. Review the work standards with the foreman and determine whether they are realistic.
    II. Tell the foreman that you will recommend him for the foreman's training course for retraining.
    III. Ask the foreman for the names of the maintainers and then replace them as soon as possible.
    IV. Tell the foreman that you expect him to meet a satisfactory level of performance.
    V. Tell the foreman to insist that his men work overtime to catch up to the schedule.
    VI. Tell the foreman to review the type and amount of training he has given the maintainers.
    VII. Tell the foreman that he will be out of a job if he does not produce on schedule.
    VIII. Avoid all criticism of the foreman and his methods.
    Which of the following suggested answers CORRECTLY lists the proper actions to be taken to solve the problem of poor performance of the foreman and his men?
    A. I, II, IV, VI   B. I, III, V, VII   C. II, III, VI, VIII   D. IV, V, VI, VIII

24. When a conference or a group discussion is tending to turn into a *bull session* without constructive purpose, the BEST action to take is to
    A. reprimand the leader of the bull session
    B. redirect the discussion to the business at hand
    C. dismiss the meeting and reschedule it for another day
    D. allow the bull session to continue

25. Assume that you have been assigned responsibility for a program in which a high production rate is mandatory. From past experience, you know that your foremen do not perform equally well in the various types of jobs given to them. Which of the following methods should you use in selecting foremen for the specific types of work involved in the program?
    A. Leave the method of selecting foremen to your supervisor
    B. Assign each foreman to the work he does best
    C. Allow each foreman to choose his own job
    D. Assign each foreman to a job which will permit him to improve his own abilities

KEY (CORRECT ANSWERS)

1.	B	11.	C
2.	B	12.	D
3.	A	13.	B
4.	D	14.	B
5.	D	15.	C
6.	B	16.	D
7.	B	17.	C
8.	B	18.	B
9.	A	19.	A
10.	D	20.	B

21. B
22. A
23. A
24. B
25. B

TEST 2

DIRECTIONS: Each question or incomplete statement is followed by several suggested answers or completions. Select the one that BEST answers the question or completes the statement. *PRINT THE LETTER OF THE CORRECT ANSWER IN THE SPACE AT THE RIGHT.*

1. A foreman who is familiar with modern management principles should know that the one of the following requirements of an administrator which is LEAST important is his ability to
    A. coordinate work
    B. plan, organize, and direct the work under his control
    C. cooperate with others
    D. perform the duties of the employees under his jurisdiction

    1._____

2. When subordinates request his advice in solving problems encountered in their work, a certain chief occasionally answers the request by first asking the subordinate what he thinks should be done.
    This action by the chief is, on the whole,
    A. *desirable*, because it stimulates subordinates to give more thought to the solution of problems encountered
    B. *undesirable*, because it discourages subordinates from asking questions
    C. *desirable*, because it discourages subordinates from asking questions
    D. *undesirable*, because it undermines the confidence of subordinates in the ability of their supervisor

    2._____

3. Of the following factors that may be considered by a unit head in dealing with the tardy subordinate, the one which should be given LEAST consideration is the
    A. frequency with which the employee is tardy
    B. effect of the employee's tardiness upon the work of other employees
    C. willingness of the employee to work overtime when necessary
    D. cause of the employee's tardiness

    3._____

4. The MOST important requirement of a good inspectional report is that it should be
    A. properly addressed   B. lengthy
    C. clear and brief   D. spelled correctly

    4._____

5. Building superintendents frequently inquire about departmental inspectional procedures.
    Of the following, it is BEST to
    A. advise them to write to the department for an official reply
    B. refuse as the inspectional procedure is a restricted matter
    C. briefly explain the procedure to them
    D. avoid the inquiry by changing the subject

    5._____

6. Reprimanding a crew member before other workers is a
   A. *good* practice; the reprimand serves as a warning to the other workers
   B. *bad* practice; people usually resent criticism made in public
   C. *good* practice; the other workers will realize that the supervisor is fair
   D. *bad* practice; the other workers will take sides in the dispute

7. Of the following actions, the one which is LEAST likely to promote good work is for the group leader to
   A. praise workers for doing a good job
   B. call attention to the opportunities for promotion for better workers
   C. threaten to recommend discharge of workers who are below standard
   D. put into practice any good suggestion made by crew members

8. A supervisor notices that a member of his crew has skipped a routine step in his job.
   Of the following, the BEST action for the supervisor to take is to
   A. promptly question the worker about the incident
   B. immediately assign another man to complete the job
   C. bring up the incident the next time the worker asks for a favor
   D. say nothing about the incident but watch the worker carefully in the future

9. Assume you have been told to show a new worker how to operate a piece of equipment.
   Your FIRST step should be to
   A. ask the worker if he has any questions about the equipment
   B. permit the worker to operate the equipment himself while you carefully watch to prevent damage
   C. demonstrate the operation of the equipment for the worker
   D. have the worker read an instruction booklet on the maintenance of the equipment

10. Whenever a new man was assigned to his crew, the supervisor would introduce him to all other crew members, take him on a tour of the plant, tell him about bus schedules and places to eat.
    This practice is
    A. *good*; the new man is made to feel welcome
    B. *bad*; supervisors should not interfere in personal matters
    C. *good*; the new man knows that he can bring his personal problems to the supervisor
    D. *bad*; work time should not be spent on personal matters

11. The MOST important factor in successful leadership is the ability to
    A. obtain instant obedience to all orders
    B. establish friendly personal relations with crew members
    C. avoid disciplining crew members
    D. make crew members want to do what should be done

12. Explaining the reasons for departmental procedure to workers tends to
    A. waste time which should be used for productive purposes
    B. increase their interest in their work
    C. make them more critical of departmental procedures
    D. confuse them

13. If you want a job done well do it yourself.
    For a supervisor to follow this advice would be
    A. *good*; a supervisor is responsible for the work of his crew
    B. *bad*; a supervisor should train his men, not do their work
    C. *good*; a supervisor should be skilled in all jobs assigned to his crew
    D. *bad*; a supervisor loses respect when he works with his hands

14. When a supervisor discovers a mistake in one of the jobs for which his crew is responsible, it is MOST important for him to find out
    A. whether anybody else knows about the mistake
    B. who was to blame for the mistake
    C. how to prevent similar mistakes in the future
    D. whether similar mistakes occurred in the past

15. A supervisor who has to explain a new procedure to his crew should realize that questions from the crew USUALLY show that they
    A. are opposed to the new practice
    B. are completely confused by the explanation
    C. need more training in the new procedure
    D. are interested in the explanation

16. A good way for a supervisor to retain the confidence of his or her employees is to
    A. say as little as possible
    B. check work frequently
    C. make no promises unless they will be fulfilled
    D. never hesitate in giving an answer to any question

17. Good supervision is ESSENTIALLY a matter of
    A. patience in supervising workers   B. care in selecting workers
    C. skill in human relations   D. fairness in disciplining workers

18. It is MOST important for an employee who has been assigned a monotonous task to
    A. perform this task before doing other work
    B. ask another employee to help
    C. perform this task only after all other work has been completed
    D. take measures to prevent mistakes in performing the task

4 (#2)

19. One of your employees has violated a minor agency regulation.
The FIRST thing you should do is
    A. warn the employee that you will have to take disciplinary action if it should happen again
    B. ask the employee to explain his or her actions
    C. inform your supervisor and wait for advice
    D. write a memo describing the incident and place it in the employee's personnel file

19._____

20. One of your employees tells you that he feels you give him much more work than the other employees, and he is having trouble meeting your deadlines.
You should
    A. ask if he has been under a lot of non-work related stress lately
    B. review his recent assignments to determine if he is correct
    C. explain that this is a busy time, but you are dividing the work equally
    D. tell him that he is the most competent employee and that is why he receives more work

20._____

21. A supervisor assigns one of his crew to complete a portion of a job. A short time later, the supervisor notices that the portion has not been completed.
Of the following, the BEST way for the supervisor to handle this is to
    A. ask the crew member why he has not completed the assignment
    B. reprimand the crew member for not obeying orders
    C. assign another crew member to complete the assignment
    D. complete the assignment himself

21._____

22. Supposes that a member of your crew complains that you are *playing favorites* in assigning work.
Of the following, the BEST method of handling the complaint is to
    A. deny it and refuse to discuss the matter with the worker
    B. take the opportunity to tell the worker what is wrong with his work
    C. ask the worker for examples to prove his point and try to clear up any misunderstanding
    D. promise to be more careful in making assignments in the future

22._____

23. A member of your crew comes to you with a complaint. After discussing the matter with him, it is clear that you have convinced him that his complaint was not justified.
At this point, you should
    A. permit him to drop the matter
    B. make him admit his error
    C. pretend to see some justification in his complaint
    D. warn him against making unjustified complaints

23._____

24. Suppose that a supervisor has in his crew an older man who works rather slowly. In other respects, this man is a good worker; he is seldom absent, works carefully, never loafs, and is cooperative.

24._____

The BEST way for the supervisor to handle this worker is to
- A. try to get him to work faster and less carefully
- B. give him the most disagreeable job
- C. request that he be given special training
- D. permit him to work at his own speed

25. Suppose that a member of your crew comes to you with a suggestion he thinks will save time in doing a job. You realize immediately that it won't work.
Under these circumstances, your BEST action would be to
- A. thank the worker for the suggestion and forget about it
- B. explain to the worker why you think it won't work
- C. tell the worker to put the suggestion in writing
- D. ask the other members of your crew to criticize the suggestion

25.____

KEY (CORRECT ANSWERS)

1.	D	11.	D
2.	A	12.	B
3.	C	13.	B
4.	C	14.	C
5.	C	15.	D
6.	B	16.	C
7.	C	17.	C
8.	A	18.	D
9.	C	19.	B
10.	A	20.	B

21.	A
22.	C
23.	A
24.	D
25.	B

PHILOSOPHY, PRINCIPLES, PRACTICES, AND TECHNICS OF SUPERVISION, ADMINISTRATION, MANAGEMENT, AND ORGANIZATION

TABLE OF CONTENTS

	Page
MEANING OF SUPERVISION	1
THE OLD AND THE NEW SUPERVISION	1
THE EIGHT (8) BASIC PRINCIPLES OF THE NEW SUPERVISION	1
I. Principle of Responsibility	1
II. Principle of Authority	2
III. Principle of Self-Growth	2
IV. Principle of Individual Worth	2
V. Principle of Creative Leadership	2
VI. Principle of Success and Failure	2
VII. Principle of Science	3
VIII. Principle of Cooperation	3
WHAT IS ADMINISTRATION?	3
I. Practices Commonly Classed as "Supervisory"	3
II. Practices Commonly Classed as "Administrative"	3
III. Practices Commonly Classed as Both "Supervisory" and "Administrative"	4
RESPONSIBILITIES OF THE SUPERVISOR	4
COMPETENCIES OF THE SUPERVISOR	4
THE PROFESSIONAL SUPERVISOR-EMPLOYEE RELATIONSHIP	4
MINI-TEXT IN SUPERVISION, ADMINISTRATION, MANAGEMENT, AND ORGANIZATION	5
I. Brief Highlights	5
A. Levels of Management	6
B. What the Supervisor Must Learn	6
C. A Definition of Supervision	6
D. Elements of the Team Concept	6
E. Principles of Organization	6
F. The Four Important Parts of Every Job	7
G. Principles of Delegation	7
H. Principles of Effective Communications	7
I. Principles of Work Improvement	7
J. Areas of Job Improvement	7
K. Seven Key Points in Making Improvements	8

	L.	Corrective Techniques for Job Improvement	8
	M.	A Planning Checklist	8
	N.	Five Characteristics of Good Directions	9
	O.	Types of Directions	9
	P.	Controls	9
	Q.	Orienting the New Employee	9
	R.	Checklist for Orienting New Employees	9
	S.	Principles of Learning	10
	T.	Causes of Poor Performance	10
	U.	Four Major Steps in On-the-Job Instructions	10
	V.	Employees Want Five Things	10
	W.	Some Don'ts in Regard to Praise	11
	X.	How to Gain Your Workers' Confidence	11
	Y.	Sources of Employee Problems	11
	Z.	The Supervisor's Key to Discipline	11
	AA.	Five Important Processes of Management	12
	BB.	When the Supervisor Fails to Plan	12
	CC.	Fourteen General Principles of Management	12
	DD.	Change	12
II.	Brief Topical Summaries		13
	A.	Who/What is the Supervisor?	13
	B.	The Sociology of Work	13
	C.	Principles and Practices of Supervision	14
	D.	Dynamic Leadership	14
	E.	Processes for Solving Problems	15
	F.	Training for Results	15
	G.	Health, Safety, and Accident Prevention	16
	H.	Equal Employment Opportunity	16
	I.	Improving Communications	16
	J.	Self-Development	17
	K.	Teaching and Training	17
		1. The Teaching Process	17
		a. Preparation	17
		b. Presentation	18
		c. Summary	18
		d. Application	18
		e. Evaluation	18
		2. Teaching Methods	18
		a. Lecture	18
		b. Discussion	18
		c. Demonstration	19
		d. Performance	19
		e. Which Method to Use	19

PHILOSOPHY, PRINCIPLES, PRACTICES, AND TECHNICS OF SUPERVISION, ADMINISTRATION, MANAGEMENT, AND ORGANIZATION

MEANING OF SUPERVISION

The extension of the democratic philosophy has been accompanied by an extension in the scope of supervision. Modern leaders and supervisors no longer think of supervision in the narrow sense of being confined chiefly to visiting employees, supplying materials, or rating the staff. They regard supervision as being intimately related to all the concerned agencies of society, they speak of the supervisor's function in terms of "growth," rather than the "improvement" of employees.

This modern concept of supervision may be defined as follows: Supervision is leadership and the development of leadership within groups which are cooperatively engaged in inspection, research, training, guidance, and evaluation.

THE OLD AND THE NEW SUPERVISION

TRADITIONAL
1. Inspection
2. Focused on the employee
3. Visitation
4. Random and haphazard
5. Imposed and authoritarian
6. One person usually

MODERN
1. Study and analysis
2. Focused on aims, materials, methods, supervisors, employees, environment
3. Demonstrations, intervisitation, workshops, directed reading, bulletins, etc.
4. Definitely organized and planned (scientific)
5. Cooperative and democratic
6. Many persons involved (creative)

THE EIGHT (8) BASIC PRINCIPLES OF THE NEW SUPERVISION

I. Principle of Responsibility
    Authority to act and responsibility for acting must be joined.
    A. If you give responsibility, give authority.
    B. Define employee duties clearly.
    C. Protect employees from criticism by others.
    D. Recognize the rights as well as obligations of employees.
    E. Achieve the aims of a democratic society insofar as it is possible within the area of your work.
    F. Establish a situation favorable to training and learning.
    G. Accept ultimate responsibility for everything done in your section, unit, office, division, department.
    H. Good administration and good supervision are inseparable.

II. Principle of Authority
The success of the supervisor is measured by the extent to which the power of authority is not used.
   A. Exercise simplicity and informality in supervision
   B. Use the simplest machinery of supervision
   C. If it is good for the organization as a whole, it is probably justified.
   D. Seldom be arbitrary or authoritative.
   E. Do not base your work on the power of position or of personality.
   F. Permit and encourage the free expression of opinions.

III. Principle of Self-Growth
The success of the supervisor is measured by the extent to which, and the speed with which, he is no longer needed.
   A. Base criticism on principles, not on specifics.
   B. Point out higher activities to employees.
   C. Train for self-thinking by employees to meet new situations.
   D. Stimulate initiative, self-reliance, and individual responsibility
   E. Concentrate on stimulating the growth of employees rather than on removing defects.

IV. Principle of Individual Worth
Respect for the individual is a paramount consideration in supervision.
   A. Be human and sympathetic in dealing with employees.
   B. Don't nag about things to be done.
   C. Recognize the individual differences among employees and seek opportunities to permit best expression of each personality.

V. Principle of Creative Leadership
The best supervision is that which is not apparent to the employee.
   A. Stimulate, don't drive employees to creative action.
   B. Emphasize doing good things.
   C. Encourage employees to do what they do best.
   D. Do not be too greatly concerned with details of subject or method.
   E. Do not be concerned exclusively with immediate problems and activities.
   F. Reveal higher activities and make them both desired and maximally possible.
   G. Determine procedures in the light of each situation but see that these are derived from a sound basic philosophy.
   H. Aid, inspire, and lead so as to liberate the creative spirit latent in all good employees.

VI. Principle of Success and Failure
There are no unsuccessful employees, only unsuccessful supervisors who have failed to give proper leadership.
   A. Adapt suggestions to the capacities, attitudes, and prejudices of employees.
   B. Be gradual, be progressive, be persistent.
   C. Help the employee find the general principle; have the employee apply his own problem to the general principle.
   D. Give adequate appreciation for good work and honest effort.
   E. Anticipate employee difficulties and help to prevent them.
   F. Encourage employees to do the desirable things they will do anyway.
   G. Judge your supervision by the results it secures.

VII. Principle of Science
Successful supervision is scientific, objective, and experimental. It is based on facts, not on prejudices.
   A. Be cumulative in results.
   B. Never divorce your suggestions from the goals of training.
   C. Don't be impatient of results.
   D. Keep all matters on a professional, not a personal, level.
   E. Do not be concerned exclusively with immediate problems and activities.
   F. Use objective means of determining achievement and rating where possible.

VIII. Principle of Cooperation
Supervision is a cooperative enterprise between supervisor and employee.
   A. Begin with conditions as they are.
   B. Ask opinions of all involved when formulating policies.
   C. Organization is as good as its weakest link.
   D. Let employees help to determine policies and department programs.
   E. Be approachable and accessible—physically and mentally.
   F. Develop pleasant social relationships.

WHAT IS ADMINISTRATION

Administration is concerned with providing the environment, the material facilities, and the operational procedures that will promote the maximum growth and development of supervisors and employees. (Organization is an aspect and a concomitant of administration.)

There is no sharp line of demarcation between supervision and administration; these functions are intimately interrelated and, often, overlapping. They are complementary activities.

I. Practices Commonly Classed as "Supervisory"
   A. Conducting employees' conferences
   B. Visiting sections, units, offices, divisions, departments
   C. Arranging for demonstrations
   D. Examining plans
   E. Suggesting professional reading
   F. Interpreting bulletins
   G. Recommending in-service training courses
   H. Encouraging experimentation
   I. Appraising employee morale
   J. Providing for intervisitation

II. Practices Commonly Classified as "Administrative"
   A. Management of the office
   B. Arrangement of schedules for extra duties
   C. Assignment of rooms or areas
   D. Distribution of supplies
   E. Keeping records and reports
   F. Care of audio-visual materials
   G. Keeping inventory records
   H. Checking record cards and books

I.   Programming special activities
   J.   Checking on the attendance and punctuality of employees

III. Practices Commonly Classified as Both "Supervisory" and "Administrative"
   A.   Program construction
   B.   Testing or evaluating outcomes
   C.   Personnel accounting
   D.   Ordering instructional materials

RESPONSIBILITIES OF THE SUPERVISOR

A person employed in a supervisory capacity must constantly be able to improve his own efficiency and ability. He represent the employer to the employees and only continuous self-examination can make him a capable supervisor.

Leadership and training are the supervisor's responsibility. An efficient working unit is one in which the employees work with the supervisor. It is his job to bring out the best in his employees. He must always be relaxed, courteous, and calm in his association with his employees. Their feelings are important, and a harsh attitude does not develop the most efficient employees.

COMPETENCES OF THE SUPERVISOR

   I.   Complete knowledge of the duties and responsibilities of his position.
   II.   To be able to organize a job, plan ahead, and carry through.
   III. To have self-confidence and initiative.
   IV.   To be able to handle the unexpected situation and make quick decisions.
   V.   To be able to properly train subordinates in the positions they are best suited for.
   VI.   To be able to keep good human relations among his subordinates.
   VII. To be able to keep good human relations between his subordinates and himself and to earn their respect and trust.

THE PROFESSIONAL SUPERVISOR-EMPLOYEE RELATIONSHIP

There are two kinds of efficiency: one kind is only apparent and is produced in organizations through the exercise of mere discipline; this is but a simulation of the second, or true, efficiency which springs from spontaneous cooperation. If you are a manager, no matter how great or small your responsibility, it is your job, in the final analysis, to create and develop this involuntary cooperation among the people whom you supervise. For, no matter how powerful a combination of money, machines, and materials a company may have, this is a dead and sterile thing without a team of willing, thinking, and articulate people to guide it.

The following 21 points are presented as indicative of the exemplary basic relationship that should exist between supervisor and employee:

1. Each person wants to be liked and respected by his fellow employee and wants to be treated with consideration and respect by his superior.
2. The most competent employee will make an error. However, in a unit where good relations exist between the supervisor and his employees, tenseness and fear do not exist. Thus, errors are not hidden or covered up, and the efficiency of a unit is not impaired.

3. Subordinates resent rules, regulations, or orders that are unreasonable or unexplained.
4. Subordinates are quick to resent unfairness, harshness, injustices, and favoritism.
5. An employee will accept responsibility if he knows that he will be complimented for a job well done, and not too harshly chastised for failure; that his supervisor will check the cause of the failure, and, if it was the supervisor's fault, he will assume the blame therefore. If it was the employee's fault, his supervisor will explain the correct method or means of handling the responsibility.
6. An employee wants to receive credit for a suggestion he has made, that is used. If a suggestion cannot be used, the employee is entitled to an explanation. The supervisor should not say "no" and close the subject.
7. Fear and worry slow up a worker's ability. Poor working environment can impair his physical and mental health. A good supervisor avoids forceful methods, threats, and arguments to get a job done.
8. A forceful supervisor is able to train his employees individually and as a team, and is able to motivate them in the proper channels.
9. A mature supervisor is able to properly evaluate his subordinates and to keep them happy and satisfied.
10. A sensitive supervisor will never patronize his subordinates.
11. A worthy supervisor will respect his employees' confidences.
12. Definite and clear-cut responsibilities should be assigned to each executive.
13. Responsibility should always be coupled with corresponding authority.
14. No change should be made in the scope or responsibilities of a position without a definite understanding to that effect on the part of all persons concerned.
15. No executive or employee, occupying a single position in the organization, should be subject to definite orders from more than one source.
16. Orders should never be given to subordinates over the head of a responsible executive. Rather than do this, the officer in question should be supplanted.
17. Criticisms of subordinates should, whoever possible, be made privately, and in no case should a subordinate be criticized in the presence of executives or employees of equal or lower rank.
18. No dispute or difference between executives or employees as to authority or responsibilities should be considered too trivial for prompt and careful adjudication.
19. Promotions, wage changes, and disciplinary action should always be approved by the executive immediately superior to the one directly responsible.
20. No executive or employee should ever be required, or expected, to be at the same time an assistant to, and critic of, another.
21. Any executive whose work is subject to regular inspection should, wherever practicable, be given the assistance and facilities necessary to enable him to maintain an independent check of the quality of his work.

MINI-TEXT IN SUPERVISION, ADMINISTRATION, MANAGEMENT, AND ORGANIZATION

I. Brief Highlights

   Listed concisely and sequentially are major headings and important data in the field for quick recall and review.

A. Levels of Management
Any organization of some size has several levels of management. In terms of a ladder, the levels are:

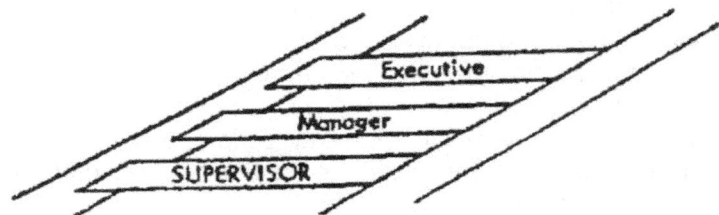

The first level is very important because it is the beginning point of management leadership.

B. What the Supervisor Must Learn
A supervisor must learn to:
1. Deal with people and their differences
2. Get the job done through people
3. Recognize the problems when they exist
4. Overcome obstacles to good performance
5. Evaluate the performance of people
6. Check his own performance in terms of accomplishment

C. A Definition of Supervisor
The term supervisor means any individual having authority, in the interests of the employer, to hire, transfer, suspend, lay-off, recall, promote, discharge, assign, reward, or discipline other employees or responsibility to direct them, or to adjust their grievances, or effectively to recommend such action, if, in connection with the foregoing, exercise of such authority is not of a merely routine or clerical nature but requires the use of independent judgment.

D. Elements of the Team Concept
What is involved in teamwork? The component parts are:
1. Members
2. A leader
3. Goals
4. Plans
5. Cooperation
6. Spirit

E. Principles of Organization
1. A team member must know what his job is.
2. Be sure that the nature and scope of a job are understood.
3. Authority and responsibility should be carefully spelled out.
4. A supervisor should be permitted to make the maximum number of decisions affecting his employees.
5. Employees should report to only one supervisor.
6. A supervisor should direct only as many employees as he can handle effectively.
7. An organization plan should be flexible.

8. Inspection and performance of work should be separate.
9. Organizational problems should receive immediate attention.
10. Assign work in line with ability and experience.

F. The Four Important Parts of Every Job
1. Inherent in every job is the *accountability* for results.
2. A second set of factors in every job is *responsibilities*.
3. Along with duties and responsibilities one must have the *authority* to act within certain limits without obtaining permission to proceed.
4. No job exists in a vacuum. The supervisor is surrounded by key *relationships*.

G. Principles of Delegation
Where work is delegated for the first time, the supervisor should think in terms of these questions:
1. Who is best qualified to do this?
2. Can an employee improve his abilities by doing this?
3. How long should an employee spend on this?
4. Are there any special problems for which he will need guidance?
5. How broad a delegation can I make?

H. Principles of Effective Communications
1. Determine the media.
2. To whom directed?
3. Identification and source authority.
4. Is communication understood?

I. Principles of Work Improvement
1. Most people usually do only the work which is assigned to them.
2. Workers are likely to fit assigned work into the time available to perform it.
3. A good workload usually stimulates output.
4. People usually do their best work when they know that results will be reviewed or inspected.
5. Employees usually feel that someone else is responsible for conditions of work, workplace layout, job methods, type of tools/equipment, and other such factors.
6. Employees are usually defensive about their job security.
7. Employees have natural resistance to change.
8. Employees can support or destroy a supervisor.
9. A supervisor usually earns the respect of his people through his personal example of diligence and efficiency.

J. Areas of Job Improvement
The areas of job improvement are quite numerous, but the most common ones which a supervisor can identify and utilize are:
1. Departmental layout
2. Flow of work
3. Workplace layout
4. Utilization of manpower
5. Work methods
6. Materials handling

7. Utilization
8. Motion economy

K. Seven Key Points in Making Improvements
1. Select the job to be improved
2. Study how it is being done now
3. Question the present method
4. Determine actions to be taken
5. Chart proposed method
6. Get approval and apply
7. Solicit worker participation

I. Corrective Techniques of Job Improvement
Specific Problems
1. Size of workload
2. Inability to meet schedules
3. Strain and fatigue
4. Improper use of men and skills
5. Waste, poor quality, unsafe conditions
6. Bottleneck conditions that hinder output
7. Poor utilization of equipment and machine
8. Efficiency and productivity of labor

General Improvement
1. Departmental layout
2. Flow of work
3. Work plan layout
4. Utilization of manpower
5. Work methods
6. Materials handling
7. Utilization of equipment
8. Motion economy

Corrective Techniques
1. Study with scale model
2. Flow chart study
3. Motion analysis
4. Comparison of units produced to standard allowance
5. Methods analysis
6. Flow chart and equipment study
7. Down time vs. running time
8. Motion analysis

M. A Planning Checklist
1. Objectives
2. Controls
3. Delegations
4. Communications
5. Resources
6. Manpower

7. Equipment
8. Supplies and materials
9. Utilization of time
10. Safety
11. Money
12. Work
13. Timing of improvements

N. Five Characteristics of Good Directions
In order to get results, directions must be:
1. Possible of accomplishment
2. Agreeable with worker interests
3. Related to mission
4. Planned and complete
5. Unmistakably clear

O. Types of Directions
1. Demands or direct orders
2. Requests
3. Suggestion or implication
4. volunteering

P. Controls
A typical listing of the overall areas in which the supervisor should establish controls might be:
1. Manpower
2. Materials
3. Quality of work
4. Quantity of work
5. Time
6. Space
7. Money
8. Methods

Q. Orienting the New Employee
1. Prepare for him
2. Welcome the new employee
3. Orientation for the job
4. Follow-up

R. Checklist for Orienting New Employees   Yes   No
1. Do you appreciate the feelings of new employees
   when they first report for work?   ___   ___
2. Are you aware of the fact that the new employee must
   make a big adjustment to his job?   ___   ___
3. Have you given him good reasons for liking the job and
   the organization?   ___   ___
4. Have you prepared for his first day on the job?   ___   ___
5. Did you welcome him cordially and make him feel needed?   ___   ___

	Yes	No

6. Did you establish rapport with him so that he feels free to talk and discuss matters with you? ___ ___
7. Did you explain his job to him and his relationship to you? ___ ___
8. Does he know that his work will be evaluated periodically on a basis that is fair and objective? ___ ___
9. Did you introduce him to his fellow workers in such a way that they are likely to accept him? ___ ___
10. Does he know what employee benefits he will receive? ___ ___
11. Does he understand the importance of being on the job and what to do if he must leave his duty station? ___ ___
12. Has he been impressed with the importance of accident prevention and safe practice? ___ ___
13. Does he generally know his way around the department? ___ ___
14. Is he under the guidance of a sponsor who will teach the right way of doing things? ___ ___
15. Do you plan to follow-up so that he will continue to adjust successfully to his job? ___ ___

S. Principles of Learning
   1. Motivation
   2. Demonstration or explanation
   3. Practice

T. Causes of Poor Performance
   1. Improper training for job
   2. Wrong tools
   3. Inadequate directions
   4. Lack of supervisory follow-up
   5. Poor communications
   6. Lack of standards of performance
   7. Wrong work habits
   8. Low morale
   9. Other

U. Four Major Steps in On-The-Job Instruction
   1. Prepare the worker
   2. Present the operation
   3. Tryout performance
   4. Follow-up

V. Employees Want Five Things
   1. Security
   2. Opportunity
   3. Recognition
   4. Inclusion
   5. Expression

W. Some Don'ts in Regard to Praise
    1. Don't praise a person for something he hasn't done.
    2. Don't praise a person unless you can be sincere.
    3. Don't be sparing in praise just because your superior withholds it from you.
    4. Don't let too much time elapse between good performance and recognition of it

X. How to Gain Your Workers' Confidence
    Methods of developing confidence include such things as:
    1. Knowing the interests, habits, hobbies of employees
    2. Admitting your own inadequacies
    3. Sharing and telling of confidence in others
    4. Supporting people when they are in trouble
    5. Delegating matters that can be well handled
    6. Being frank and straightforward about problems and working conditions
    7. Encouraging others to bring their problems to you
    8. Taking action on problems which impede worker progress

Y. Sources of Employee Problems
    On-the-job causes might be such things as:
    1. A feeling that favoritism is exercised in assignments
    2. Assignment of overtime
    3. An undue amount of supervision
    4. Changing methods or systems
    5. Stealing of ideas or trade secrets
    6. Lack of interest in job
    7. Threat of reduction in force
    8. Ignorance or lack of communications
    9. Poor equipment
    10. Lack of knowing how supervisor feels toward employee
    11. Shift assignments

    Off-the-job problems might have to do with:
    1. Health
    2. Finances
    3. Housing
    4. Family

Z. The Supervisor's Key to Discipline
    There are several key points about discipline which the supervisor should keep in mind:
    1. Job discipline is one of the disciplines of life and is directed by the supervisor.
    2. It is more important to correct an employee fault than to fix blame for it.
    3. Employee performance is affected by problems both on the job and off.
    4. Sudden or abrupt changes in behavior can be indications of important employee problems.
    5. Problems should be dealt with as soon as possible after they are identified.
    6. The attitude of the supervisor may have more to do with solving problems than the techniques of problem solving.
    7. Correction of employee behavior should be resorted to only after the supervisor is sure that training or counseling will not be helpful.

8. Be sure to document your disciplinary actions.
9. Make sure that you are disciplining on the basis of facts rather than personal feelings.
10. Take each disciplinary step in order, being careful not to make snap judgments, or decisions based on impatience.

AA. Five Important Processes of Management
1. Planning
2. Organizing
3. Scheduling
4. Controlling
5. Motivating

BB. When the Supervisor Fails to Plan
1. Supervisor creates impression of not knowing his job
2. May lead to excessive overtime
3. Job runs itself—supervisor lacks control
4. Deadlines and appointments missed
5. Parts of the work go undone
6. Work interrupted by emergencies
7. Sets a bad example
8. Uneven workload creates peaks and valleys
9. Too much time on minor details at expense of more important tasks

CC. Fourteen General Principles of Management
1. Division of work
2. Authority and responsibility
3. Discipline
4. Unity of command
5. Unity of direction
6. Subordination of individual interest to general interest
7. Remuneration of personnel
8. Centralization
9. Scalar chain
10. Order
11. Equity
12. Stability of tenure of personnel
13. Initiative
14. Esprit de corps

DD. Change

Bringing about change is perhaps attempted more often, and yet less well understood, than anything else the supervisor does. How do people generally react to change? (People tend to resist change that is imposed upon them by other individuals or circumstances.

Change is characteristic of every situation. It is a part of every real endeavor where the efforts of people are concerned.

1. Why do people resist change?
   People may resist change because of:
   a. Fear of the unknown
   b. Implied criticism
   c. Unpleasant experiences in the past
   d. Fear of loss of status
   e. Threat to the ego
   f. Fear of loss of economic stability

2. How can we best overcome the resistance to change?
   In initiating change, take these steps:
   a. Get ready to sell
   b. Identify sources of help
   c. Anticipate objections
   d. Sell benefits
   e. Listen in depth
   f. Follow up

II. Brief Topical Summaries

   A. Who/What is the Supervisor?
      1. The supervisor is often called the "highest level employee and the lowest level manager."
      2. A supervisor is a member of both management and the work group. He acts as a bridge between the two.
      3. Most problems in supervision are in the area of human relations, or people problems.
      4. Employees expect: Respect, opportunity to learn and to advance, and a sense of belonging, and so forth.
      5. Supervisors are responsible for directing people and organizing work. Planning is of paramount importance.
      6. A position description is a set of duties and responsibilities inherent to a given position.
      7. It is important to keep the position description up-to-date and to provide each employee with his own copy.

   B. The Sociology of Work
      1. People are alike in many ways; however, each individual is unique.
      2. The supervisor is challenged in getting to know employee differences. Acquiring skills in evaluating individuals is an asset.
      3. Maintaining meaningful working relationships in the organization is of great importance.
      4. The supervisor has an obligation to help individuals to develop to their fullest potential.
      5. Job rotation on a planned basis helps to build versatility and to maintain interest and enthusiasm in work groups.
      6. Cross training (job rotation) provides backup skills.

7. The supervisor can help reduce tension by maintaining a sense of humor, providing guidance to employees, and by making reasonable and timely decisions. Employees respond favorably to working under reasonably predictable circumstances.
8. Change is characteristic of all managerial behavior. The supervisor must adjust to changes in procedures, new methods, technological changes, and to a number of new and sometimes challenging situations.
9. To overcome the natural tendency for people to resist change, the supervisor should become more skillful in initiating change.

C. Principles and Practices of Supervision
1. Employees should be required to answer to only one superior.
2. A supervisor can effectively direct only a limited number of employees, depending upon the complexity, variety, and proximity of the jobs involved.
3. The organizational chart presents the organization in graphic form. It reflects lines of authority and responsibility as well as interrelationships of units within the organization.
4. Distribution of work can be improved through an analysis using the "Work Distribution Chart."
5. The "Work Distribution Chart" reflects the division of work within a unit in understandable form.
6. When related tasks are given to an employee, he has a better chance of increasing his skills through training.
7. The individual who is given the responsibility for tasks must also be given the appropriate authority to insure adequate results.
8. The supervisor should delegate repetitive, routine work. Preparation of recurring reports, maintaining leave and attendance records are some examples.
9. Good discipline is essential to good task performance. Discipline is reflected in the actions of employees on the job in the absence of supervision.
10. Disciplinary action may have to be taken when the positive aspects of discipline have failed. Reprimand, warning, and suspension are examples of disciplinary action.
11. If a situation calls for a reprimand, be sure it is deserved and remember it is to be done in private.

D. Dynamic Leadership
1. A style is a personal method or manner of exerting influence.
2. Authoritarian leaders often see themselves as the source of power and authority.
3. The democratic leader often perceives the group as the source of authority and power.
4. Supervisors tend to do better when using the pattern of leadership that is most natural for them.
5. Social scientists suggest that the effective supervisor use the leadership style that best fits the problem or circumstances involved.
6. All four styles—telling, selling, consulting, joining—have their place. Using one does not preclude using the other at another time.

7. The theory X point of view assumes that the average person dislikes work, will avoid it whenever possible, and must be coerced to achieve organizational objectives.
8. The theory Y point of view assumes that the average person considers work to be a natural as play, and, when the individual is committed, he requires little supervision or direction to accomplish desired objectives.
9. The leader's basic assumptions concerning human behavior and human nature affect his actions, decisions, and other managerial practices.
10. Dissatisfaction among employees is often present, but difficult to isolate. The supervisor should seek to weaken dissatisfaction by keeping promises, being sincere and considerate, keeping employees informed, and so forth.
11. Constructive suggestions should be encouraged during the natural progress of the work.

E. Processes for Solving Problems
1. People find their daily tasks more meaningful and satisfying when they can improve them.
2. The causes of problems, or the key factors, are often hidden in the background. Ability to solve problems often involves the ability to isolate them from their backgrounds. There is some substance to the cliché that some persons "can't see the forest for the trees."
3. New procedures are often developed from old ones. Problems should be broken down into manageable parts. New ideas can be adapted from old one.
4. People think differently in problem-solving situations. Using a logical, patterned approach is often useful. One approach found to be useful includes these steps:
   a. Define the problem
   b. Establish objectives
   c. Get the facts
   d. Weigh and decide
   e. Take action
   f. Evaluate action

F. Training for Results
1. Participants respond best when they feel training is important to them.
2. The supervisor has responsibility for the training and development of those who report to him.
3. When training is delegated to others, great care must be exercised to insure the trainer has knowledge, aptitude, and interest for his work as a trainer.
4. Training (learning) of some type goes on continually. The most successful supervisor makes certain the learning contributes in a productive manner to operational goals.
5. New employees are particularly susceptible to training. Older employees facing new job situations require specific training, as well as having need for development and growth opportunities.
6. Training needs require continuous monitoring.
7. The training officer of an agency is a professional with a responsibility to assist supervisors in solving training problems.

8. Many of the self-development steps important to the supervisor's own growth are equally important to the development of peers and subordinates. Knowledge of these is important when the supervisor consults with others on development and growth opportunities.

G. Health, Safety, and Accident Prevention
1. Management-minded supervisors take appropriate measures to assist employees in maintaining health and in assuring safe practices in the work environment.
2. Effective safety training and practices help to avoid injury and accidents.
3. Safety should be a management goal. All infractions of safety which are observed should be corrected without exception.
4. Employees' safety attitude, training and instruction, provision of safe tools and equipment, supervision, and leadership are considered highly important factors which contribute to safety and which can be influenced directly by supervisors.
5. When accidents do occur, they should be investigated promptly for very important reasons, including the fact that information which is gained can be used to prevent accidents in the future.

H. Equal Employment Opportunity
1. The supervisor should endeavor to treat all employees fairly, without regard to religion, race, sex, or national origin.
2. Groups tend to reflect the attitude of the leader. Prejudice can be detected even in very subtle form. Supervisors must strive to create a feeling of mutual respect and confidence in every employee.
3. Complete utilization of all human resources is a national goal. Equitable consideration should be accorded women in the work force, minority-group members, the physically and mentally handicapped, and the older employee. The important question is: "Who can do the job?"
4. Training opportunities, recognition for performance, overtime assignments, promotional opportunities, and all other personnel actions are to be handled on an equitable basis.

I. Improving Communications
1. Communications is achieving understanding between the sender and the receiver of a message. It also means sharing information—the creation of understanding.
2. Communication is basic to all human activity. Words are means of conveying meanings; however, real meanings are in people.
3. There are very practical differences in the effectiveness of one-way, impersonal, and two-way communications. Words spoken face-to-face are better understood. Telephone conversations are effective, but lack the rapport of person-to-person exchanges. The whole person communicates.
4. Cooperation and communication in an organization go hand in hand. When there is a mutual respect between people, spelling out rules and procedures for communicating is unnecessary.
5. There are several barriers to effective communications. These include failure to listen with respect and understanding, lack of skill in feedback, and misinterpreting the meanings of words used by the speaker. It is also common

practice to listen to what we want to hear, and tune out things we do not want to hear.
   6. Communication is management's chief problem. The supervisor should accept the challenge to communicate more effectively and to improve interagency and intra-agency communications.
   7. The supervisor may often plan for and conduct meetings. The planning phase is critical and may determine the success or the failure of a meeting.
   8. Speaking before groups usually requires extra effort. Stage fright may never disappear completely, but it can be controlled.

J. Self-Development
   1. Every employee is responsible for his own self-development.
   2. Toastmaster and toastmistress clubs offer opportunities to improve skills in oral communications.
   3. Planning for one's own self-development is of vital importance. Supervisors know their own strengths and limitations better than anyone else.
   4. Many opportunities are open to aid the supervisor in his developmental efforts, including job assignments; training opportunities, both governmental and non-governmental—to include universities and professional conferences and seminars.
   5. Programmed instruction offers a means of studying at one's own rate.
   6. Where difficulties may arise from a supervisor's being away from his work for training, he may participate in televised home study or correspondence courses to meet his self-development needs.

K. Teaching and Training
   1. The Teaching Process
   Teaching is encouraging and guiding the learning activities of students toward established goals. In most cases this process consists of five steps: preparation, presentation, summarization, evaluation, and application.

   a. Preparation
   Preparation is two-fold in nature; that of the supervisor and the employee. Preparation by the supervisor is absolutely essential to success. He must know what, when, where, how, and whom he will teach. Some of the factors that should be considered are:
   1) The objectives
   2) The materials needed
   3) The methods to be used
   4) Employee participation
   5) Employee interest
   6) Training aids
   7) Evaluation
   8) Summarization

   Employee preparation consists in preparing the employee to receive the material. Probably the most important single factor in the preparation of the employee is arousing and maintaining his interest. He must know the objectives of the training, why he is there, how the material can be used, and its importance to him.

b. Presentation
In presentation, have a carefully designed plan and follow it. The plan should be accurate and complete, yet flexible enough to meet situations as they arise. The method of presentation will be determined by the particular situation and objectives.

c. Summary
A summary should be made at the end of every training unit and program. In addition, there may be internal summaries depending on the nature of the material being taught. The important thing is that the trainee must always be able to understand how each part of the new material relates to the whole.

d. Application
The supervisor must arrange work so the employee will be given a chance to apply new knowledge or skills while the material is still clear in his mind and interest is high. The trainee does not really know whether he has learned the material until he has been given a chance to apply it. If the material is not applied, it loses most of its value.

e. Evaluation
The purpose of all training is to promote learning. To determine whether the training has been a success or failure, the supervisor must evaluate this learning.
In the broadest sense, evaluation includes all the devices, methods, skills, and techniques used by the supervisor to keep himself and the employees informed as to their progress toward the objectives they are pursuing. The extent to which the employee has mastered the knowledge, skills, and abilities, or changed his attitudes, as determined by the program objectives, is the extent to which instruction has succeeded or failed.
Evaluation should not be confined to the end of the lesson, day, or program but should be used continuously. We shall note later the way this relates to the rest of the teaching process.

2. Teaching Methods
A teaching method is a pattern of identifiable student and instructor activity used in presenting training material.
All supervisors are faced with the problem of deciding which method should be used at a given time.

a. Lecture
The lecture is direct oral presentation of material by the supervisor. The present trend is to place less emphasis on the trainer's activity and more on that of the trainee.

b. Discussion
Teaching by discussion or conference involves using questions and other techniques to arouse interest and focus attention upon certain areas, and by doing so creating a learning situation. This can be one of the most

valuable methods because it gives the employees an opportunity to express their ideas and pool their knowledge.

- c. Demonstration
  The demonstration is used to teach how something works or how to do something. It can be used to show a principle or what the results of a series of actions will be. A well-staged demonstration is particularly effective because it shows proper methods of performance in a realistic manner.

- d. Performance
  Performance is one of the most fundamental of all learning techniques or teaching methods. The trainee may be able to tell how a specific operation should be performed but he cannot be sure he knows how to perform the operation until he has done so.
  As with all methods, there are certain advantages and disadvantages to each method.

- e. Which Method to Use
  Moreover, there are other methods and techniques of teaching. It is difficult to use any method without other methods entering into it. In any learning situation, a combination of methods is usually more effective than any one method alone.

Finally, evaluation must be integrated into the other aspects of the teaching-learning process.

It must be used in the motivation of the trainees; it must be used to assist in developing understanding during the training; and it must be related to employee application of the results of training.

This is distinctly the role of the supervisor.

Basic Fundamentals of Automotive Vehicles

Contents

	PAGE
I. TYPES OF AUTOMOTIVE VEHICLES	1
II. WEIGHT DISTRIBUTION AND LOAD SECURING METHODS	1
III. AUTOMOTIVE VEHICLE OPERATION	5
IV. OPERATOR'S MAINTENANCE	23
V. LUBRICATION	27
VI. TIRES	31

Basic Fundamentals of Automotive Vehicles

This chapter provides general information on starting, operating, and maintaining automotive equipment for hauling materials, equipment, passengers, and fuels. It includes information on the capabilities, gross limits, and utilization of automotive equipment. Also covered are safety precautions to be observed when operating or working near automotive equipment, inflating and changing tires, and handling, loading, hauling, and offloading materials, equipment, and fuels. Knowledge of the information in this chapter and its application to the job will enable you to perform your duties more efficiently.

I. TYPES OF AUTOMOTIVE VEHICLES

PASSENGER CARRYING VEHICLES

The most common types of passenger carrying vehicles are automobiles, buses, carryalls, station wagons, and ambulances. These vehicles are used to transport light cargo and personnel.

HAULING VEHICLES

The most common standard trucks are classified by weight-carrying capacity and by body type. The weight-carrying capacity may be referred to as light trucks, from 1/2 to 2 tons; medium trucks, from 1 1/2 to 2 1/2 tons; and heavy duty trucks, from 2 1/2 to 5 tons.

A body-type classification may refer to the principal purpose for which the truck is used (hauling of cargo), or to the physical character of the particular body (stake, van, or dump).

TRUCK-TRACTOR AND SEMITRAILER

Besides standard trucks, industry uses many truck-tractors with semitrailers. Truck-tractors used to tow semitrailers may be gasoline or diesel engine powered, and range in capacity from 5 tons through 15 tons. Semitrailers are made in a variety of body types such as personnel carrying, fuel tank, cargo van, stake, bitumen tank, and low-bed (equipment hauling). Low-bed trailers of several lengths and widths up to 75-ton capacity are also used.

FUEL HANDLING VEHICLES

Fuel handling vehicles are classified as *fuel tank trucks* or *fuel tank semitrailers.* Each vehicle has distinguishing characteristics (model, size, and capacity). The purpose of fuel handling vehicles is to load, haul, and discharge fuel to other vehicles, aircraft, or fuel depots.

II. WEIGHT DISTRIBUTION AND LOAD SECURING METHODS

Distribution of cargo has definite bearing on the life of tires, axles, frame, and other parts of the vehicles. The fact that a truck or trailer is not loaded beyond its gross vehicle weight capacity does not mean that the individual tires and axles may not be overloaded by faulty distribution of the cargo.

As an aid to properly loading a truck or semitrailer, the center of the payload must be determined. In a truck, the position of the center of payload is the center of the body, or the point midway between the rear of the driver's cab and the tailgate. In a truck-tractor semitrailer unit, the position of the center of the payload is roughly the center of the semitrailer body, because the tractor's front wheels seldom carry any of the payload. When loading, it is important that the maximum capacity of the vehicle is not exceeded over any one of the axles and, if possible, that loads are distributed so that there is a less-than-maximum axle loading. No vehicle will be loaded over its rated capacity without direct authorization.

The trend of vehicle manufacturers is to rate trucks in terms of maximum gross vehicle weight instead of by tonnage capacities. This has resulted in poor utilization of trucks because of loading below rated capacities. It has also caused confusion, in many instances as to the maximum pounds of payload that may be transported in trucks rated in tonnage capacities.

The maximum permissible payload of a truck is determined by deducting the curb weight and weight of the driver (175 lbs.) from the manufacturer's gross vehicle weight rating. The maximum gross vehicle weight rating for a specified operating condition applies only when the tires and equipment on the truck are in accordance with the manufacturer's recommendations for the specified operating condition, which is referred to as *ideal*, *moderate*, or *severe*,

Ideal conditions mean that the truck is operated over improved, level roads, such as asphalt or concrete, at constant, relatively moderate speeds, with no adverse weather or road conditions. Under these conditions, recommended payload equals 100 percent of maximum permissible payload.

Moderate conditions mean that the truck is operated at high speeds over improved highways, such as asphalt or concrete, with or without long or steep grades, or at moderate speeds over semi-improved roads with gravel or equivalent surfacing, in gently rolling country with few steep grades and no adverse weather or road conditions. Under these conditions, recommended payload equals 80 percent of maximum permissible payload.

Severe conditions means that the vehicle is operated off the highway on rough or hilly terrain or over unimproved or pioneer access roads with deep ruts, holes, or steep grades; or where traffic has created deep holes or ruts in heavy snow covering normally good city streets or highways. Under these conditions, the recommended payload equals 64 percent of maximum permissible payload.

It is important that the payload weight be properly distributed over the body so that the percentage of weight carried by the front axle and that carried by the rear axle will be in the ratio for which the vehicle was designed.

A knowledge of the following terms will give you a better understanding of payload weight distribution for vehicles.

Gross Vehicle Weight (GVW) means the total weight of the loaded truck. It is the sum of the weights of the chassis, accessories, equipment attachments, cab, body, full complement of fuel, lubricants and coolant, payload, and driver.

Curb weight is the weight of the empty truck - without payload and driver - including fuel tank, cooling system, and crankcase filled. It also includes the weight of tools, spare wheel, and all other equipment specified as standard.

Dry chassis weight means the weight of the chassis complete with cowl, but not including weight of cab, body or fifth wheel, spare wheel, tire assembly with carrier, fuel, lubricants, coolant, tools, payload, operator, and frame reinforcement where required.

Payload allowance means the maximum weight of material that can be transported.

Check material for damage before and during the loading operation. Do not accept damaged material unless the damage is noted on the dispatch order or written acknowledgement of the damage is received from the supply department.

Physical dimensions, capacities, weight limitations, and load distribution of trucks and trailers vary greatly. These variations preclude the covering of all types of loads. Therefore, the methods and procedures described here must be considered typical.

There are conditions which can cause load movement while in transit. However, almost all load movement can be prevented by proper blocking and bracing. All loads must be balanced in the vehicle lengthwise and crosswise before the vehicle is operated. Precautions must be taken to prevent vertical movement because of sudden stops or travel over rough terrain as vertical movement can cause the breakdown of good blocking and bracing. If the load is not placed tightly or is out of alignment, the unbalanced loading will cause unequal pressures. The use of bulkheads, separation gates, dividers (lengthwise and crosswise), layer separations, runners, blocks, cleats, and strapping, properly fabricated and applied, will prevent most load movement.

The truck and trailer combination can be adapted to transport various types of materials such as fragile, bulky, compact, dense, and rough items, and high center of gravity items. In order to accommodate the variety of items you must plan the load, properly prepare the truck or trailer, and secure the load to the vehicle. This will prevent any possibility of the load shifting or falling off the vehicle, shifting and contacting other traffic, fouling underpasses, culverts, bridge abutments, and creating a hazard to pedestrians. Securing the load can be accomplished by staying the load with proper lines, or chains secured by tie-down or binders. Use appropriate gear such as paper, cloth, or other type filler to protect fragile items from damage by chafing (rubbing together).

If the truck or trailer is not enclosed or covered, use tarpaulins to cover the cargo and prevent exposure, damage, loss of cargo, or littering.

When transporting pipe, lumber, or other unusually long loads which extend beyond the truck body, attach a red flag to the end of the load and use a red light to mark the end of the load when traveling at night.

Before operating a truck or trailer loaded with unusually heavy, long, or odd-sized materials, ensure that the load weight and dimensions are within the prescribed state and local regulations. If oversize or overweight vehicles are required to be used for a particular job, obtain special permits prior to moving such loads or vehicles on public highways.

When transporting explosives or material interstate, adhere to all instructions, state and local laws, and I.C.C. regulations.

PRINCIPLES OF OPERATION OF PASSENGER CARRYING VEHICLES

You should have knowledge about how components are assembled to make up the automotive chassis consisting of the engine, frame, power train, wheels, steering and braking systems.

Passenger carrying vehicles which include automobiles, buses, carry-alls, station wagons, and ambulances are all similar in their principles of operation although some assemblies and components will be different in body styles, types, and sizes.

PRINCIPLES OF OPERATION OF HAULING VEHICLES

A typical <u>dump</u> truck is equipped with a dump body which has a struck capacity of 5 cubic yards, and is hinged to the rear of a subframe which is mounted directly on the truck chassis. The hoist assembly used to raise and lower the dump body is comprised of a pair of double-acting hydraulic cylinders, a positive-displacement gear-type hydraulic pump, a hydraulic oil reservoir, and connecting

high pressure-type hoses. The hydraulic pump is driven by a propeller shaft connected to the power-take-off. Operation of the hoist assembly is controlled by the dump body control lever located to the left of the driver's seat.

By disengaging the vehicle clutch and shifting the dump body control lever to either position other than <u>neutral,</u> the power-take-off and hoist pump engages. When moving the control lever to the <u>power-up</u> position and engaging the clutch, the dump body will raise (when the dump body reaches its limit of travel, it automatically stops). Upon moving the control lever to the <u>power-down</u> position, the dump body will lower. Moving the control lever to the <u>neutral</u> position and locking it will secure the dump body.

Another hauling vehicle used is the <u>truck-tractor</u> and <u>semitrailer</u> combination. This combination is unique in the manner in which the semitrailer and truck-tractor are attached to perform the hauling services for which they are intended. A large part of the weight of the semitrailer in this combination is supported by a connection, called the <u>fifth wheel,</u> the remaining weight is supported by the wheels of the semitrailer. The trailer braking system (usually air) is coupled to the towing vehicle by a flexible hose and a detachable coupling. The trailer braking system is usually designed so that it will keep the trailer in place when the couplings are disconnected. The trailer is also equipped with a landing gear which is a retractable support under the front end of the semitrailer. This gear is used to hold up the front end when it is uncoupled from the truck-tractor. When semitrailers are coupled and uncoupled, it is important that operation of the landing gear be coordinated with operation of the fifth wheel lock. If the landing gear is elevated before the fifth wheel connection is fully locked, the front end of the semitrailer will drop to the ground when the truck-tractor is driven away, with the possibility of damaging both the load and the semitrailer. Before the semitrailer is uncoupled, the brake couplings should be disconnected so that the semitrailer brakes are applied to prevent it from moving.

The method of connecting the truck-tractor to the semitrailer is by means of a fifth wheel. The upper fifth wheel plate is securely attached to the underside of the front end of the semitrailer frame. Permanently attached to the center of the upper fifth wheel plate is a kingpin by which the truck-tractor pulls the semitrailer after the upper fifth wheel is attached to the truck-tractor lower fifth wheel. The kingpin is locked into position by a kingpin lock which is a ring on the lower fifth wheel that clamps around this kingpin. The kingpin lock is operated by a hand lever that extends to the side of the lower fifth wheel and can be released by pulling it out when the semitrailer is to become detached from the truck-tractor.

PRINCIPLES OF OPERATION OF FUEL HAULING VEHICLES

A typical <u>fuel tank</u> truck is equipped with a tank body divided into compartments. Each compartment has a manhole and filler cover assembly, bottom sump or well, discharge valves with screen assemblies and drainpipe. The drainpipes end in a manifold in the equipment compartment. The compartment also houses a delivery pump, a discharge valve control assembly, a pump delivery line gate valve, automatic dump valve drain tube valves, a gravity line gate valve, a filter separator, a pressure gate, a meter, a water separate chamber, and a grounding cable.

The delivery pump is powered by the transfer power takeoff, which is controlled by the transfer power shifting lever located in the driver's compartment. The lever is moved backward to the <u>engaged</u> position to engage the power takeoff which causes the pump to operate. The lever is moved forward to the <u>disengaged</u> position to disengage the power takeoff and stop the pump.

The discharge valve control operating levers control the discharge valves located at the bottom of each tank compartment. Pulling back on a lever opens a discharge valve and permits the flow of fuel into the piping system. Squeezing the trip rod operating handle mounted on the lever, and moving the lever forward, locks the compartment valve and shuts off the flow of fuel.

In an emergency, the discharge valve control remote control lever, located on the left side of the discharge valve control operating lever bank, provides a means of locking all discharge valves. Pulling the handle causes a release lever to trip the operating levers and locks the valves.

III. AUTOMOTIVE VEHICLE OPERATION

The sole source of complete and authentic information on operating a given automotive vehicle is the operator's manual issued by the manufacturer.

The information given in this section describes the prestart checks, starting checks, and operating procedures which are typical of automotive vehicles used.

PRESTART CHECKS

Before operating any vehicle, be sure that it is ready for the run. A prestart check should begin as you approach your vehicle. Take a look at it. Does its overall appearance seem normal? Oftentimes you will be able to tell from this first look if your vehicle has a broken spring or other exterior defects.

As you continue with the prestart check, move around to the front of your vehicle and raise the cap. If the coolant level is not visible, add coolant. Continual lowering of the level of coolant indicates a possible leak in the cooling system. In freezing weather, test the antifreeze solution in the radiator with a hydrometer. If necessary, add enough antifreeze to the coolant to prevent freezing at predicted minimum temperatures. Be sure to report a leaking cooling system on the Operator's Trouble Report so that corrective action can be taken by the maintenance shop.

Next check the level of the lubricating oil in the crankcase. It should be at or near the full mark on the dipstick. If it is not, add sufficient oil to raise the level to full. If the oil is dirty and gritty when rubbed between the fingertips, it will have to be changed.

Fan belts should be checked for defects in the belt, and excessive looseness or tightness. When found to be defective, the belts must be replaced. When found to be too loose or too tight, adjust according to the manufacturer's specifications.

Battery water level must be checked. If the level is not visible, add battery water to the level required. Check for loose battery wire connections, and tighten if required. Have worn or frayed battery wires replaced by the maintenance shop.

Close the hood, making sure that it latches properly.

Check the fuel tank. Most fuel tank gages register when the ignition switch is turned on. If the fuel gage is not working properly, and you have no way of knowing how much fuel is in the tank, fill it up. Running out of fuel could be very inconvenient and embarassing. Be sure to report improper operation of the fuel gage on the Operator's Trouble Report, so that corrective action can be taken by the maintenance shop.

Leaks found during your checks can often be corrected by tightening bolts, filler plugs, and line connections. If these steps fail to stop a leak, report the trouble for corrective action by the maintenance shop.

As you check the wheels and tires, be sure the tire pressure is as recommended (usually stenciled on each fender of the vehicle) by using either a tire gage or a tire air-hose that is equipped with a gage. Be particularly alert for uneven tread wear; this condition may indicate misalignment, need for balancing, or improper inflation. You may replace the tire at the tire shop, but balancing or alignment will be handled by the maintenance shop. When inspecting the wheels, see that the wheel flange bolts are in place and properly secured.

As you continue your prestart checks, examine the vehicle body for missing components, dents, doors that close improperly, and door windows and windshield glass that are cracked or broken. Next look under the vehicle to check the drive shaft, rear end, and rear axles for leaks or other obvious defects. Any discrepancies must be reported on the Operator's Trouble Report, so that corrective action can be taken by the maintenance shop.

When you have completed the external portion of the prestart checks, get into the cab and check the lights by turning on the light switch and observing whether the headlights are burning on both high and low beam. Have someone observe whether the stoplights on the rear of the vehicle go on when you apply the brakes. As you inspect the lights, wipe the glass lenses with a cloth. A film of mud or dust can cut light beams considerably. If the vehicle has special lights, such as turn signals, fog lights, and spotlights, they, too, must be in good working condition. Test the horn, check seat belts, and inspect the rear view mirror for damage. Before moving on, check the condition of the windshield wiper blades. In addition, check the vehicle's brakes, making sure that the brake lines are not broken or leaking, and that the parking brake cable and assembly are in working order. If any item needs to be adjusted, repaired, or replaced, note the trouble on the Operator's Trouble Report, so that corrective action can be performed by the maintenance shop.

A prestart check will be slightly different for each type vehicle, but the basic principles apply to all. At first, these checks may seem like a long and useless procedure. Once you have established a routine, however, you will find that the complete check requires only a few minutes. Many times this check will save you hours of trouble in the field or on the road.

STARTING CHECKS BEFORE OPERATION

After starting the engine, but before putting the vehicle or equipment into motion, make a few additional checks. First, and most important, make certain that you get an oil pressure indication. This indication may be below operating range at first, but be certain that it is registering. If your equipment has an oil pressure low warning light, make certain the light does not remain on more than several seconds after the engine is started. If the light does not go out after several seconds of engine operation, stop the engine and call a mechanic. Occasionally, a defective system causes the light to stay on, but in either case you will need the mechanic.

Your vehicle or equipment ammeter should also register a positive charge as the engine starts to run. This may be indicated by an ammeter which begins to register in a positive direction or by a red light which goes out when the charging begins. You should also check the temperature indicator, which should start to move upward on its scales as the engine warms up. In addition, check the windshield wipers to see if they are operating properly.

DURING OPERATIONS CHECKS

When a vehicle or piece of equipment is not operating properly, there are various symptoms by which the malfunction can be identified. You should be able to recognize these symptoms immediately and stop the machine before damage results. We have already mentioned the starting checks for oil pressure and the electrical system. Now let's look at some of the troubles that may occur during operation.

Temperature. The operating temperature of your piece of equipment is a measure of its mechanical condition. An engine that is running too hot or too cold is not functioning properly, and the cause of the high or low temperature should be determined immediately. If there is trouble in the cooling system, the engine, in most cases, will overheat.

Before you run your piece of equipment into the repair shop or call a mechanic, make a few checks to see if you can locate the trouble. First, check the radiator. If the water is low, refill. In addition, check to see if there are leaves or other matter clogging air passages of the radiator grill. Check the oil level. An insufficient amount of oil can cause overheating. Loose, slipping water pump belts and fan belts will cause overheating; check and tighten them if they are slipping.

If you eliminate these possible causes of overheating, and the temperature is still not normal, it is time to call a mechanic.

Oil Pressure. As mentioned earlier, you should make certain that oil pressure registers when the engine is started. High pressure readings may be observed while the engine is warming up in cold weather, before the oil has reached operating temperature. After a brief warmup period, the gage indicator should return to normal. Do not forget, however, to keep constant check on oil pressure throughout the day. If the pressure should drop, stop the engine and notify a mechanic.

There are a number of things that can cause low oil pressure. Diluted lubricating oil will cause a drop in pressure. If the oil is at the proper level, but is thin and lacks body, it may have been diluted with fuel leaking past the piston rings. The crankcase should be drained and refilled with the proper grade of oil. If frequent oil dilution or low oil pressure continues after changing the oil, your engine needs further services of a mechanic. As mentioned before, on rare occasions the trouble will be in the pressure gage rather than in the engine proper.

Electrical System. If your piece of equipment has a generator and battery, the ammeter indicates the condition of the electrical system. If the ammeter shows a discharge when the engine is running and all electrical accessories such as lights have been turned off, there is something wrong with the system; call a mechanic. Some vehicles have a warning light instead of an ammeter; if this light comes on and stays on during engine operation (except when the engine is idling), this too is an indication of trouble in the electrical system.

Smoking. Whenever you are operating motorized equipment and you see smoke coming from the exhaust pipe, there is trouble of some sort. The most common causes of smoking in a gasoline engine are worn pistons, rings, or cylinders, and faulty fuel mixtures. Smoking caused by worn engine parts is usually coupled with high oil consumption and calls for a major overhaul.

There are a number of mechanical troubles that will cause a diesel to smoke. If the engine is running too cool, the exhaust will form a cloud of white smoke. If the radiator is equipped with adjustable shutters, close them until the engine reaches the proper operating temperature. If the engine does not have shutters, place a partial covering over the radiator to bring the temperature up. Another cause of smoky exhaust is a clogged air cleaner. Follow the maintenance instructions printed on the air cleaner.

If the engine is allowed to idle for considerable periods, there will be more fuel injected into the cylinder than will burn, and consequently it will smoke. Do not idle the engine for long periods.

If the engine is subjected to loads that cause it to slow or lug down, it will begin to smoke. The remedy is to keep the engine revved up and to use the proper gear to handle the load. If you eliminate these causes of smoking and the engine still smokes, it is probably due to injectors, valves, fuel pumps, or worn piston rings; any of these conditions means a repair job for the mechanics.

Wheel Trouble. If you are operating automotive equipment, your hands on the steering wheel will tell you if the vehicle pulls to the right or to the left. You will feel vibrations caused by unbalanced wheels. When you apply the brakes, you will be able to feel whether the wheel is pulled to the right or to the left; thus you will know whether the front wheel brakes are operating evenly.

When you feel the vehicle pull to one side, stop and check the tires. If the tires are evenly inflated and the vehicle still pulls to one side, you should have the wheel alignment and the wheels checked by a mechanic. Your hands on the wheel will also tell you if the vehicle turns hard and whether the play in the steering wheel is excessive.

Transmission and Differential. Transmission difficulties may be characterized by shifting difficulty, gears jamming, and by unusual noises from the area where the transmission is located. This is true of a vehicle having either a manual or an automatic transmission. About the only thing that an equipment operator can do is to check the level of lubricant; if the transmission is low on lubricant, fill it to the proper level.

Differential trouble can often be recognized by noise from the differential area. However, noise from defective universal joints, rear wheel bearings, tires, or mufflers are sometimes mistaken for differential trouble. Stop the vehicle if noise occurs. For the purpose of operational maintenance with respect to differentials, an equipment operator has the responsibility of seeing that lubricant is at the proper level and bringing it up to the proper level if it is low. If there is differential trouble and you find that the level is not low, you should turn the job of locating and correcting the trouble over to a mechanic.

Brake Troubles. If your equipment is fitted with airbrakes, be aware of the air pressure indicator reading at all times. The reading may be too high; a high reading would probably indicate a faulty gage, a governor out of adjustment, or a defective governor. The most usual trouble with airbrakes is too little pressure. Low pressure can indicate a number of things, but most commonly it indicates a defective air safety valve, a governor out of adjustment, or an excessively worn compressor.

The air pressure gage is only one of the possible means by which you will discover trouble. Some of the other airbrake troubles are that they release too slowly, grab, or brake unevenly.

On hydraulic brakes, a soft, spongy pedal indicates either improper adjustment of air in the system. A pedal that goes to, or nearly to, the floorboard calls for immediate attention by a mechanic. Stops that require excessive pressure on the pedal, and brakes that are overly sensitive and grab when only slight pressure is applied to the pedal are other troubles that mean work for the mechanic.

Be sure that your brakes are in the best possible condition; your life may depend on them.

Clutches. If the clutch does not completely disengage when the pedal is entirely depressed, or if the clutch takes hold too near the floorboard, you should report the condition to a mechanic.

Vibration. On most of the equipment you operate, you will feel a certain amount of vibration; an unusual amount of vibration should not have to shake you out of your seat to make you realize that something is wrong. Unbalanced wheels, a cylinder that is not firing, a bent drive shaft, and other mechanical defects will cause excessive vibration.

After operating a piece of equipment for a period of time, you should be so aware of its characteristic sounds and its feel that you will be able to detect the slightest variation from normal operation. You may not be able to diagnose the mechanical symptoms, but you should be able to recognize trouble when it starts.

OPERATING PASSENGER CARRYING AND HAULING VEHICLES

After completing all prestarting and starting checks, and ensuring everything is in order, place the transmission in neutral or park and start the engine. Before you pull onto the road, be sure that it is clear enough for you to do so safely.

If your vehicle has an automatic transmission, set the transmission lever at D (Drive) or push in the D button. Release the emergency brake and speed up the engine by depressing the accelerator about one quarter of the way toward the floorboard. The vehicle should accelerate in Low smoothly. At a speed of about 18 to 25 mph under normal acceleration, the transmission should shift automatically into Drive. On some vehicles you must release the accelerator momentarily to let the transmission shift into Drive. A faint click in the transmission indicates the shift to the higher gear.

With a standard transmission, depress the clutch pedal, shift into first (low) gear, release the emergency brake, and engage the clutch slowly and smoothly while speeding up the engine a bit with the accelerator. Let the vehicle get up to about 10 to 15 mph before shifting into second gear, and to about 20 to 25 mph before shifting into third or high gear. Depress the clutch pedal before each shift, and release it smoothly after shifting.

On many vehicles with standard transmission, the gear shift lever is mounted on the steering column. Refer to the vehicle instruction manual for gear shifting directions.

Up and Down Grade. In starting a vehicle with a standard transmission up a grade from a stationary position, keep the emergency brake on to prevent the vehicle from rolling backward. Push in the clutch, shift into low, then ease off on the clutch pedal. As the clutch begins to take hold, release the emergency brake slowly, at the same time, increasing the speed of the engine. If these operations are performed carefully, the vehicle should start smoothly. Shift the vehicle into second only when it has reached enough speed to continue upgrade without laboring or jerking. You may not be able to shift from second to high until the end of the grade. If the grade is very steep, you may have to use low gear all the way up.

Downgrade always use the same gear that would be used going upgrade. Depress the clutch, shift into neutral, accelerate the engine to a speed that will pull the vehicle in a lower gear, then shift into the lower gear. If the procedure is efficiently carried out, the shift will be virtually noiseless.

UNDER NO CIRCUMSTANCES SHOULD THE VEHICLE COAST DOWNGRADE IN NEUTRAL. A vehicle out of gear is out of control except, possibly, when the brakes are applied. Even then the vehicle may pick up speed in excess of its braking ability, and you risk not only burning up the brakes, but having a serious accident as well.

Low Range and Double-Clutching. Heavy trucks may be equipped also with a two-speed rear axle and have what is known as a low range. By shifting to this low range, you tap the extra engine power that is needed to start an extremely heavy load, in rough driving, and in steep climbing. Under normal driving conditions, you would use the normal range.

No matter what kind of load the truck is carrying, start out in low gear, not in second. Together, the low range and low gear give maximum starting power. Take your time and accelerate smoothly in each gear before shifting to the next higher gear. Under some road or load conditions, the series of shifts from low to high may require as much as a mile of travel.

The transmissions of some trucks and buses are constructed in a form which makes it necessary to double-clutch to prevent the clashing and grinding of gears when shifting. Double-clutching adjusts engine speed to vehicle speed in a particular gear.

Double-clutching requires some practice. If you can possibly arrange to do so, take a truck around a given area with a supervisor or other experienced equipment operator to instruct you.

```
DOUBLE-CLUTCHING FROM A LOWER
        TO A HIGHER GEAR

• Push in clutch pedal
• Take foot off gas pedal
• Shift into neutral
• Let out clutch pedal
• Wait momentarily
• Push in clutch pedal again
• Shift to higher gear
• Let out clutch pedal
• Depress gas pedal
```

```
DOUBLE-CLUTCHING FROM A HIGHER
        TO A LOWER GEAR

• Push in clutch pedal
• Take foot off gas pedal
• Shift into neutral
• Let out clutch pedal
• Accelerate engine
• Push in clutch pedal again
• Shift to lower gear
• Let out clutch pedal
• Depress gas pedal
```

Steering. Proper steering is a matter of keeping your hands on the wheel, your eyes on the road, and your mind on safe driving. It also means keeping the vehicle on your side of the road, avoiding holes and obstructions, and passing other vehicles safely.

If your vehicle steers hard, pulls to the right or left, or the front wheels shimmy, try to find the cause of the trouble at once. It may be due to nothing more than underinflated tires, or it may be caused by the wheels being out of balance or alignment. It may also mean that some part of the steering mechanism needs adjusting, or repair.

If not accustomed to power steering, you may have difficulty at first in guiding this type of vehicle, because its steering mechanism responds more readily than one with conventional steering. Under power steering, a mere finger nudge of the steering wheel will turn the vehicle from its path.

Backing. Not all driving is forward. You will also have to back into loading platforms and parking spaces and into position for shovel loading and other jobs on construction projects. Backing must be done with skill and caution. If the rear view of your vehicle is restricted, have someone direct you. Otherwise, get out frequently to check whether the way is clear. NOTE: The operator is responsible for all backing accidents.

Curves. Speeding under any conditions is dangerous and unsafe, but speeding on curves is extremely dangerous for at least four reasons: it increases the hazard of skidding; it heightens the _ possibility of load shifting; it wears tires away very fast; and the vehicle may run off the road or overturn.

It is not easy to state at what speed you can safely round a curve. The maximum safe speed depends on the arc of the curve, the width of the road, and the condition of its surface. Many curves are posted with safe speed limit signs, but on many, YOU still must judge how fast to take them.

In approaching a curve, SLOW DOWN as soon as it comes into view, then accelerate enough to keep the vehicle pulling steadily. If the road ahead curves frequently, maintain a speed moderate enough to keep the vehicle on an even keel, using the highest gear possible. Avoid using the brakes. NEVER try to pass another vehicle on a curve. Stay on your own side of the center line.

Skids. To avoid skids, watch for obstructions, pavement breaks, holes, shoulder edges, and loose gravel that might grab your wheels. Beware of wet roads, roads strewn with leaves, roads full of mud or slush, and railroad and trolley tracks.

To prevent going into a skid, cut down your speed, and increase the distance between your vehicle and the one ahead. Do not accelerate too fast or the wheels may spin; drive in as high a gear as possible. The higher the gear, the less the tendency to skid. Should you get into a skid, however, turn the wheels IN THE DIRECTION OF THE SKID, stay in gear with the clutch engaged, and accelerate slightly to help straighten the course of the vehicle. DO NOT APPLY THE BRAKES; you will only increase the skid by locking the wheels. If any slowing is necessary, it should be done in a lower gear.

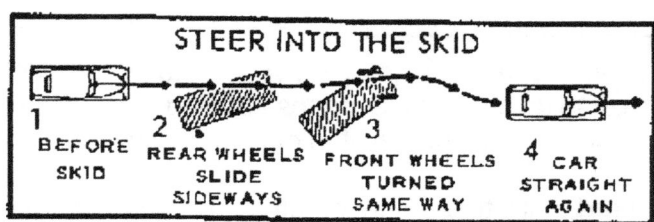

Off and On The Shoulder. Getting off and on the shoulder is a common occurrence on narrow roads and in congested traffic, and it usually is not difficult to get back on the road. However, if the shoulder is lower than the road, first change to a lower gear without braking. Second, instead of scrapping or tearing away the side walls of your tires by trying to creep back upon the road gradually, proceed slowly until you are able to get back by making a sharp angle turn to the left.

OPERATING TRUCK TRACTOR AND SEMITRAILER

Before setting out with a truck tractor and semitrailer, you must know the procedures for coupling and uncoupling the truck tractor from the semitrailer. To couple the truck tractor to the semitrailer, proceed as follows:

1. Place wheel chocks in front of and behind the trailer wheels.

2. Make sure the fifth wheel lock is open; then back the tractor close enough to the trailer to permit coupling of the brake lines.

3. Connect the brake hoses in the proper order by first connecting the truck tractor <u>service</u> air line hose to the trailer, followed by the <u>emergency</u> air line hose.

4. Open the cutout valve to allow pressure to build up in the reserve tank on the trailer.

5. Apply pressure to the trailer brakes, if they are operated independently. If the trailer brakes are not operated independently, proceed as described below.

    a. For vacuum-operated brakes, turn off the service line valve and disconnect the hose; this should automatically apply pressure to the trailer brakes.

    b. For air-operated brakes, turn off the emergency line valve and disconnect the hose; this should automatically apply pressure to the trailer brakes.

6. Back the tractor under the trailer until the fifth wheel engages the trailer kingpin and locks. If the tractor is not in line to engage the trailer kingpin and must be repositioned, uncouple the airhose before moving the tractor to avoid breaking the hose.

7. When the fifth wheel and the kingpin are locked, test security of the hookup. Remove the chocks, place the tractor in first gear, engage the clutch, and move the tractor forward slightly while applying pressure to the brakes.

8. If the trailer is properly connected, stop the tractor and set the hand brake; double check all couplings, reconnect the air brake hose, and open the air valve.

9. Connect the trailer electrical power line; check for proper operation of lights and, where applicable, heating or refrigeration equipment.

10. Raise the trailer parking legs, and release the trailer parking brake.

11. Before moving the tractor, check the brakes for proper functioning and for adequate air pressure; minimum operating air pressure is 60 pounds.

To uncouple a truck tractor from a semitrailer, proceed as follows:

1. Set the tractor hand brake.

2. Apply pressure to the trailer brakes by disconnecting the hose lines, as described above, step 5.

3. Disconnect the trailer electrical power lines and secure them to the tractor.

4. Place wheel chocks in front of and behind the trailer wheels and set the trailer parking brake.

5. Lower trailer parking legs; be sure the ground is firm enough to prevent the parking legs from sinking.

6. Place the fifth wheel hook lock handle in the release position; move the tractor foward slightly, leaving the trailer kingpin partly in the fifth wheel slot.

7. Recheck the trailer supports; if trailer is secure, move the tractor away from the trailer.

<u>Safe Operation.</u> In driving a tractor-trailer, watch for obstructions. Since a trailer body is often considerably higher than a truck body, you must allow for this height and watch out for viaducts, tree limbs, extended roofs OVER loading docks, and other obstructions. Also watch weight limitations on bridges. A tractor-trailer usually is longer than a truck; therefore, you must drive it carefully to avoid cutting in on other motorists.

<u>Braking, Stopping, and Parking.</u> With independently operated trailer brakes, apply the trailer brakes FIRST, gradually and smoothly, to avoid locking the wheels and skidding. As speed is reduced, apply the truck or tractor brakes to spread the braking load on all wheels. With synchronized brakes, both tractor and trailer brakes are operated by one foot pedal like the brakes on automobiles.

In making emergency stops, be sure the trailer brakes are applied either first or simultaneously with - never after - the tractor brakes. Attempting to stop without using the trailer brakes will cause the trailer load to push the tractor forward, and possibly push it into whatever you are trying to avoid.

In the event of any stop where you leave your cab, set your parking brake. This applies to all automotive equipment. If you have operated tractor-trailer units, you know that you can hold the unit on a grade by setting the trailer brake. Holding your rig on the grade by setting the trailer brake is all right AS LONG AS YOU ARE IN THE CAB, but DON'T set the trailer brake and LEAVE the cab. The engine on your rig may die and cause the air pressure to drop off. If this happens, your trailer brakes will release, and you will have a runaway rig.

<u>Turning and Backing.</u> In turning a tractor-trailer, remember that the outside turning circle of the complete unit is the same as that of the tractor, and that the trailer wheels cut inside the path of the tractor.

At first, it might seem that backing would be a difficult operation. Actually, the hinged-in-the-middle feature of tractor-trailer units makes them easier to handle in cramped quarters than conventional trucks.

If you wish to back your automobile or truck to the right, you would naturally turn the steering wheel to the right. To back your semitrailer to the right, you turn your steering wheel to the left. This action pushes the front of the semitrailer to the left and steers the semitrailer wheels to the right.

If you have to make a right-hand back into an alley (sometimes called a <u>blind back</u>), drive the unit past the alley entrance, keeping it far enough from the curb so that the tractor can head slightly to the right as you come to a stop.

Before you start to back, check behind the trailer from both sides of the cab to be sure of your distance, and that traffic is clear. Turn the steering wheel to the LEFT to push the semitrailer around and back it to the right. As you continue to back slowly, keep the tractor wheels turned to the left and continue to check clearances from the right-hand door of the cab. As the trailer swings into the alley (with clearance on all sides), turn the steering wheel to the RIGHT and continue to back the semitrailer into the alley.

As the unit gets into line, straighten the front wheels and back down the alley, watching at all times to see that the semitrailer does not veer to either side. If the semitrailer angles to the left wall, adjust it to the right by turning your steering wheel to the left. If the semitrailer veers to the right, adjust it to the left by turning your steering wheel to the right.

A left-hand back is easier, because you can see the trailer from the driver's side of the cab. Of course, the direction you turn the steering wheel is just the opposite to a right-hand back.

Remember that to back the semitrailer to the right you turn the steering wheel to the left; and to back the semitrailer to the left, you turn the steering wheel to the right.

A skidding tractor-trailer unit is handled in a slightly different manner than a conventional vehicle. Turn your wheels immediately in the direction of the skid, accelerate slightly and (ONLY if the tractor is equipped with independent controlled brakes), apply the trailer brakes off and on gently so that the wheels will not lock. The trailer will then act as a drag and tend to pull both units back in line.

If the trailer starts to skid, handle it like a conventional vehicle, that is, do not apply brakes and turn in direction of skid.

BUSES

When operating buses to transport personnel, you will have responsibilities in addition to those concerning the operation of trucks and trailers.

Whether you operate a small shuttle bus on the base or a large passenger bus through a community from installation to installation, you are expected to observe a schedule of arrivals and departures, and to account for your runs.

Operation. The following rules for the operation of buses are supplementary to those applying to all motor vehicles:

1. Only operators with satisfactory records of safe driving will be assigned to drive buses.

2. Operators must be trained to stop, start, and operate buses smoothly and without jerks or sudden changes in acceleration.

3. Operators must not put vehicle in motion with the doors open,

4. Operators must not close the doors of a bus until passengers are completely clear of the bus when discharging, or fully inside and off the steps when entering the bus.

5. When making a turn or upon approaching a sharp curve, operators must reduce speed and use care to avoid injuring passengers.

6. The bus operator must give his attention to the road when driving and will not carry on unnecessary conversation with the passengers while the vehicle is in motion.

7. Operators of fare-charging buses will not make change while the bus is in motion.

<u>Regulations.</u> The driver of a school bus is required to exercise all precautions listed above in addition to the following special precautions:

1. <u>Speed.</u> No school bus will be driven at a speed greater than that authorized by the laws of the state in which the vehicle is being operated. When children are on the bus, the speed must be not more than 45 miles per hour.

2. <u>Orderly Conduct.</u> Passengers will be under the authority of and directly responsible to the operator of the bus, and the operator will be held responsible for the orderly conduct of the passengers.

3. <u>Regular Stops .</u> Pick up or discharge of any passenger except at regular stops designated is prohibited.

4. <u>Railroad Crossings.</u> Before crossing any railroad track or tracks, you must stop the bus within 50 feet but not less than 15 feet from the nearest rail of such railroad; while stopped, listen and look in both directions along the track for any approaching train; do not proceed until such precautions have been taken and until you have ascertained that the course is clear.

5. <u>Crossing Street.</u> Whenever a school bus stops to discharge passengers who must cross the street or highway in order to reach their destination, such passengers must cross in front of the bus, except when laws regulating local traffic prohibit this. In case of separated lanes with a median strip, the rule applies to both roadways. The bus must not be started until passengers desiring to cross have done so.

6. <u>Escorting Children.</u> The operator of a school bus must not permit pupils to cross a street or highway until they can do so safely; and he will, if necessary, secure the bus, dismount, and act as their escort.

The following precautions apply to operation of semitrailer buses:

1. <u>Passengers</u>

    a.   Standing in moving vehicles is prohibited except where handholds or straps are provided for each standee.

    b.   No passenger will be permitted to ride on running boards or with arms or legs extended outside the vehicle, or seated on fenders, top of cab, cab shields, or in door wells.

c. No passenger will be permitted to get on or off while the vehicle is in motion.

2. Exit-Entrance

a. Exit-entrance on semitrailer buses without doors should be equipped with a heavy gage safety chain across the opening 36 inches above floor level. Chains should be attached by a secure latching arrangement which will permit easy latching and unlatching.

b. The following signs must be posted at or near the inside of the exit and entrance of semitrailer buses not equipped with doors:

SITTING OR STANDING ON STEPS OR IN DOOR WELLS IS PROHIBITED

SAFETY CHAIN MUST BE LATCHED WHILE BUS IS IN MOTION

DUMP TRUCK OPERATION

During dumping operations, the truck should be on level ground or inclined uphill with front of truck facing downward. When the truck is in position, release the lower latches of the tailgate with the hand lever at the front left corner of the body. Now engage the power control with the dump body control lever, located in the cab. With the control lever at the farthest forward position, accelerate the engine moderately; do not race it. Hydraulic pressure will begin to hoist the dump body.

As the body rises, the load will slide backward under the open tailgate. If the load piles up and blocks the tailgate, place the truck in low gear and move it forward until there is more space to dump the remainder of the load. Do not change the position of the body control lever. If the load does not slide out easily, have someone dislodge it with a long hand shovel (taking care not to stand in the immediate dumping area). When dumping a load containing rocks or other large solids, the tailgate should be latched at the bottom, but unfastened at the top so that the tailgate can drop down and the load can drop. To spread a load over a large area, shift the truck into low gear and drive it slowly forward while dumping.

You can hold the body in any position by returning the control lever to position C. When dumping is completed, lower the body by returning the control lever to position A. Then close the tailgate latches.

TANK TRUCK OPERATION

Tank trucks are used to haul and dispense fuels or other types of liquids. A tank truck is equipped with a stainless steel, 1,200-gallon tank body, which is divided into two 600-gallon compartments. The fuel delivery system is equipped with an upright filter/separator and meter. Since there are only two tank compartments, the discharge valve control has two operating levers. There is a speed control linkage assembly which controls speed of the engine, power takeoff, and delivery pump.

The filter/separator is equipped with three filter elements, three go-no-go fuses, a pressure gage, and an automatic dump (drain) valve. The primary function of the filter element is to collect solid contaminants and separate water from the fuel.

The go-no-go fuses shut off the fuel flow if water or solid contaminants exceed a safe level; the shutoff of flow indicates that the filters are not operating properly. The malfunction must be located and corrected, and the fuses must be replaced before operation is continued.

The pressure gage reflects the condition of each of the filter elements and go-no-go fuses. When the pressure differential between the inlet pressure and the outlet pressure (gage handle in position 1) exceeds 20 psi, or when pressure differential between the inlet pressure and the internal pressure (gage handle in position 2) exceeds 15 psi, filter elements must be replaced. When pressure differential between outlet pressure and internal pressure (gage handle in position 3) exceeds 15 psi, replace the go-no-go fuses.

The automatic dump (drain) valve is float-operated. The float sinks in fuel but rises in water. When water is present in the valve housing, the float rises, the valve opens, and the water drains away through the valve drain tube. Open the automatic dump (drain) valve during fueling operations. Check pressure differential every day that equipment is in use; check it while the pump is operating, and record the readings.

When operating the fuel tank truck for discharging of fuels, follow instructions prescribed in the manufacturer's operating manual or the directions on the inside of the equipment compartment door. The general instructions which follow are typical.

Close the meter drain valve, delivery pump drain cock, and filter/separator drain valve. Open the automatic dump (drain) valve. Enter the driver's compartment and start the engine; depress the clutch, and put the transfer shift lever in neutral; place the transfer power takeoff shift lever in the engaged position; then place the transmission gearshift lever in fourth gear position, and release the clutch.

> CAUTION: Allowing the engine to run with transmission engaged and the transfer shift lever in neutral without the transfer power takeoff in the engaged position will cause bearing failure in the transfer case. Be sure to shift the transmission gearshift lever to neutral when not operating the power takeoff.

After the vehicle has been made ready, return to the fuel handling control compartment and set the remote hand throttle to allow the engine to operate at 700 rpm when the fuel dispensing pump is engaged. Move the discharge valve control operating lever of the tank compartment to be discharged to the open position; and be sure, before pumping operations begin, to attach the grounding wire to the vehicle being serviced. Open the pump delivery line hose and squeeze the nozzle operating lever and discharge the fuel. After discharging the fuel, close the pump delivery line gate valve, and move the discharge valve control operating lever to the closed position. Close the automatic dump valve drain tube valve and turn the hand throttle to the closed position. Return to the driver's compartment; depress

the clutch and place the transmission gearshift lever in neutral; then place the transfer power takeoff shifting lever to disengaged, and stop the engine.

When changing from one type of fuel to another, drain and flush the fuel compartment, pump filter/separator, service lines, manifold, meter, gage, and dispensing hoses and nozzles.

Remember, all pumping mechanisms are not controlled and operated in the same manner. You will find that each make or model will operate differently. If you are in doubt as to the proper pump operation and maintenance procedures, study the caution and instruction plates located near the pump and control mechanisms.

Drivers of fuel tank trucks must observe safe driving practices as listed below.

Drive defensively, and make allowances for other drivers.

Make turns only from proper lanes, and signal intent to other drivers. Never leave the proper lane except when necessary and then only when safe to do so.

Avoid excessive speeds at all times and especially on rough terrain, in gravel, and on curves. Be alert for passing or approaching traffic.

Drive downgrade in the same gear that would be used to drive upgrade.

Move completely off the road, if possible, when necessary to park. Set brakes, and chock wheels if stopping on a grade. Set flags during day and set flares or reflectors at night.

Stop at all railroad crossings, and be especially watchful in the case of multiple tracks.

Keep vehicle moving to prevent accumulations of vapor if a small leak develops in route. Arrange to discharge load at nearest point.

Ask for assistance if a large amount of fuel is escaping, such as might be the case if the vehicle is damaged. Immediately secure the engine, cordon the area, and obtain firefighting and security support.

Reduce refueling stops to a minimum under load. Stop the engine while refueling the prime mover.

Avoid driving past a fire or near the route until it is safe to do so.

Never smoke on or about tank vehicles used for hauling flammable liquids. Carry no matches on such vehicles.

Examine tires occasionally on long hauls for tire pressure and for damage that could cause an accident.

HAND SIGNALS

When you plan to turn, slow down, or stop, you must let the drivers approaching you and the drivers following you know well in advance what you intend to do.

The hand signals for these maneuvers are shown below. Instead of hand signals, mechanical directional signals may be used if your vehicle is so equipped. When operating vehicles in congested areas such as construction sites, docking areas, and pick-up and delivery areas, the hand signals depicted should be used.

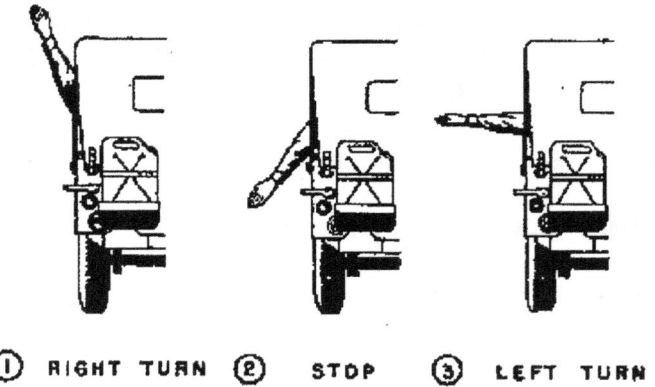

① RIGHT TURN ② STOP ③ LEFT TURN

HAZARDOUS CONDITIONS

Speed should always be reduced for night-time driving. Too many drivers try to drive just as fast at night as they do in the daytime.

Night driving is two to three times more dangerous than day driving. Fatigue and sharply reduced vision are the primary causes for increased danger. The steady hum of the motor and the darkness on the road ahead tend to lull us to sleep at the wheel. Wide-awake driving is necessary at all times and especially at night, since we can see objects only a limited distance ahead. After-dark driving requires different skills and extra care for safe driving.

Listed below are requirements and practices applicable to night driving which should be carefully observed:

1. When you meet a vehicle at night, you must lower your headlight beams when within 500 feet of the approaching vehicle.

2. Lower your headlight beams when following another vehicle within 200 feet.

3. Lower your headlight beams when you are driving on well-lighted streets.

4. Use your lower headlight beams when driving in a fog, and reduce your speed. Driving with your high beams in a fog is like shining your lights on a mirror — light is reflected back into your eyes and blinds you.

5. Avoid looking directly into the lights of vehicles that you are meeting. Instead, watch the right-hand edge of the road.

6. Keep your headlights properly adjusted so that the lower beams are not aimed upward into the approaching driver's eyes.

7. Keep your windshield clean.

8. Slow down when facing the glare from approaching headlights.

9. Be sure you can stop whenever necessary within the vision distance of your vehicle's headlights, and watch continually and carefully for pedestrians along the roadside.

10. Use your headlights during the period from one-half hour after sunset to one-half hour before sunrise, and whenever visibility is reduced.

When overtaking and passing other vehicles on the road, observe the common rules of passing. Use extreme caution whenever passing a vehicle as the view immediately beyond the other vehicle is blocked on that side. The greater the speed of the vehicle ahead, the more road space and time will be required to overtake and pass the vehicle.

Listed below are restrictions for overtaking and passing:

1. Do not pass to the right of another vehicle, except on multiple-lane divided highways (more than two lanes of traffic moving in one direction) and only then if such passing is permitted; use extreme caution in such instances.

2. Do not pass at an intersection or railroad crossing.

3. Do not pass on a hill or curve, except on multiple-lane, divided highways.

4. Do not pass a vehicle that is signaling to turn or to move into your lane of traffic, or one that has started to overtake and pass another vehicle.

5. Do not pass when the center line of the road is solid on your side.

6. Do not pass where the highway is divided by two solid lines.

7. Do not pass when the single center line is solid.

Rain, snow, ice, or fog affect visibility, stopping distance, maneuverability, and vehicle control. Follow these suggestions for driving under such conditions:

1. Adjust the speed of the vehicle to existing conditions.

2. For normal conditions, allow at least one car length between vehicles for every 10 mph that you are traveling. Increase the normal safe distance between vehicles to allow for wet conditions.

3. Use tire chains or snow tires on ice or snow; however, they are only an aid to increase traction and will not eliminate the necessity for added caution.

4. Slow down when approaching bridges, overpasses, and shady areas in the road; surfaces in such areas often freeze before regular roadway surfaces and remain frozen longer.

5. Keep the outside of the windshield and windows clear of snow, ice, and frost at all times, and use the vehicle defroster to improve visibility; use extreme caution when driving in fog.

6. Apply brakes with a light pumping action to prevent skidding and use engine compression to help control the vehicle.

7. Signal well in advance to warn others of an intended stop or turn.

Superhighways, designed for high speed driving, require drivers to be more skillful and alert to avoid accidents. When entering expressways, yield to all traffic. While traveling, allow necessary distance between vehicles for safe stopping; avoid highway hypnosis by making rest stops and opening vents or windows; and never exceed the posted speed. During emergencies, get the vehicle off the roadway; use flasher lights or flares behind the vehicle to warn other motorists; and look behind for oncoming or passing traffic before opening vehicle doors. When leaving expressways, get in the proper lane well before the turn-off, and use turn signals to warn other drivers.

When driving through water, reduce speed to prevent brake drums, engine, and ignition from getting wet. Test the brakes for effectiveness immediately after leaving the water. If water has entered the brake drums and wet the linings, drive at a very slow speed while gently applying sufficient pressure on the brake pedal to cause a slight drag, thereby squeezing the brake linings against the drums and forcing the water out of the linings.

Snow and Ice. Snow and ice severely limit the traction of any vehicle. To increase traction, put chains on all driving wheels. When moving over fresh snow, maintain a slow, steady speed. Rapid acceleration is likely to cause skidding, or cause the wheels to dig in. If your vehicle becomes stuck in a hole in the snow, rocking it back and forth by shifting from forward to reverse may enable you to start again. Brakes, when used, should be applied lightly and released quickly if skidding begins. If you are driving hauling equipment that includes a trailer, apply only the trailer brakes, or at least apply them first.

Hard packed snow or ice is even more dangerous to drive on than newly fallen snow. Snow tires are not much help on ice, as they add little or no traction and give you a false feeling of security. Deflating the tires a bit will assist in preventing skidding.

Mud, Sand, and Swamps. When approaching a stretch of sticky soil or of muddy or swampy ground, put chains on the rear wheels to save yourself a lot of distress. If chains are not available, and the going looks rough, go into the necessary low gear. Engage the front-wheel drive, if the vehicle has one. Size up the road ahead so that once you start you can keep going. As far as possible, avoid ruts, holes, and edges that may cause side slips and swaying loads. Speed should be maintained, but do not spin the wheels. If the wheels start to lose traction, decrease speed but stay in the same gear. If the vehicle should become hopelessly bogged down, do not spin the wheels and burn up the tires, and do not overtax the equipment. Instead disengage the clutch at once, and get out and look the situation over. How to get out of bad situations depends on circumstances.

You may be able to back out and select a better way through. If you have wheel mats, use them. You may be able to jack up one wheel and place brush, boards, rocks, or similar material under it, enabling you to pull out. You may be able to dig your way out by digging a ditch in the direction that the wheels are expected to move. When the wheels are in deep ruts, ditches dug at an angle to the ruts may be necessary to assist the wheels back to a straddle position over the rut.

Of course, if a suitable tow truck is available, use it to get out of trouble. If your piece of equipment is equipped with a winch, use it to pull yourself out.

If the truck has dual wheels, use two tow ropes and six strong stakes. Drive two stakes into the ground the same distance apart as the wheels. Drive these stakes in front of the truck, if the best route out is forward, and behind if the best route out is backward. Use the other four stakes as anchors. The loop ends of the tow ropes are secured to the wheels by passing them between the duals, out through the spokes, and over the hub. The ropes are then attached to the anchor stakes. When this is done, the vehicle can move out on its own power by allowing the tow ropes to wind up between the dual wheels.

If stuck in sand, chicken wire on heavy burlap or canvas tarpaulins staked to the surface will aid greatly in supporting the load of the truck - and usually will get you out. In some cases, sand is somewhat encrusted below the surface and the vehicle will continue to creep forward even though the wheels spin. As long as the vehicle continues to move, the wheels may be kept spinning slowly, allowing your vehicle to dig its way out. Do not allow the vehicle to develop a differential jump; should this occur, STOP VEHICLE and try another solution. You may have to let some of the air out of your tires to pull through a stretch of sand but, as a general rule, it is bad practice to run on underinflated tires. In going through sand, as in going through other tough spots, it is essential to maintain momentum and keep going. Changing of gears must be avoided by selecting the proper gear before entering the sand.

Fording. Before you start through water, whether fording or crossing a stretch of flooded highway, be sure that the water is not so deep that it will drown out your motor. Also make sure that the surface under the water will support your vehicle. As a rule, nothing is gained by attempting to use momentum in crossing streams or other water. Cross slowly in a low gear. If there is any danger of water surging or splashing into the fan, disconnect it before crossing. After crossing the stream, apply the brakes intermittently until dry, enough to hold. At the first opportunity, wheels, crank-case, universal joint, differential, transmission, and other parts submerged should be checked to determine that no water has entered.

SECURING

When returning to the equipment pool area at the end of the day's run, top off fuel tanks, check oil and coolant levels, and position vehicle in a safe manner. Let engine idle, check instrument readings, secure footbrake or handbrake, place transmission in neutral, secure engine by turning off ignition switch, complete daily trip ticket, roll up windows, secure doors, block vehicle if required, drain air tanks (if so equipped), and turn in required reports to the dispatcher,

IV. OPERATOR'S MAINTENANCE

Every equipment operator is required to perform certain daily maintenance services on his vehicle as a matter of routine. The faithful performance of these services does much to prolong the life of the vehicle, to avoid major repairs and overhaul, and to assure the equipment operator that his vehicle will perform consistently and dependably. *Operator's maintenance* is the term that describes the required inspection, service, lubrication, and adjustments performed by an operator to keep power tools and equipment in a safe operable condition, in order to prevent personnel injuries, mechanical malfunctions, and curtailment of production or progress.

FAN BELTS

Worn or loose fan belts are often the cause of engine overheating, especially when the engine is operating in low or second gear. Excessive looseness or tightness can be determined by applying the manufacturer's specified pressure to the belt at a point midway between the fan and the generator pulleys and determining that the deflection is within the range specified for the vehicle.

If it.is necessary to adjust the fan belt, first look at the type of device used to provide the fan takeup and follow the manufacturer's adjusting procedures.

IGNITION AND ELECTRICAL SYSTEMS

Ignition troubles are often a major cause of improper engine performance. When an ignition tuneup is required, it includes checking the battery, cleaning and inspecting all wires and terminals, cleaning or replacing and adjusting spark plugs, checking ignition timing, and adjusting breaker points. These are important jobs in an ignition tuneup, but you are only required to check the battery and clean and inspect all wires and terminals. An experienced mechanic using proper equipment will adjust and check timing and ignition breaker points, and clean or replace and adjust spark plugs to the manufacturer's specifications.

BATTERY AND BATTERY CONNECTIONS

The storage battery supplies power for all electrical accessories. The condition of the battery is the first concern in accessory maintenance. Check the battery periodically for water, and see that the battery terminals are tight and free from corrosion. If the battery fails to supply sufficient power to turn the starter or to operate other electrical units on a vehicle, report this malfunction to the maintenance section for corrective action.

Most electrical troubles can be traced to poor ground connections, loose wire connections, and worn or frayed wires that cause short circuits, rather than to a defective battery.

Tightening a loose wire connection is a simple operation; a worn, frayed, or broken wire should be taped to make temporary repairs ONLY. The vehicle should be taken to the shop where a mechanic will replace the wire with a new one.

COOLING SYSTEM

You will need to drain the coolant from the cooling system occasionally to remove sediment and rust scales and for periodic radiator flushing. Be sure all the coolant is removed. The manufacturer's maintenance manuals will show you the locations of drain cocks and plugs, which are usually found in the lowest points of the systems.

When refilling a cooling system that has been drained, allow water to pass through the engine and out the drain openings before closing them. When the water is clear and flows freely from the openings, close them securely and fill the cooling system slowly. Never add water faster than it can circulate through the various branches of the system, since water overflowing from the cap may give a false indication of a full system. Do not add water to the cooling system of an overheated engine; allow the engine to cool first. If you must add water before you are sure the engine is cool, run the engine and add water very slowly. Cold water in an overheated engine may crank a cylinder block or cause other serious damage to engine parts.

WHEELS AND TIRES

You should become familiar with the recommendations of tire manufacturers on the proper use and care of tires on vehicles. Probably one of the most common mistakes is incorrect tire pressure. To keep vehicles operating continuously and efficiently, you must follow the procedures recommended by the manufacturer for inspecting and inflating tires. To get the maximum life from a tire, you must maintain proper tire pressure to match the load the vehicle will carry at its actual operating speed. You must make periodic pressure checks on cold tires (before running equipment), and make visual inspection of tires for tread cuts, sidewall snags, and wear. Check wheel rims for splits, metal fatigue, and out-of-round condition.

When tires are to be removed, take the equipment to the tire shop, where special tools and personnel are available to replace or repair the tires. You will be required to help the tire repair personnel to disassemble and repair the tire. Detailed procedures on this will be given later in the chapter.

BRAKE SYSTEMS

When inspecting hydraulic brakes, ensure that the proper level of hydraulic fluid is maintained in the master cylinder reservoir, and check the system for leaks and worn parts. Be sure to add the kind of hydraulic fluid recommended by the manufacturer, because some brake systems are made with natural rubber seals and others with synthetic seals. Unless the recommended fluid is used, the seals will deteriorate quickly and the hydraulic brakes will not operate.

Dust and dirt that accumulates around the filler plug opening can also affect brake operation. A small particle of dust or dirt that may find its way into the operating mechanism can close a vent or prevent a valve from seating properly. See that all dust and dirt are removed before you uncover the master cylinder and add fluid. Add enough fluid so that the level reaches just below the filler plug opening. After filling the reservoir, see that the vent at the top of the reservoir is open and the filler plug is tight.

Leaks and loose joints in the brake system not only allow fluid to escape but also permit air to enter. Air in the hydraulic system can be felt by the soft, springy action of the brake pedal, and must be removed by bleeding to obtain a solid pedal. When bleeding becomes necessary, take the vehicle to the maintenance shop, where special tools and personnel are available to correct the situation.

When inspecting and servicing airbrake systems, the most common problem you will find is leaking air lines. The air line hoses and couplings should be checked for leaks and wear, particularly those connecting a truck and trailer. Replace worn hoses and tighten hose connections and couplings. The cutout cocks provided at the tractor hose connections are often responsible for air loss. These tapered valves should be checked often and kept tightly closed. When no trailer is being towed, they often jar open. Be sure these valves are closed tightly, but are free to open when trailer brakes are required. A little penetrating oil will free a binding cutout cock.

The drain cock at each air reservoir should work freely. Reservoirs should be drained daily to remove water that accumulates from condensation.

BODY AND FRAME

The mobility of trailers results in frequent shipment of vehicles, with consequent likelihood of damage to the body and frame during shipment. Of course, accidents are another cause of body and frame damage.

During the operator's maintenance, he will inspect the body and frame of the vehicle. He will look for damaged portions of the body and report the damage so that repairs can be made by the body shop personnel. These body repairs include straightening body panels, replacing body parts, and repainting.

If damage to the frame is detected by your inspection, this will also be reported and the body shop personnel allowed to repair the damage, if they are equipped to do so. If they do not have the equipment, the vehicle must be sent to a larger repair facility equipped with frame straightening machines.

LUBRICATING OIL SYSTEM

Check the oil level and, if necessary, add additional oil for a _full_ gage or dipstick reading. Do not overfill.

If the oil feels gritty to the fingers or has no body, it has lost its effective lubricating qualities and must be changed.

Oil changes should also be made in accordance with the manufacturers' lubrication and maintenance schedules. On most of your equipment, the grade and quantity of the oil to be used will be found on the lubricating charts.

Drain the oil only after the engine has run and is warmed up. This warmup period will thin the oil and stir up the sludge and foreign matter in the oil pan. After replacing with new oil, recheck the oil level to be certain that the oil column reaches the _full_ mark on the dipstick. Then run the engine for a few minutes to ensure no leaks exist, particularly around the oil filter and the oil drain plug. Get into the habit of looking at the ground or pavement over which the vehicle has been parked, for any oil spots that may indicate leakage.

Changing oil filter elements periodically will be part of your job. Usually the filter elements are changed at the same time the oil is changed in the crankcase. On new engines, it may be changed (1) after the first 500 miles; (2) according to the manufacturer's instructions; or (3) according to shop policy. The filter element should be replaced with the type recommended by the manufacturer. Be sure to remove the old gasket and see that the new gasket under the cover or in the crankcase is properly fitted, and that there are no oil leaks. Always check these points immediately after starting the engine.

FUEL SYSTEM

The fuel system consists of the fuel tank, fuel pump, carburetor, intake manifold, and fuel lines or tubes connecting the tank, pump, and carburetor.

Fuel tanks give little or no trouble, and as a rule require no servicing other than an occasional draining and cleaning. If, during inspection, you should find the fuel tank either punctured or leaking, report the trouble, leaving the repairs or replacement to the repair shop where there are proper servicing facilities. All fuel leaks will be considered cause for immediate shutdown.

If the presence of gasoline in the crankcase is observed, it is a good indication of a diaphragm leaking within the fuel pump. Usually, the mechanics will replace the pump or repair it using a repair kit for this purpose.

Inspect the fuel lines and connections, observing that the lines are placed away from the exhaust pipes, mufflers, and manifolds so that excessive heat will not cause vaporlock. Make sure fuel lines are attached to the frame, engine, and other units so that the effects of the vibration will be minimized. Fuel lines should be free of contact with sharp edges which might cause wear. In places of excessive movement, as between the vehicle frame and rubber-mounted engine, short lengths of gasoline-resistant flexible tubing are used. Occasionally, road vibration may loosen and break lines, and they can become pinched or flattened by flying rocks. Such damage could interfere with the flow of fuel.

A certain amount of scale forms within the fuel lines and sometimes causes a stoppage.

When, in the course of your daily maintenance services of the fuel system, you observe operational troubles with the carburetor, report the troubles, leaving the adjustments, repairs, or replacement of the carburetor with the maintenance personnel equipped to handle these troubles.

V. LUBRICATION

As you may recall, lubricants act as cooling agents, sealing agents, cleaning agents, and reduce friction and wear. This section discusses the procedures of lubrication.

Periodic lubrication prolongs the usefulness of a vehicle. Proper lubrication is more than merely placing a grease gun on a fitting and pulling the trigger. It means selecting the correct lubricants and applying them in a sufficient amount and in the proper places. The experienced equipment operator uses neither too much nor too little lubricant.

Lubrication, then, is a thorough job of oiling and greasing. The lube rack will likely carry several approved standard lubricants. This standardization of lubricants eliminates the variation and confusion in manufacturer's brand names and quality designations, and makes readily available a few standard lubricants.

Familiarize yourself with the lubrication chart of the vehicle with which you are working. These charts show what to lubricate, and where.

Of course, you must learn to use grease guns properly, as well as other dispensers of oils and grease.

Remember that grease on the outside of a fitting does not lubricate, and oil or grease in puddles or gobs around the grease rack can cause serious injury. So look for and remove spilled oil or grease that drops from chassis parts. Better yet, while lubricating a piece of equipment, remove all excessive grease from the fittings and wipe up lubricants that fall to the floor.

DISPENSING LUBRICANTS

Grease guns and dispensers operate either by hand or are air operated. You have probably used the hand-operated muzzle-loader type of grease gun. This grease gun can be taken apart to load it with grease. It is generally used in places hard to reach with a pressure gun, or in lubricating water pumps and other accessories requiring a special lubricant. Lubricants used for most chassis parts, however, are forced through the fittings by guns operated by air pressure.

Crankcase oil is generally dispensed with measured containers or with a hand- or air-operated pumping system. Hand- or air-operated systems normally have meters that register the amount of oil dispensed, Gear box lubricants are generally dispensed by some type of hand-or air-operated pumping system. Be sure you use the right lubricant dispensers. To prevent mistakes, each dispenser is marked to show the grade and type of lubricant it contains.

Before using the lubrication gun, all fittings which are to be lubricated MUST be properly cleaned to avoid forcing dirt into the bearing.

The proper technique for using the lubrication gun is essential. Improper use of the gun can damage the hydraulic coupler jaws and can also damage the fitting. Damaged coupler jaws will prevent proper sealing with fittings. To prevent damage, press the coupler straight onto the clean fitting.

CAUTION: Care must be exercised when using a high pressure lube gun on certain lube points. Excessive pressure can damage or *blow off* the grease seals and/or dust caps. To prevent this damage, apply grease by one or two quick pulls on the trigger; this prevents excess pressure building up in the seals.

After a vehicle is lubricated, clean and fill the grease guns. Then check them to see if they are working properly. Next see that they and other lubricating equipment are stowed in their proper places. Take an inventory of your tools to be sure they are not carried away on the vehicle frame or running board.

CHASSIS LUBRICATION

Most chassis lubrication fittings are located on the front suspension and steering mechanisms. The importance of proper chassis lubrication cannot be overstressed. This lubrication should always be performed in accordance with the manufacturer's lubrication charts.

Frozen fittings will not readily accept lubricants because the friction surface containing the fitting has dry and dirty working surfaces. Some relative motion in the connection is needed to permit

the lubricant to enter the frozen fitting. Vertical rocking of the vehicle is the usual method of providing this relative motion in the coupling. In some extreme cases, it may be necessary to disassemble the unit being greased in order to properly lubricate it. NEVER pass up a frozen fitting.

BODY LUBRICATION

To lubricate the hood, apply a few drops of oil on the fastener-and-release mechanism, coat the fastener pins and hooks with a light application of dry stick lubricant, and close the hood.

Car doors and trunk lids are lubricated by applying a drop or two of oil to the door latch and trunk lid mechanisms. Also apply a few drops of oil to the hinges and swing the door back and forth or raise and lower the lid to spread the lubricant over the contacting surfaces; wipe off any excess lubricant.

The door striker assembly is lubricated by applying a light coating of dry stick lubricant to all sliding surfaces and a few drops of oil to all bearing surfaces. Apply a drop or two of oil around the edge of the cylinder face and to the outer surface of pushbutton latches and press the pushbuttons several times to distribute the lubricant. Wipe off any excess oil and lubricants.

Never use oil to lubricate locks since it collects dust and lint. Inject graphite directly into the keyhole and work the lock several times to distribute the graphite in the tumbler mechanism.

A dry stick lubricant is best used for sliding weather-stripping surfaces of ashtrays, hinged visors, glove compartments, and other hinged units within the vehicle. Hinged surfaces outside of the vehicle may be lubricated lightly with oil. Always remember that the few minutes it requires to oil these various items will, in most cases, eliminate their failure.

Generator Service. Periodic lubrication service is required by most generators. A few generators have sealed bearings which require no lubrication. The generator should be lubricated only at those intervals specified by the manufacturer's lubrication chart.

Distributor Service. The distributor requires service lubrication at three points - the shaft bearing, the centrifugal spark advance mechanism, and the cam. The shaft bearing is lubricated through either an oil cup, grease fitting, or grease cup. Some distributors are equipped with a removable access plug to the shaft bearing reservoir.

The automatic spark centrifugal advance mechanism may be lubricated through a small, round felt wick located at the top of the distributor shaft. Apply two or three drops of motor oil to the

felt wick. With your fingertip, apply a light film of high temperature type grease to the cam. CAUTION: Excess lubricant on the cam may be thrown over to the points and cause ignition failure.

Steering Gear Service. The fluid level in the gear housing should be checked at every chassis lubrication. You should clean around the fill plug on top of the steering gear housing before removing the fill plug. Do not disturb the adjusting screw locknut adjacent to the fill plug. Check the lubricant level and add lubricant, if necessary, to bring the lubricant level to the bottom of the fill plug hole. You then replace the fill plug.

Three points require lubrication in power steering systems. The gear housing is serviced as above on the linkage type of power steering. As you may recall, the linkage type of power steering system has the power cylinder and control valve connected to the steering linkage and a steering gear of conventional design. Additional lubrication fittings under the car may be found on the power cylinder or the power cylinder attachment points in the linkage type. The fluid reservoir is serviced at each chassis lubrication by cleaning the area, removing the dipstick or reservoir cover, checking the oil level, and replacing the dipstick or cover after adding oil if necessary. Power systems can become inoperative due to dirt in the system, so use care to prevent dirt from entering the reservoir during service operations.

Brake Service. The fluid level in the hydraulic brake master cylinder should be checked at every chassis lubrication. The fluid level must be visually checked at the reservoir. Pumping the brake pedal does not constitute a complete check. Service the master cylinder by cleaning the area around the fill plug, removing the fill plug, checking the fluid level and refilling the master cylinder reservoir to within half an inch below the fill hole, and replacing the gasket and fill plug. Always use the hydraulic fluid recommended by the manufacturer's lubrication chart. The use of inferior brake fluid or one which contains mineral oil will result in deterioration of the rubber seal, making it necessary to completely overhaul the brake system and flush all brake lines.

FAN BELT ADJUSTMENTS

There are many types of fan belts and many procedures used for adjusting them. It is beyond the scope of this manual to present information on all types of fan belts. Therefore, the following information presented should familiarize you with fan belt adjustments in general.

Check the fan belt (sometimes called a drive belt) tension by applying the manufacturer's specified pressure to the belt at a point midway between the fan and the generator pulley. Belt deflection at this point should be as specified. If belt deflection is found to be more or less than specified, adjust tension as follows:

1. Loosen generator-to-adjusting-arm capscrew.

2. Insert end of pry bar between crankcase and generator so that the lower end of the bar will bear against crankcase.

3. Pull upper end of pry bar away from engine with a pull of approximately 50 pounds, and keep handle in this position; then tighten the generator-to-adjustment-arm capscrew. This procedure will place belts under proper tension and allow for specified belt deflection.

HANDBRAKE ADJUSTMENT

In most automotive vehicles, the handbrake has its own hookup. Either external-contracting brake bands are located on the drive shaft or some type of mechanical linkage operates the rear wheel brakes.

Handbrake controls consist of a handbrake lever connected by linkage to the brake shoe lever at the rear of the transfer case. The handbrake is properly adjusted when it will hold the vehicle on an incline with the handbrake lever moved one-third of the way in reverse, or if application of the brake at a speed of 10 mph stops the vehicle within a reasonable distance.

To increase braking action of the handbrake, turn the knurled end of the handbrake lever clockwise. To decrease braking action (to prevent dragging of the brake shoes), turn the knurled end counterclockwise. If braking action cannot be increased sufficiently by turning the knurled end clockwise, turn the knurled end counterclockwise, adjust linkage tension at the brake shoe lever, and then turn the knurled end clockwise until the correct brake adjustment is obtained. To adjust linkage at brake shoe lever, hold adjusting nut on transfer end of linkage, loosen locknut, turn adjusting nut clockwise on linkage, and tighten locknut.

VI. TIRES

Pneumatic tires and inner tubes are designed to provide traction and cushion the shocks of the road or terrain. Traction is provided by the natural friction of the rubber upon contact with the road or terrain, aided by the tread design of the tire. Cushioning is provided largely by the air within the tube, or the tire itself if of tubeless design. Both tires and tube are flexible enough to *give* when a bump or chuck hole is struck, and they are able to resume their former shape immediately.

CHANGING A TIRE

A word of CAUTION before you lift a vehicle with a jack to change a tire: If you are to jack either of the rear wheels, place a block or stone in front of both front wheels to keep the vehicle from rolling forward and off the jack; if you jack either of the front wheels, place the block or stone behind both rear wheels.

To remove the wheel, remove the hubcap, which snaps into spring clips. Then remove the five or six hub bolts or nuts that fasten the wheel to the wheel hub. Wheels on the right side are fastened with right-hand thread bolts or nuts, and those on the left side with left-hand thread bolts or nuts to eliminate the tendency to loosen with wheel rotation. In raising the wheel from the ground, be careful not to push the vehicle off the jack. The spare wheel and tire should be placed on the vehicle immediately.

Removing dual disk wheels to change tires on heavy vehicles is not too difficult. Generally, both disks are fastened together by two nuts on each hub bolt - one nut for each wheel. Either single or dual wheels can be securely mounted on the same hub with this arrangement. Outer nuts must be loosened first, freeing the outer wheel disk from the hub. Loosening the outer nuts, which thread over the inner nuts, unfastens the outer wheel disk. In removing dual disk wheels, you will find left-hand threads on both inner and outer nuts on the left wheels and right-hand threads on those of the right wheels. Reverse the procedure to mount and tighten the wheels.

On trucks having spoke wheels, the tire and tube are removed with the rim. After removing the clamps which secure the rim on the spoke spider, the rim with the tire and tube can be lifted off. If the spoke wheel has two rims and tires, the second rim and tire can be lifted off after the spacer separating the rims is removed. In replacing the tires, the inner rim should be placed so that the valve stem can be reached easily for periodic inflation.

A tire demounter should be used to remove a tire from the rim.

In mounting a tubed tire, inflate the tube until it is almost round. Put the inside bead of the tire on the rim and insert the tube into the tire with the valve at the red (balance) mark on the tire. Guide the valve stem through the valve hole. Be sure the valve stem is pointed in the right direction if you are mounting the tire for use on dual wheels. And if it is a rubber stem, see that the stem enters the hole without bending.

The first bead will slide in rather easily, but the second bead may offer a little trouble. Use the tire irons, and work both ways from the stem to slide both tire beads in the rim walls. DO NOT PINCH THE TUBE. Use a rubber mallet (NOT a hammer) to strike the center of the tread around the tire to help seat the second bead and the tube properly. On other than drop center rims, see that the lock rings are securely fastened.

Inflate the tire slowly alter mounting it on the rim. See that the tire beads fit snugly against the rim flanges, and that lock rings are turned face down and remain in the locked position. Serious accidents can result from failure to observe these precautions. Too much pressure applied at once can cause a lock ring to fly off the rim or the tire itself to be blown off and seriously injure personnel. Inflate tires inside a steel tire cage. This will confine the tire enough to keep it from striking you in case either it or the ring bursts its fittings.

TUBELESS TIRES

Most of the lighter and heavier vehicles now are equipped with tubeless tires. Instead of being sealed in an inner tube, the air in these tires is sealed in a space between the outer casing and the rim. Both this space and the point of contact of the tire against the rim must be airtight. The rim, on which the valve for inflating the tire is mounted, becomes a part of the air retaining chamber. When using tire irons, exercise care not to tear or otherwise injure the sealing ribs or beads on the tire being repaired.

Before replacing a tubeless tire, examine the rim carefully for dents, roughness, and rust, any of which may impair or break the air seal. Straighten out any dents with a hammer, and use steel wool to clean the bead seat area of any rust or grit. If the rim is badly bent or out of round, a new wheel should be installed on the vehicle.

Removing and remounting a tubeless tire are similar to the operations for tubed tires. If the tire seal is broken or defective, it will be necessary to use a tube inside the tire. Otherwise, the tire will lose air, and you will have to inflate it frequently. Some tubeless passenger car tires must be removed from the rear of the rim to prevent stretching the bead wires too far and causing them to break. If in doubt about any other details of changing tubeless tires, follow the tire manufacturer's instructions, or consult with your supervising petty officer.

ROTATING TIRES

Rotating tires is recommended by the manufacturer. If several tires show more wear than others, or if the mileage is approaching another mile interval, you will rotate all the vehicle's tires in the following manner:

1. On automobiles having a spare tire, the left front tire should be moved to the left rear, the right front to the spare, the two rears to the opposite front wheels, and the spare to the right rear.

2. On automobiles having no spare, move the front tires to the rear on the same side, and move the rear to the opposite front wheels.

3. On vehicles having six tires (dual tires on rear), new tires should normally be mounted on the front wheels for one-third of their life, then moved to the outside rear wheels for another third, and finally shifted to the rear inside wheels. A few service conditions which demand maximum traction on rear wheels may require that new tires, or tires with relatively good treads, be mounted on the rear wheels.

CAUSES OF TIRE WEAR

Pneumatic tires have been installed on many items of equipment to increase mobility and efficiency. However, unless tires are properly cared for, much of this efficiency and mobility is lost to the user.

Probably the greatest factor in prolonging the life of pneumatic tires is proper inflation. Correct tire pressure cannot be checked by kicking the tire. It requires the use of a pressure gage. Tire pressure checks should be made prior to the vehicle being moved. This can be accomplished during the *Before Operation Services.* (Don't forget to check the spare tire.) If the pressure is neglected, the results can be costly. Tire pressure should be stenciled on the dash or fenders.

Abnormal wear from improper tire inflation can be divided into four categories. These are: overinflation, overinflation-impact injury, underinflation, and underinflation injury. Let's look at each of these in detail, and learn how to get maximum life from our tires.

Overinflation stretches the tire and permits only the center section of the tread to come in contact with the road. Since the wear is concentrated on the central part of the tread, the indication of overinflation is wear in the center of the tread. An overinflated tire has no give and is constantly subjected to hard jolts, causing the drive wheels to bounce and spin, literally abrasing the rubber. There is also less tire to road surface contact with an overinflated tire, and this causes a safety hazard in both braking and sliding.

An overinflated tire is more susceptible to impact injury because the cords are stretched tight. In this condition, the tire will not give or flex and distribute the shock over a great area of the ply cords.

The external indication of an underinflated tire is more wear on the edges than in the center of the tread. Underinflation causes excessive movement and scuffing between the tire and the road, which in turn results in faster tread wear. There may be occasions when chains are not available and tire pressures must be lowered to get better traction in sand, ice, mud, and snow. When this occurs, prescribed pressures for these conditions should be maintained to prevent tire damage.

The excessive flexing and movement of the ply cords cause a tire to get hot resulting in separation of cords and rubber. When the cords are separated from the body, the tire is permanently damaged and must be replaced. This replacement is a direct result of operator neglect and not fair wear and tear. While the tire must be removed from the wheel to properly identify this condition, in many instances radial cracks will appear on the outer wall of the tire which will serve as a warning that the tire has been operated underinflated.

All uneven tire wear is not caused by improper inflation. Wear of this type can be caused by wheels out of line or improperly balanced, excessive toe-in or toe-out, or improper camber. Uneven tire wear can also be caused by operating a vehicle with the front wheel drive engaged on dry hard surfaced roads. When uneven tire wear occurs, the mechanical defects must be corrected immediately and the tires rotated.

The proper selection and mounting of tires for dual assemblies is extremely important. Mismatched tires cause uneven distribution of the load which defeats the purpose of the duals. In this case, the larger tire carries the greater load, subjecting it to excessive wear and early failure. Also, the smaller tire wears more rapidly than normal. It scuffs along without sufficient road traction causing excessive wear. Since you are not always able to match sizes of tires exactly, except with new tires, certain tolerances are allowed. The larger of the two duals should always be mounted on the outside so that they will conform to the *crown* of the road and shoulder the load more evenly.

Directional bar tread is commonly used on road graders and other earthmoving equipment. The bars and open center pattern are designed to permit each bar to dig in deep, take a firm hold, and give maximum traction in soft, muddy, or slippery surfaces. Since this is a directional tread tire, it must be mounted on live axles so the point of the *V* comes in contact with the ground first. When the directional tire is mounted in this manner, it is *self-cleaning.* It forces the dirt and mud out to the side. When the directional tread tire is mounted on a towed vehicle or on a dead axle, it is mounted so that the open part of the 7 meets the ground first.

An insignificant little thing, but absolutely necessary, is the valve cap. This cover keeps dirt, water, and grit out of the valve and provides the final seal against air escaping from the tube. For speed and convenience in inflating, valve stems should be readily accessible. They should be positioned to prevent rubbing against the brake drum and to extend through the wheel hand holes. Ends of valves on front wheels and inside duals point away from the vehicle. Valves on outside duals point toward the vehicle. On dual wheels, valves are placed 180° apart for convenience in checking pressure and inflating.

Rims and rim flanges should be checked regularly to be sure that they are in good condition and fit properly. Since the flange comes in direct contact with the bead which supports the tire, flanges that are bent, broken, chipped, or of the wrong size put a terrific strain on the bead and lead to early tire failure.

Most of the larger wheels and rims used on equipment are the lockring type. The use of the lockring makes tire changing much easier and faster than on the one piece rim of the same size. The principle of the lockring is simple, requiring only that the lockring be firmly seated in the gutter of the rim base. When this is done, the tire and wheel will perform equally as well as the one piece riri. While there is a high safety factor built into the tire and rim assembly, danger results from carelessness or negligence in assembly. Before starting the inflate, make sure that all rim parts are correctly assembled and interlocking. It is recommended that inflation cages, safety chains, or some other safety device be used during inflation. Rims and lockrings should be inspected periodically for damage. A damaged rim or lockring should be replaced immediately as this will create a safety hazard and may ruin a tire. A displaced lockring may spring loose and can result in serious injury or death to personnel who may be in the vicinity.

When should we replace worn tires? This is a very important question because tires worn beyond the prescribed limit cannot be recapped. If you cannot grip the tread with your thumb and index finger, ask your supervisor for technical assistance to determine if replacement is required. When the tread design is worn off in the center so that the tire is smooth across the center, the tire should be replaced.

Make careful checks for damage due to vehicle obstructions. Spring clips, fender bolts, exhaust pipes, etc. may be set in a satisfactory location when the vehicle is at a standstill. But under unusual operating conditions, the body movement may cause these units to contact the tire and cause severe abrasion. The tires of low bed trailers and trailer-mounted air compressors are highly susceptible to this type damage.

Rocks or dry caked mud should be removed from between dual assemblies as soon as possible. Extensive tire damage can also be caused by snow and ice packed between duals or under fenders and cross braces in winter operation. Any such materials coming in contact with tires while they are in operation can cause severe cuts or abrasions.

FUNDAMENTALS OF AUTOMOTIVE POWER TRAINS AND CHASSIS

CONTENTS

		Page
I.	POWER TRAIN COMPONENTS	1
II.	BRAKE SYSTEMS	12
III.	SUSPENSION SYSTEMS	19
IV.	FRAME	22

BASIC FUNDAMENTALS OF AUTOMOTIVE POWER TRAINS AND CHASSIS

The mechanism that transmits the power of a vehicle's engine to the wheels and accessory equipment is called the power train. In a simple situation, a set of gears or a chain and sprocket could perform this task, but automotive vehicles are not designed for simple operating conditions. They are designed to have pulling power as well as to move at high speeds, to travel in reverse as well as forward, and to operate on rough terrain as well as on smooth roads. To meet these varying demands, a number of units have been added including clutches, transmissions, propeller shafts, universal joints, differentials, and live axles.

The chassis is the assembly of mechanisms that make up the major operating part of the vehicle. It usually includes everything except the vehicle body. This assembly includes the engine, the frame which supports the engine and the power train, the steering and braking systems, and the suspension system.

This chapter provides information on the various components, or subassemblies, that make up the automotive power train and chassis. In effect, it establishes the relationship between these various parts and shows how they work together in the automotive vehicle. To maintain and service these components, or subassemblies, you must know where to find them on a vehicle. You must also understand their purpose and how they operate. This chapter contains a general discussion of these subject; the operation and maintenance manuals which accompany each piece of equipment will give you more detailed information.

I. POWER TRAIN COMPONENTS

The common elements of the power train system assembled in a typical vehicle are shown in the following figure. The main components of the power train are described as follows:

CLUTCH.
By means of the clutch, the operator can disconnect the engine from the remainder of the power train. This is essential when starting the engine, thus allowing the vehicle to stand motionless while the engine is running. It also allows gradual engagement of the engine to the power train and gear ratio changing to meet varying road conditions.

TRANSMISSION.
An internal combustion engine cannot develop appreciable torque at low speeds; it develops maximum torque only at one speed, and the crankshaft of an engine must always rotate in the same direction. Because of these limitations, a transmission is necessary in automotive vehicles. The transmission provides the mechanical advantage that enables the engine to propel the vehicle under adverse conditions of the load. It also provides the operator with a selection of vehicle speeds while the engine is held at speeds within the effective torque range, and it allows disengaging and reversing the flow of power from the engine to the wheels.

PROPELLER SHAFT.
A propeller shaft is used to transfer the power from the transmission located near the front of the vehicle to the differential near the rear.

UNIVERSAL JOINTS.

It is necessary to provide flexibility in the power train if springs are to be used on the vehicle. As the load is increased or decreased, and as the vehicle travels over uneven surfaces, the vertical distance between the transmission output shaft and the axle will change. This flexibility is provided by the use of universal joints which permit transfer of torque at an angle.

SLIP JOINTS.

As the load is changed, and as the vehicle travels over uneven ground, the distance from the axle to the transmission varies. Slip joints allow for this variation.

DIFFERENTIAL.

A differential is required to compensate for the difference in distance the rear wheels travel when the vehicle rounds a turn. The differential permits application of power to the rear wheels while allowing each wheel to turn at a different speed when the vehicle is rounding a curve.

AXLES.

An axle is a shaft supporting a vehicle on which the wheels turn. A *live axle* is one that supports part of the weight of a vehicle and also drives the wheels connected to it. A *dead axle* is one that carries part of the weight of a vehicle, but does not drive the wheels. The usual front axle of a vehicle is a dead axle and the rear axle is a live axle. In four-wheel drive vehicles, both front and rear axles are live axles, and in six-wheel drive vehicles, all three axles are live axles.

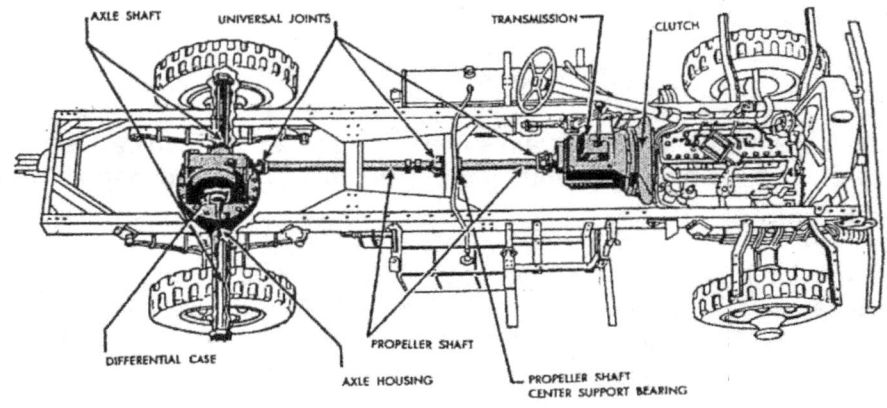

TYPICAL POWER TRAIN

THE CLUTCH

A clutch in an automotive vehicle is the mechanism in the power train that connects the engine crankshaft to, or disconnects it from, the transmission and thus the remainder of the power train. Since the internal combustion engine does not develop a high starting torque, it must be disconnected from the power train and allowed to operate without load until it develops enough torque to overcome the inertia of the vehicle when starting from rest. The application of the engine power to the load must be gradual to prove smooth engagement and to lessen the shock on the driving parts. After engagement, the clutch must transmit all the engine power to the transmission without slipping. Further, it is desirable to disconnect the engine from the power train during the time the gears in the transmission are being shifted from one gear ratio to another.

Clutches are located in the power train between the engine and the transmission assembly.

Clutches transmit power from the clutch driving plate to the driven member by friction. In the disk clutch, the driving plate or member, which is secured to the engine flywheel, is gradually brought into contact with the driven member (disk), which is attached to the transmission input shaft. The contact is made and held by strong spring pressure controlled by the operator with the clutch pedal. With only light spring pressure, there is little friction between the two members and the clutch is permitted to slip. As the spring pressure increases, friction also increases, and less slippage occurs. When the operator removes his foot from the clutch pedal and full spring pressure is applied, the speed of the driving plate and driven disk is the same, and all slipping stops. There is then a direct connection between the flywheel and transmission input shaft.

Malfunction Detection. Several types of clutch troubles that may be encountered during vehicle operation are: slipping, chattering or grabbing when engaging, spinning or dragging when engaged, and clutch noises. As an operator, you would explain the malfunction on the Operator's Trouble Report and turn the report into the maintenance shop for corrective action.

Clutch Lubrication. Although some clutches do not require lubrication, there are other types of clutches that require it at periodic intervals. The clutch-pedal control shaft and clutch linkage are among some of the lubricating points that would be greased at normal regular servicing intervals in accordance with the manufacturer's lubrication manual.

MANUAL TRANSMISSIONS

The transmission is part of the power train. It is located in the rear of the engine between the clutch housing and the propeller shaft. The transmission transfers engine power from the clutch shaft to the propeller shaft, and allows the operator a means of varying the gear ratio between the engine and the rear wheels.

Dual ratio, or two-speed, rear axles are sometimes used on trucks. They contain two different gear ratios which can be selected at will by the driver, usually by a manual-control lever. A dual-ratio rear axle serves the same purpose as the auxiliary transmission, and like the latter, it doubles the number of gear ratios available for driving the vehicle under the various loads and road conditions.

Operator's Maintenance. It is the operator's responsibility to check with the manufacturer's instruction manual for instruction on the proper type and amount of recommended lubricant to be used in the transmission case. You must maintain the lubricant at the proper level. The normal level of lubricant to be placed in a transmission is usually at the bottom of the filler plug opening. By maintaining the proper level, gear teeth are protected, foaming is reduced, and thus the transmission will continue to perform properly.

Malfunction Detection. Several types of transmission troubles that may be encountered in vehicle operation are: hard shifting into gears, transmission slips out of *first* or *reverse*, transmission slips out of *second*, transmission slips out of high, no power through transmission, transmission noisy in gear, gear clash in shifting, and oil leaks. As an operator, you would explain the malfunction on the Operator's Trouble Report enabling the mechanic to check out the possible cause of trouble reported.

AUTOMATIC TRANSMISSION

The transmissions described previously are manual transmissions; that is, they require a clutch and a lever for shifting gears. The automatic transmission is used in almost all types of automotive and construction equipment. Automatic transmissions are composed of a fluid coupling or hydraulic torque converter and a system of planetary gears controlled automatically.

<u>Fluid Couplings</u>. Fluid couplings are widely used with automatic transmissions. By slipping at idling speeds and by holding to increase power as engine speed increases, fluid couplings act as a sort of automatic clutch. There is no mechanical connection between the engine and transmission, but power is transmitted through the use of oil.

The principle of fluid drive can best be illustrated through the use of a pair of electric fans facing each other. If one fan is operated with power, the air blast from this fan will cause the other fan to rotate.

There is considerable power loss through slippage at low speeds, but at intermediate or high driving speeds the power loss is very small. It ranges from 1 percent at 25 miles per hour to one-quarter percent at 60 miles per hour.

<u>Torque Converters</u>. A torque converter is a special form of fluid coupling. It is one of the most common types of automatic transmissions and is widely used in the latest models of automotive and construction equipment.

The torque converter consists of three basic elements: the pump (driving member), the turbine (driven member), and the stator (reaction member). All of these members have curved vanes. The stator is placed between the load and the power source to act as a fulcrum and is secured to the torque converter housing. The pump throws out oil in the same direction in which the pump is turning. As the oil strikes the turbine blade, it forces the turbine to rotate, and the oil is directed toward the center of the turbine. Then the oil leaves the turbine and moves in a direction opposite to that of the pump. As the oil strikes the stator, it is redirected to flow in the same direction as the pump, thereby adding its force to that of the pump. Torque is multiplied by the velocity and direction given to the oil by the pump, plus the velocity and direction of the oil entering the pump from the stator.

<u>Planetary Gears</u>. Automatic transmissions use a system of planetary gears to enable the torque from the torque converter or fluid coupling to be used as efficiently as possible.

Planetary units are the heart of the modern automatic transmission. An understanding of the power flow through the planetary units is essential to an understanding of the operation of the automatic transmission.

Four basic parts make up the planetary gear system. These basic parts are the sun gear, the ring (or internal) gear, the planet pinions, and the planet carrier.

The sun gear is so named because it is the center of the system. The term *planet* is used to describe these pinions and gears because they rotate around the sun gear. The ring gear, or internal gear, is so called because of its shape and because it has internal teeth.

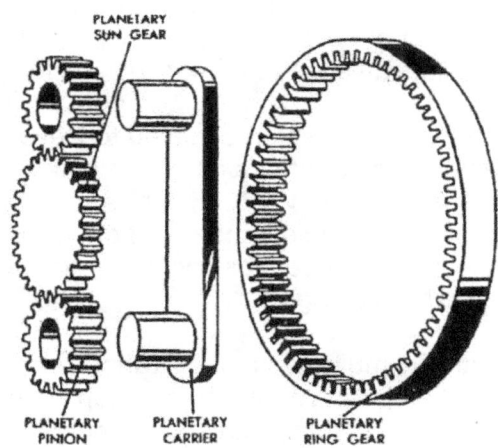

There are several advantages inherent in the planetary gear system. One of the advantage is the compactness of the system. Another advantage is that there is more tooth contact to carry the load, in that each gear of the planetary system is usually in contact with at least two other gears of the system. The gears are always in mesh. There can be no tooth damage due to tooth clash or partial engagement. The big advantage is the one which makes it so popular: namely, the ease of shifting gears. Planetary gear sets in automatc transmissions are shifted without any skill on the part of the driver.

There are various ways in which power may be transmitted through the planetary gear set. shaft from the engine may be connected to drive the sun gear, it may be connected to drive the planet carrier, or it may be connected to drive the ring gear. The propeller shaft also may be connected to any of these members. However, only power can be transmitted in the planetary gear system when (1) the engine is delivering power to one of the three member, (2) the propeller shaft is connected to one of the other members, and (3) the remaining member is held against rotation. All three conditions must be satisfied for power to be transmitted in the system. Automatic transmissions provide the means for holding a member through hydraulic servos or spring pressure.

Operation. Most automatic transmissions are basically the same. They combine a fluid torque converter with a planetary gear set, and control the shifting of the planetary gears with an automatic hydraulic control system.

To start the engine, the selector lever must be in the Neutral or Park positon. It is good practice to apply the service brakes before starting the engine and keep them applied after the engine is running. In the automatic transmission, the fluid torque converter is attached to the engine crankshaft and serves as the engine flywheel. This means that whenever the engine runs, engine power flows into the converter and drives the converter output (turbine) shaft. There is no neutral in the torque converter. Neutral is provider in the planetary gear set by the release of bands and clutches.

With the engine running, you can *feel* the transmission go into gear and into neutral as the selector level is moved from Park or Neutral to Drive, Low, or Reverse. If the engine is running at fast (cold) idle, the vehicle will start to move as soon as the transmission goes into gear, unless the parking or service brakes are applied. If the engine is idling at normal (hot) idle, the vehicle will not move. You can, however, *feel* the transmission go into gear. Part of this *feel* is the audible decrease in engine rpm. The engine is now running under a load. The torque converter and the planetary gear set are actually transmitting engine torque to the driveshaft. The torque applied, however, is not sufficient to move the vehicle.

For all normal forward driving, the selector is moved to Drive. As the throttle is advanced from the idle position, the vehicle will start off smoothly and accelerate steadily. The transmission is designed to operate at a steady-throttle position. Most drivers depress the accelerator pedal to definite position and hold it there steadily until the desired speed is attained. Depending on the accelerator pedal position, the transmission will upshaft automatically to intermediate and then to high.

The transmission automatically multiplies and/or transmits engine torque to the driveshaft as driving conditions demand. The speeds at which the coupling point and the gear shifts occur are controlled partially by the driver. The driver has only a partial control in the Drive position, because the transmission in the Drive position will shift the planetary gear set into the higher gear to prevent engine overspeeding regardless of throttle position.

The transmission can multiply engine torque as much as 5.4 times. The torque converter can multiply engine torque as much as 2.2 times. The planetary gear set in low gear multiplies the torque converter output torque 2.46 times. The maximum engine torque multiplication in the transmission is 2.2 x 2.46 or 5.41 times. This means that the transmission can receive an engine output torque of 100 ft-lbs and deliver 541 ft-lbs torque to the driveshaft. Of course, frictional losses have to be subtracted from the 541 ft-lbs.

The driver can force downshaft the transmission from high to intermediate at speed up to about 65 mph. A detent on the downshift linkage warns the driver when the carburetor is wide open. Accelerator pedal depression through the detent will bring in the downshift.

With the throttle closed, the transmission will downshift automatically as the vehicle speed drops to about 10 mph. With the throttle open at any position up to the detent, the downshifts will come in automatically at speeds about 10 mph and in proportion to throttle opening. This prevents engine lugging on steep hill climbing.

When the selector lever is moved to L (low) with the transmission in high, the transmission will downshift to intermediate or to low depending on the road speed. At speeds below about 25 mph, the downshift will be from high to low.

With the selector in Low position, the transmission cannot upshift. On some vehicles the Low position is called Hill Control, since low gear provides maximum engine braking. When maximum engine braking is desired, the transmission must not upshift, because an upshift will reduce engine braking effort. When the selector is moved to Reverse, the hydraulic control system shifts the planetary gear set to reverse. When the selector lever is moved to Park, a spring force is applied against a pawl to engage the parking pawl with a parking gear on the output shaft. When the pawl is engaged, the transmission output shaft (and, therefore, the rear wheels) is mechanically locked to the transmission main case.

In summary:
1. An automatic transmission has the torque converter to act as an automatic clutch. This automatic clutch permits the vehicle to stand still at engine idle, but automatically

goes to work at a full-throttle start so that the transmission can take maximum engine torque, multiply it more than four times and deliver it to the driveshaft.
2. It is practically impossible to *kill* the engine under any driving condition.
3. At a start, engine speed is fast and vehicle speed is slow. With a steady throttle, engine speed remains fairly constant while vehicle speed increases to 65 mph. You found that the torque converter and planetary gear set *know* when engine torque should be multiplied, how much to multiply it, and when to transmit it to the driveshaft.
4. The ratio changes (shifts) occur at full-engine torque within a fraction of a second and without extreme harshness.

Operator's Maintenance. Periodic service by the operator includes checking the transmission oil level when the engine is idling and at normal operating temperature, the vehicle is level, and the transmission control lever is in Park. Remove dipstick and note oil level. If it is low, and sufficient transmission fluid (the oil used in all automatic transmission is special and is composed of mineral oil and additives). In the transmission, it is used as a combination power-transmission medium, hydraulic control fluid, heat transfer medium, bearing surface lubricant, and gear lubricant. In all cases, the manufacturer's recommendations should be followed when servicing and filling the transmission with transmission fluid.

Caution: Do not overfill the transmission because overfilling will cause foaming and shifting troubles.

Malfunction Detection. Several types of automatic transmission troubles that may be encountered during vehicle operation are: No drive in any selected position; engine speed accelerates on standstill starts but vehicle acceleration lags; engine speed accelerates during upshifts; transmission will not upshift; upshift harsh; closed throttle (coast) downshift harsh; will not downshift; vehicle creeps excessively in drive; vehicle creeps in neutral; no drive in reverse, improper shift points; unusual transmission noise; and oil leaks. As an operator, you must explain the malfunction on the Operator's Trouble Report and turn the report into the maintenance shop for corrective action.

AUXILIARY TRANSMISSIONS

Auxiliary transmissions are mechanisms mounted in the rear of the regular transmission to provide an increased number of gear ratios. The types most commonly used, normally have only a low and a high (direct) range, incorporated into a transfer assembly. The low range provides an extremely low gear ratio on hard pull. At all other times, the high range is used, and the power passes through the main shaft. Gears are shifted by a separate gearshift lever in the driver's cab.

Transfer Cases. Transfer cases are placed in the power trains of vehicles driven by all wheels. Their purpose is to provide the necessary offsets for additional propeller shaft connections to drive the wheels.

Transfer cases in heavier vehicles have two speed positions and a declutching device for disconnecting the front driving wheels. Two speed transfer cases serve also as auxiliary transmissions.

Some transfer cases are quite complicated. When they have speed changing gear, declutching device, and attachment for three or more propeller shafts, they are even larger than the main transmission.

Some transfer cases contain an overrunning sprag unit (or units) on the front output shaft. (A sprag unit is a form of overrunning clutch; power can be transmitted through it in one direction but not in the other.) On these transfer cases, the transfer is designed to drive the front axle slightly slower than the rear axle. During normal operation, when both front and rear wheels turn at the same speed, only the rear wheels drive the vehicle. However, if the rear wheels should lose traction and begin to slip, they tend to turn faster than the front wheels. As this happens, the sprag unit automatically engages so that the front wheels also drive the vehicle. The sprag unit simply provides an automatic means of engaging the front wheels in drive whenever additional tractive effort is required. There are two types of sprag-unit-equipped transfers: a single-sprag-unit transfer and a double-sprag unit transfer. Essentially, both types work in the same manner.

Power Takeoffs. Power takeoffs are attachments in the power train used for obtaining power to drive auxiliary accessories. They are attached to the transmission, auxiliary transmission, or transfer case.

Malfunction detection and operator maintenance for auxiliary transmissions are similar to those for the manual transmission.

PROPELLER SHAFT ASSEMBLY

The propeller shaft assembly consists of a propeller shaft, a slip joint, and one or more universal joints. This assembly provides a flexible connection through which power is transmitted from the transmission to the live axles.

The propeller shaft may be solid or tubular. A solid shaft is somewhat stronger than the hollow or tubular shaft of the same diameter, but the hollow shaft is stronger than a solid shaft of the same weight. Hollow shafts are used in the open.

A slip joint is provided at one end of the propeller shaft to take care of end play. The driving axle, being attached to the springs, is free to move up and down while the transmission is attached to the frame and cannot move. Any upward or downward movement of the axle, as the spring are flexed, shortens or lengthens the distance between the axle assembly and the transmission. To compensate for this changing distance, the slip joint is provided at one end of the propeller shaft.

The usual type of slip joint consists of a splined stub shaft, welded to the propeller shaft, which fits into a splined sleeve in the universal joint.

A universal joint is a connection between two shafts that permits one to drive the other at an angle. Passenger vehicles and trucks usually have universal joints at both ends of the propeller shaft.

Universal joints normally do not require any maintenance other than lubrication. Some universal joints (U-joints) have grease fittings and should be lubricated when the vehicle has a preventive maintenance inspection. Others may require disassembly and lubrication periodically. When lubricating U-joints that have grease fittings, use a low pressure grease gun to avoid damaging seals.

FINAL DRIVES

A final drive is that part of the power train that transmits the power delivered through the propeller shaft to the drive wheels or to sprockets, in the case of tracklaying equipment. Because it is encased in the rear axle housing, the final drive is usually referred to as a part of the rear axle assembly. It consists of two gears called the ring gear and pinion. These are beveled gears, and they may be spur, spiral, or hypoid.

The function of the final drive is to change by 90 degrees the direction of the power transmitted through the propeller shaft to the driving axles. It also provides a fixed reduction between the speed of the propeller shaft and the axle shafts and wheels. In passenger car this reduction varies from about 3 to 1 to 5 to 1. In trucks, it can vary from to 1 to as much as 11 to 1.

The gear ratio of a final drive having bevel gears is found by dividing the number of teeth on the driven or ring gear by the number of teeth on the pinion. In a worm gear final drive, the gear ratio is found by counting the number of revolutions of the worm gear required for one revolution of the driven gear.

Most final drives are of the gear type. Hypoid gears are used in passenger cars and light trucks to eliminate the rear seat propeller shaft tunnel or to permit a lower body design. They permit the bevel driven pinion to be placed below the center of the ring gear, thereby lowering the propeller shaft. Worm gears allow a large speed reduction and are used to a limited extent on larger trucks. Spiral bevel gears are similar to hypoid gears. They are used in both passenger cars and trucks to replace spur gear that are considered too noisy.

DIFFERENTIALS

Associated with the final drive and contained in the rear axle housing is the differential. The purpose of the differential is easy to understand when you compare a vehicle to a company of men marching in mass formation. When the company makes a turn, the men in the inside file must take short steps, almost marking time, while men in the outside file must take long steps and walk a greater distance to make the turn. When a motor vehicle turns a corner, the wheels on the outside of the turn must rotate faster and travel a greater distance than the wheels on the inside. This causes no difficulty for front wheels of the usual passenger car because each wheel rotates independently. However, in order to drive the rear wheels at different speeds, the differential is needed. It connects the individual axle shaft for each wheel to the bevel drive gear. Therefore, each shaft can turn at a different speed and still be driven.

To overcome the situation where one spinning wheel might be undesirable, some trucks are provided with a *differential lock*. This is a simple dog clutch, controlled manually or automatically which locks one axle shaft to the differential case and bevel drive gear. Although this device forms a rigid connection between the two axle shafts and makes both wheels rotate at the same speed, it is used, very little. Too often the driver forgets to disengage the lock after using it. There are, however, automatic devices for doing almost the same thing. One of these, which is rather extensively used today, is the high-traction differential. This does not work, however, when one wheel loses traction completely. In this respect, it is inferior to the differential lock.

With the no-spin differential, one wheel cannot spin because of loss of tractive effort and thereby deprive the other wheel of driving effort. For example, one wheel is on ice and the other wheel is on dry pavement. The wheel on ice is assumed to have no traction. However, the wheel on dry pavement will pull to the limit of its tractional resistance at the pavement. The wheel on ice cannot spin because wheel speed is governed by the speed of the wheel applying tractive effort.

AXLES

A live axle is one that supports part of the weight of a vehicle and also drives the wheels connected to it. A dead axle is one that carries part of the weight of a vehicle but does not drive the wheels.

In 4-wheel drive vehicles, both front and rear axles are live axles, and in 6-wheel drive vehicles, all three axles are live axles. The third axle, part of a *bogie drive* is joined to the rearmost axle by a trunnion axle. The axle trunnion is attached rigidly to the frame. Its purpose is to help in distributing the load on the rear of the vehicle to the two live axles which it connects.

There are four types of live axles used in automotive and construction equipment. They are: plain, semifloating, three-quarter floating, and full floating.

The plain live axle, or nonfloating rear axle, is seldom used in construction equipment today. The axle shafts in this assembly are called nonfloating because they are supported directly in bearings located in the center and ends of the axle housing. In addition to turning the wheels, these shafts carry the entire load of the vehicle on their outer ends. Plain axles also support the weight of the differential case.

The semifloating axle that is used on most passenger cars and light trucks has its differential case independently supported. The differential carrier relieves the axle shafts from the weight of the differential assembly and the stresses caused by its operation. For this reason, the inner ends of the axle shafts are said to be floated. The wheels are keyed or bolted to outer ends of axle shafts and the outer bearings are between the shafts and the housing. The axle shafts, therefore, must take the stresses caused by turning or skidding of the wheels. The axle shaft in a semifloating live axle can be removed after the wheel and brake drum have been removed.

The axle shafts in a three-quarter floating axle may be removed with the wheels, which are keyed to the tapered outer ends of the shafts. The inner ends of the shafts are carried as in semifloating axle. The axle housing, instead of the shafts, carries the weight of the vehicle because the wheels are supported by bearings on the outer ends of the housing. However, axle shafts must take the stresses caused by the turning, or skidding, of the wheels. Three-quarter floating axles are used in some trucks but in very few passenger cars.

The full floating axle is used in most heavy trucks. These axle shafts may be removed and replaced without removing the wheels or disturbing the differential. Each wheel is carried on the end of the axle tube on two ball bearings or roller bearings and the axle shafts are bolted to the wheel hub. The wheels are driven through a flange on the ends of the axle shaft which is bolted to the outside of the wheel hub. The bolted connection between axle and wheel does not make this assembly a true full floating axle, but nevertheless, it is called a floating axle. A true full floating axle transmits only turning effort, or torque.

MAINTENANCE

There are very few adjustments that must be made to the power train during normal operations. As an operator, your primary duties will be limited to lubrication of the power train. You can reduce repairs by proper lubrication and periodic inspection of these power train units.

Proper lubrication depends upon the use of the right kind of lubricants which must be put in the right places in the amounts specified by the lubrication charts. The charts provided with the vehicle will show what units in the power train will require lubrication, and where they are located.

In checking the level of the lubricant in gear cases, keep these two important points in mind:

First, always carefully wipe the dirt away from around the inspection plug and then use the proper size wrench to remove the inspection plugs. A wrench too large will round the corners and prevent proper tightening of the plug. For the same reason, never use a pipe wrench or a pair of pliers for removing plugs.

Secondly, be sure the level of the lubricant is right—usually just below or on a level with the bottom of the inspection hole. Before checking the level, allow the vehicle to stand for a while on a level surface so the gear oil can cool and find its own level. Gear oil heated and churned by revolving gears expands and forms bubbles. Although too little gear oil in the gear boxes is responsible for many failures of the power train, do not add too much gear lubricant. Too much oil causes extra maintenance.

Excessive oil or grease can find its way past the oil seals or gear cases. It may be forced out of a transmission into the clutch housing and result in a slipping clutch; or it may get by the rear wheel bearings from the differential housing to cause brakes to slip or grab. Always clean differential and live axle housing vents to prevent leaking seals.

Universal joints and slip joints at the ends of propeller shafts are to be lubricated if fittings are provided. Some of these joints are packed with grease when assembled, others have grease fittings. Do not remove these plugs until you consult the manual or your chief for instructions.

Some passenger cars and trucks have a leather boot or shoe covering the universal and slip joints. The boot prevents grease from being thrown from the joints and it also keeps dirt from mixing with the grease. A mixture of dirt and grease forms an abrasive that will wear parts in a hurry. Never use so much grease on these joints that the grease will be forced out of the boot. The extra grease will be lost and the added weight of the grease will tend to throw the propeller shaft out of balance.

When you are to give a vehicle a thorough inspection, inspect the power train for loose gear housings and joints. Look for bent propeller shafts that are responsible for vibrations, and examine the gear housing and joints for missing crews and bolts. Check to see that the U-bolts fastening the springs to the rear axle housing are tight. A loose spring hanger can throw the rear axle assembly out of line, and place additional strain on the propeller shaft and final drive. When making these inspections, always check the steel lugs for tightness.

After tightening the gear housing, loose connections, and joints, road test the vehicle to see if the various units in the power train are working properly. Shift the gears into all operating speeds and listen for noisy sounds. Report all improper operation of the power train units on the Operator's Trouble Report enabling the mechanic to check out possible causes.

DRIVING WHEELS

Wheels attached to live axles are the driving wheels. The number of wheels and number of driving wheels is sometimes used to identify equipment. Wheels attached to the outside of the driving wheels make up dual wheels. Dual wheels give additional traction to the driving wheels and distribute the weight of the vehicle over a greater area of road surface. They are considered as single wheels in describing vehicles. For example, a 4x2 (four by two) could be a passenger car or a truck having four wheels with two of them driving. A 4x4 indicates a vehicle having four wheels with all four driving. In some cases, these vehicles will have dual wheels in the rear. You would describe such a vehicle as a 4x4 with dual wheels.

A 6x4 truck, although having dual wheels in the rear, is identified by six wheels, four of them driving. Actually, the truck has ten wheels but the wheel attached to each driving wheel could be removed without changing the identity of the truck. If the front wheels of this truck were driven by a live axle, it would be called a 6x6.

II. BRAKE SYSTEMS

Good brakes are an absolute necessity for the safe operation of a motor vehicle. The modern day vehicle is capable of moving at extremely high speeds, and this results in an ever increasing demand for more efficient braking systems. Braking systems must not only be able to stop the vehicle, but must stop it in as short a distance as possible.

Friction is the resistance to relative motion between two surfaces in contact with each other. Thus, when a stationary surface is forced into contact with a moving surface, the resistance to relative motion or the rubbing action between the two surfaces will slow down the moving surface. In nearly all brake systems, the brake drums provide the moving surface and the brake shoes provide the stationary surface. The friction between the brake drums and the brake shoes slows the drum, wheel, and the friction between the tires and the road surface slows the vehicle, eventually bringing it to a complete stop.

INDIVIDUAL BRAKES

On modern equipment individual service brakes are provided for each wheel and are operated by a foot pedal. The equipment also has an emergency or parking brake. The parking brake is operated by a separate pedal or a hand lever.

Individual brakes are classified into three types: external contracting brake, internal expanding brake, and disk brake.

<u>External Contracting Brakes</u>. External contracting brakes are sometimes used for parking brakes on motor vehicles and for controlling the speed of auxiliary equipment drive shafts.

In operation, the brake band (or shoe) of an external contracting brake is tightened around the rotating drum by moving the brake lever. The brake hand is made of comparatively thin, flexible steel, shaped to fit the drum, with a frictional lining riveted to the inner surface. This flexible brake band cannot withstand the high pressure required to produce the friction that will stop a heavily loaded or fast moving vehicle, but works well as a parking brake.

In an external contracting brake, the brake band is anchored opposite the point where the pressure is applied. In addition to supporting the band, the anchor proves a means for adjusting brake lining clearance. Other adjusting screws and bolts are provided at the ends of the band.

<u>Internal Expanding Brakes</u>. Internal expanding brakes are used almost exclusively as wheel brakes. This type of brake permits a more compact and economical construction. The brake shoe and brake operating mechanism are supported on a backing plate or brake shield which is attached to the vehicle axle. The brake drum, attached to the rotating wheel, acts as a cover for the shoe and operating mechanism and furnishes a frictional surface for the brake shoe.

In operation, the brake shoe of an internal expanding brake is forced outward against the drum to produce the braking action. One end of the shoe is hinged to the backing plate by an anchor pin, while the other end is unattached and can be moved in its support by the operating mechanism. When force from the operating mechanism is applied to the unattached end of the shoe, the shoe expands and brakes the wheel. A retracting spring returns the shoe to the original position when braking action is no longer required.

The brake-operating linkage alone does not provide sufficient mechanical advantage for positive braking. Some means of supplementing the physical application of the braking system has to be used to increase pressure on the brake shoes. A self-energizing action is very helpful in accomplishing this, once setting of the shoes is started by physical effort. While there are variations of this action, it is always obtained by the shoes themselves, which tend to revolve with the revolving drum.

When the brake shoe is anchored (see figure below) and the drum revolves in the direction shown, the shoe will tend to revolve with the drum when it is forced against the drum. As a result, the shoe will exert considerable pressure against the anchor pin. Since the pin is fixed to the brake shield, this pressure will tend to wedge the shoe tightly in between the pin and the drum as shown. As the initial braking pressure is increased on the cam, the wedging action increases and the shoe is forced still more tightly against the drum to increase the friction. This self-energizing results in more braking action than could be obtained with the actuating pressure alone. Brakes making use of this principle to increase pressures on the braking surfaces are known as self-energizing (or servo) brakes.

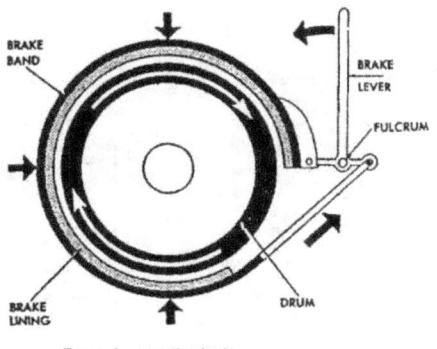

External contracting brake

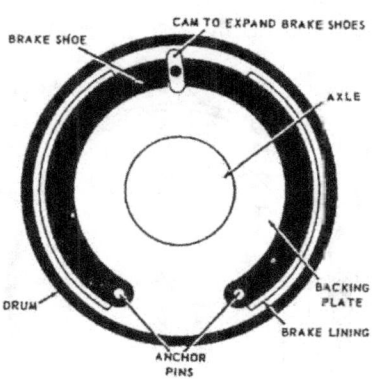

Internal expanding brake

It is most important that the operator control the total braking action at all times; therefore, the self-energizing action should increase only upon application of additional "actuating" pressure at the brake pedal. The amount of self-energizing action available depends mainly on location of the anchor pin. As the pin is moved toward the center of the drum, wedging action increases until a point is reached where the shoe will automatically lock. The pin must be located outside this point so that the operator can control the braking.

When two shoes are anchored on the bottom of the backing plate, self-energizing action is effective on only one shoe. The other shoe tends to revolve away from its pivot, which reduces its braking action. When the wheel is revolving in the opposite direction, the self-energizing action is produced on the opposite shoe.

Two shoes are usually mounted so that self-energizing action is effective on both. This is accomplished by pivoting the shoes to each other and leaving the pivot free of the backing plate. The only physical effort required is for operating the first, or primary, shoe. Both shoes then apply additional pressure to the braking surfaces with no increase in the pressure on the operating linkage. The anchor pins are fitted into slots in the free ends of the brake shoes. This method of anchoring allows the movement of the shoes necessary to expand against the drum when the shoes are forced against the drum, and the self-energizing action of the primary shoe is transmitted through the pivot to the secondary shoe. Both shoes will tend to revolve with the drum and will be wedged against the drum by the one anchor pin. The other anchor pin will cause a similar action when the wheel is revolving in the opposite direction.

The operating mechanism for wheel brakes differs with the brake systems, and so do the brake shoe adjusting devices. The brake drums and brake shoes, however, are similar in all wheel brakes.

Most modern automotive brakes have a self-adjusting feature that automatically adjust the brakes when they need it as a result of brake lining wear.

<u>Disk Brakes</u>. The disk brake has a metal disk instead of a drum, and a pair of flat pads instead of curved brake shoes. The figure below shows a sectional view of a typical disk brake assembly. The two flat pads are located on the two sides of the disk. The assembly in which the flat pads are held is called the caliper assembly. In operation, the pads are forced against the two sides of the disk by the movement of pistons in the caliper assembly. The pistons are actuated by hydraulic pressure from the master cylinder. The effect is to clamp the rotating disk between the stationary pads as illustrated below. This is the same action you get when you pick up a piece of paper; our fingers and thumb clamp on both sides of the paper to hold it. In the same way, the pads apply friction to the disk and attempt to stop its rotation. This provides the braking action.

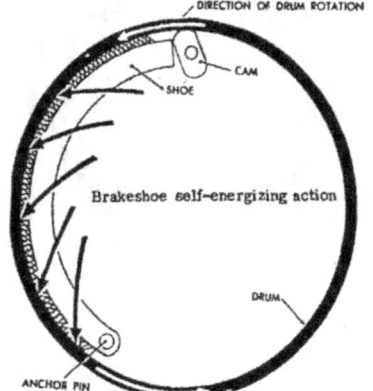

Sectional view of disk brake in released and applied position.

MECHANICAL HANDBRAKES

In most automotive vehicles, the handbrake has its own hookup. Either external contracting brake bands are located on the drive shaft or some type of mechanical linkage operates the rear wheel brakes.

HYDRAULIC BRAKE SYSTEMS

A hydraulic brake system is primarily a liquid connection or coupling between the brake pedal and the individual brake shoes and drums. The system consists of one master cylinder connected by pipes and flexible tubing to the wheel cylinders. The wheel cylinders control the movement of the brake shoes at each wheel.

The brake fluid in hydraulic systems is composed of alcohol and caster oil or glycerin. This liquid neither freezes nor boils at temperatures encountered in year-round operations. When the brake pedal in a hydraulic brake system is depressed, the hydraulic fluid forces the pistons in the wheel cylinder against the brake shoes. The shoes expand against the brake drum and stop the vehicle. Hydraulic brakes are self-equalizing brakes. If the actuating pistons were all the same size, each brake in the hydraulic system would receive an identical hydraulic force when the brakes are applied because a force exerted at any point upon a closed liquid is distributed equally through the liquid in all directions. Some brake systems have larger wheel cylinders in the front than in the rear. This is because, when stopping, more of the vehicle's weight is felt in front and, therefore, more front wheel braking effort is required.

The mechanical advantage of any brake system is the relation between the pressure applied by the operator on the brake pedal to the pressure exerted on the braking surfaces.

The master cylinder has two functions. It is a reservoir for the brake fluid, and it contains the piston and the valves which change mechanical force to hydraulic pressure when the brake pedal is depressed. The pressure on the brake pedal moves the piston within the master cylinder, forcing the brake fluid from the master cylinder through tubing and flexible hose to the wheel cylinders. As pressure on the pedal is increased, greater hydraulic pressure is built up within the brake cylinders, and thus greater force is put forth against the ends of the brake shoes. When pressure on the pedal is released, the springs on the brake shoes return the wheel cylinder pistons to their released positions. This action forces the brake fuid back through the flexible hose and tubing to the master cylinder.

Most older model cars are equipped with the single system master cylinder. This system is, however, being replaced with dual system master cylinders.

The operation of a dual system master cylinder is basically the same as a single master cylinder. The dual system master cylinder, however, has two pistons, two separate fluid reservoirs, and two output ports. Thus, the dual system master cylinder has two separate hydraulic pressure systems. One of the hydraulic systems normally is connected to the front brakes, and the other system is the rear brakes. If either the front or rear hydraulic system fails, the other system remains operational.

The master cylinder, like other parts in the brake system, is subject to wear, leaks, and deposits or corrosion on the cylinder wall and piston. Master cylinder reservoir fluid level should be checked periodically and clean brake fluid added, as needed, to maintain fluid level approximately ½" from the top of the reservoir.

The brake lines transmit fluid and pressure from the master cylinder to the wheel cylinders, which in turn change the hydraulic pressure into mechanical force. The wheel cylinders are mounted on the brake backing plate. Inside each cylinder are two pistons that move in opposite directions by hydraulic pressure, which pushes the brake shoes against the brake drum. The brake shoes are made of iron, steel, or cast aluminum. They support the brake lining and transmit force to the lining, which is attached to the face of the shoe and make contact with the inner surface of the brake drums. During contact with one another the lining and the drum create the frictional surface that gives the braking effect.

AIRBRAKE SYSTEMS

Air, like all gases, is easily compressed. Compressed air exerts pressure and this pressure will be equal in all directions. Air under pressure can be conveniently stored and carried through lines or tubes. Considerable force is available for braking since operating air pressure may be as high as 100 psi. All brakes on a vehicle, and on a trailer (when one is used), are operated together by means of a brake valve.

The compressor is driven from the engine crankshaft or one of the auxiliary shafts. The three common methods of driving the compressor from the engine are gear, belt, and chain.

The compressor may be lubricated from the engine crankcase or be self-lubricated. Cooling may be either by air or liquid from the engine.

The purpose of the compressor governor is to automatically maintain the air pressure in the reservoir between the maximum pressure desired (100-105 psi) and the minimum pressure required for safe operation (80-85 psi) by starting and stopping compression.

The two steel tanks which are components of most air brake systems are called reservoirs. These tanks are used to cool, store, and remove moisture from the air and give a smooth flow of air to the brake system.

A safety valve consists of an adjustable spring-loaded ball check valve in a body. It is used to protect the system against excessive pressures and is usually mounted on a reservoir. The safety valve is normally set at 150 psi but can be varied to suit the vehicle requirements.

A pressure gauge is attached to any line which registers reservoir pressure and is mounted to the dashboard of the vehicle.

The brake valve is the operator's control of the air brake system. When the brake valve is engaged, air from the reservoir flows through the valve to the brakes. The three types of brake valves used in the air brake systems are pedal, treadle, and hand. When you press the pedal of an airbrake system, air under pressure in a reservoir is released to the brake lines by an air valve. This air goes to the brake chambers located close to the wheel brakes, which contain flexible diaphragms. The force of the air admitted to these chambers cause the diaphragms to operate the brake shoes through a mechanical linkage.

An air pressure gage will let you know if you have proper air pressure within the reservoir (60 lbs. pressure is minimum). This gage is usually found on the instrument panel of a truck or bus. If the pressure fails to build up or exceeds the maximum limits after building up, secure the truck until the fault is corrected.

Independent control of trailer brakes is valuable under adverse conditions when it is sometimes desirable to apply the brakes on the trailer without applying the brakes on the truck or tractor. The independent trailer control valve, conveniently located in the cab, provides the operator with perfect control of his trailing load at all times.

VACUUM BRAKES

In the vacuum brake system, depressing the brake pedal opens a valve between the power cylinder, which contains a piston, and the intake manifold to which the power cylinder is connected. To apply the brakes, air is exhausted from the cylinder ahead of the piston, while atmospheric pressure acts on the rear side of the piston to exert a powerful pull on the rod attached to the piston.

When the brake valve is closed, the chamber ahead of the piston is shut off from the intake manifold and is open to the atmosphere. The pressure is then the same on both sides of the piston; therefore, no pull is exerted upon the pull rod. The brake shoe return springs then release the brakes and return the piston to its original position in the power cylinder.

Hydrovac is a trade name for a one-unit vacuum power braking system. It combines into one assembly a hydraulic control valve, a vacuum power cylinder and a hydraulic slave cylinder. This assembly is connected to both the master cylinder and the wheel brakes, eliminating the need for mechanical connections with the brake pedal.

When you press the brake pedal, fluid is forced from the master cylinder through the check valve to the slave cylinder and on to the wheel cylinders. The foot pedal pressure, acting through the master cylinder, acts also against the slave cylinder piston, assisting the vacuum pistons and push rods to press upon the brake shoes.

OPERATOR MAINTENANCE

Periodic brake service by the operator includes the use of proper brake fluid; checking brake fluid level; inflating tires properly; checking for loose connections or parts; checking for leaks in the system; draining air reservoirs daily; and checking the self-contained lubricating oil system of air compressors daily.

MALFUNCTION DETECTION

The types of brake trouble that may be encountered in vehicle operation are: brake pedal goes to the floorboard with no resistance; one brake drags; all brakes drag; vehicle pulls to one side when braking; soft or spongy pedal; excessive pedal effort required; noisy brakes; air in the system; loss of brake fluid; brakes heat up during driving and fail to release; leaky brake cylinder; grabbing brake action; and brake pedal can be depressed without slowing the vehicle. As an operator, you must explain the malfunction on the Operator's Trouble Report and turn it into the maintenance shop for necessary correction.

STEERING MECHANISMS

All steering mechanisms have the same basic parts. The steering linkage ties the front wheels together and connects them to the steering gear case at the lower end of the steering column, which in turn connects the gear case to the steering wheel.

The arms and rods of the steering linkage have ball or ball and socket ends to provide a swivel connection between them. These jointed ends are provided with grease fittings, dust seals or boots, and many of them have end-play adjustment devices. These joints and devices must be adjusted and lubricated regularly.

The tie-rod is usually located behind the axle and keeps the front wheels in proper alignment. To provide for easier steering and maximum leverage, the tie-rod may be separated into two lengths and connected to the steering gear near the center of the vehicle.

The drag link between the steering arm and the pitman arm may be long or short, depending on the installation.

The pitman arm, splined to the shaft extending from the steering gear case, moves in an arc, its position depending on which way the steering wheel is turned. It is approximately vertical when the front wheels are straight ahead. Therefore, the length of the drag link is determined by the distance between the steering arm and the vertical position of the pitman arm. Unlike the tie-rods, the length of the drag link is not adjustable.

The steering gear case contains the gears that control the movement of the pitman arm and steering linkage.

POWER STEERING

Power steering has been used for a number of years on heavy-duty applications, but it is only in recent years that power steering has been applied to any extent on automotive vehicles. The principle of power steering is very simple. A booster arrangement is provided which is set in operation when the steering wheel is turned. The booster then takes over and does most of the work of steering. Power steering has used compressed air, electrical mechanisms, and hydraulic pressure. Hydraulic pressure is used on the vast majority of power-steering mechanisms today.

In the hydraulic power-steering system, a continuously operating pump provides hydraulic pressure. As the steering wheel is turned, valves are operated to admit this hydraulic pressure to a cylinder. Then, the pressure causes a piston to move—and the piston does most of the steering work.

There are actually two general types of power-steering systems. In one, the integral type, the power operating assembly is located in the steering gear case. In the other, the linkage type, the power operating assembly is part of the steering linkage.

In the linkage-type power-steering system, the power cylinder or booster cylinder is not part of the steering gear. Instead, the power cylinder is connected into the steering linkage. In addition, the valve assembly is included in the steering linkage, either as a separate assembly or united with the power cylinder.

WHEEL ALIGNMENT

Steering control depends greatly upon the position of the wheels in relation to the rest of the vehicle and the surface over which it travels. Any changes from the specified setting of the wheels affect steering and the riding control of the vehicle. Therefore, the proper wheel alignment is important for vehicle control.

Steering geometry is the term manufacturers use to describe steering and front wheel alignment. Steering geometry includes pivot inclination, wheel caster, wheel chamber, toe-in and toe-out. These terms refer to angles in the front wheel alignment which may change because of driving over rough terrain, striking stationary objects, and accident damage.

OPERATOR MAINTENANCE

Doing maintenance servicing by the operator, the service that the steering linkage normally requires is periodic lubrication of the connecting joints between the links which contain bushings.

When vehicles are equipped with manually operated steering, check the steering gear housing for sufficient lubrication and add recommended manufacturer's gear lubricant, if necessary. For vehicles equipped with power steering, check belt tension which can cause low oil pressure and hard steering. Check fluid level. If the fluid level is low, add fluid to bring it up to the recommended level. Use only special power steering fluid recommended. If the level is low, the possibility exists that there is a leak. Check all hose and power-steering connections for signs of leaks. Leakage may occur at various points in the power-steering unit if the seals are defective. Report conditions to the maintenance shop for replacement of any defective seal, or it may only be necessary to tighten the connections to eliminate leaks.

MALFUNCTION DETECTION

The types of steering trouble that may be encountered in vehicle operation are: excessive play in the steering system; hard steering; vehicle wanders; vehicle pulls to one side when braking; front wheel shimmy at low speeds; front-wheel tramps (high speed shimmy); steering kickback; tires squeal on turns; improper tire wear; and noises. As an operator, you would explain the malfunction on the Operator's Trouble Report and turn it into the maintenance shop for corrective actions.

III. SUSPENSION SYSTEM

A suspension system is a system of anchoring and suspending the wheels or tracks from the frame by means of springs. The suspension system is an important feature of military vehicles; it supports the weight and allows them to be driven under varying loads and speed conditions over bumpy roads and rough terrain without great risk of damage.

The usual components of a suspension system are the springs and shock absorbers. Some suspension systems also have torsion bars.

SPRINGS

Springs support the frame and the body of the vehicle, as well as the load the vehicle carries. They allow the wheels to withstand the shocks of uneven road surfaces and provide a flexible connection between the wheels and the body. The best spring is the one which absorbs road shock rapidly and returns to its normal position slowly. Such a spring, however, is very rare, if not an impossibility. Extremely flexible, or soft springs, allow too much movement of the vehicle superstructure, while still, hard springs do not allow enough movement.

The springs do no support the weight of the wheels, rims, tires, and axles. These parts make up the unsprung weight of the vehicle. The unsprung weight decreases the action of the springs and is, therefore, kept to a minimum to permit the springs to do the job of supporting the vehicle frame and load.

The three types of spring suspension usually found in vehicles are: the longitudinal, the lengthwise mounting, which is the most common; the independent, which is generally used in front suspensions; and transverse, which is the crosswise mounting.

The multiple leaf spring consists of a number of steel strips or leaves of different lengths, fastened together by a bolt through the center. Each end of the largest or master leaf is rolled in an eye which serves as a means of attaching the spring to the spring hanger and spring shackle. Leaf rebound clips surround the leaves at two or more intervals along the spring to keep them from separating on the rebound after the spring has been depressed. The clips allow the spring leaves to slide but prevent them from separating and throwing the entire rebound stress on the master leaf. Thus, the spring acts as a flexible beam. Leaf springs may be suspended lengthwise (parallel to the frame), or cross-wise.

When installed lengthwise, both ends of the spring are attached to the frame and the center is clamped to the axle or spring seat. In some trucks and cars the rear springs are clamped under the axle, instead of over it to lower the center of gravity. A low center of gravity will help prevent a heavily loaded truck from upsetting.

Springs installed crosswise have the ends attached to the axle, and the frame rests on the center of the spring. Torque arms or radius rods are required with this type of spring suspension to absorb the driving thrust of the wheels. The driving thrust and brake action of wheels tend to twist the springs from the spring hangers and shackles connecting them to the frame or axles.

Spring hangers are fittings to which the spring ends are attached. A bolt or pin passes through the bushing in the spring eye and is secured to the spring hanger on the frame. The bushing and shackle bolt or pin, therefore, provide the bearing surface which supports the load on the spring.

The spring bushings may be made of bronze or rubber. They may be pressed or screwed into the spring eye, depending on the design. The steel bolts or pins that pass through the bushing are also either plain or threaded. Threaded bushings and shackle bolts offer a greater bearing surface and are replaced more easily when they become worn.

When a leaf spring is compressed, it must straighten out or break. Therefore, spring shackles are required at one or both ends of the spring. Spring shackles provide a swinging support and allow the spring to straighten out when compressed. One shackle is used in either the front or rear support of springs installed lengthwise. Two shackles are used in supporting springs installed crosswise.

You will see many types of spring shackles. The link shackle and U-shackle are the most common. Link shackles are used in heavy vehicles, and the U-type is more common for use on passenger cars and light trucks.

You will find link shackles used to support a transverse spring on the dead front axle of some wheeled tractors. Most wheeled tractors do not even have springs, and all load cushioning is obtained through large, low pressure tires.

Track-type tractors are equipped with one large leaf spring supported without spring shackles. It is fastened to the engine support and rests on the frames supporting the tracks and rollers. Brackets on the track frames keep the spring from shifting. The main purpose of the spring is to relieve the running gear of stresses during operation.

Some vehicles are equipped with leaf springs at the rear wheels only; others are so equipped both front and rear.

Coil springs are most generally used on independent suspension systems. They provide a very smooth riding quality. Their use has normally been limited to passenger vehicles. Recently, however, they have been used to a limited extent on trucks. The spring seat and hanger, shaped to fit the coil ends, hold the spring in place. Spacers made of rubberized fabric are placed at each end of the coil to prevent squeaking. The rubber bumper, mounted in the spring supporting member, prevents metal to metal contact when the spring is compressed. Most vehicles are equipped with coil springs at the two front wheels, while some other have them at both front and rear.

SHOCK ABSORBERS
Springs alone are never satisfactory in a light vehicle suspension system. A stiff spring gives a hard ride because it does not flex and rebound when the vehicle passes over a bump. On the other hand, too flexible a spring rebounds too much, and the vehicle rides roughly. To smooth the riding qualities of the vehicle, shock absorbers are used. They prevent excessive jolting of the vehicle by balancing spring stiffness and flexibility. They allow the springs to return to rest slowly after having been compressed. Although single-acting shock absorbers check only spring rebound, double-acting shock absorbers check spring compression as well as spring rebound, permitting the use of the more flexible springs.

FRONT AXLE SUSPENSION
Most passenger car front wheels are individually supported with independent suspension systems. The ones you are likely to encounter are the coil spring and the torsion bar suspension systems. These are used with independent front axles and shock absorbers.

REAR AXLE SUSPENSION
Driving wheels are mounted on a live driving axle that is suspended by springs attached to the axle housing. Leaf springs are generally used for suspending live axles. Coil springs are used on a number of passenger cars with torque tube drive.

OPERATOR MAINTENANCE
Under normal operation, and given proper maintenance, suspension systems would not need adjustments or replacement for many miles. The spring assemblies of the suspension system should be checked regularly to ensure that shackles are tight and that bushings within the shackles are not worn excessively or frozen tight. Occasionally, spraying lubricating oil on the spring leaves helps to prevent squeaking at the ends of the spring leaves. Following the lubrication chart furnished for a particular vehicle, check and lubricate the front suspension system including linkage, kingpin, and ball joints. During your checks you may find shock absorber bushings worn; if so, it is best to have the bushings replaced, or in some instances a complete replacement of the shock absorbers is needed.

MALFUNCTION DETECTION
Some types of suspension troubles that may be encountered in vehicle operation are: hard steering, vehicle wander, vehicular pulls to one side during normal driving, front-wheel shimmy, front-wheel tramp (high speed shimmy), steering kickback, hard or rough ride, sway on

turns, spring breakage, sagging springs, and noises. As an operator, you would explain the malfunction on the Operator's Trouble Report and turn the trouble report into the maintenance shop for corrective action.

IV. FRAME

The chassis is the assembly of mechanisms that make up the major operating part of the vehicle. It is usually assumed to include everything except the vehicle body. The individual operating assemblies are mounted on the frame, which must be strong enough to support the weight of the vehicle and its rated load without distortion. The frame must be rigid enough to keep the units of the vehicle in proper alignment and to protect them against the stresses and strains of road and surface shocks.

The frame is generally constructed of cold-rolled open-hearth steel, but sometimes of alloy steel to lighten the weight of the vehicle. The side members or rails are the heaviest parts of the frame. The cross members are fixed to the side members rigidly enough to prevent weaving and twisting of the frame. Angular pieces of metal called gusset plates are riveted or welded at the point where members are joined for added strength.

The number, size, and arrangement of cross members depend on the type of vehicle for which the frame is designed. Usually, a front cross member supports the radiator and front end of the engine as well as stiffens the frame. The rear cross members furnish support for the fuel tanks and rear trunk on passenger cars, and the two-bar connections for trucks. Additional cross members are added to the frame to support the rear of the engine and power train and to secure the rigidity required.

The cross members of most small vehicles are designed in either X or K form. The front cross members are wider and of heavier construction than the back members because they support the engine and the front wheels. The side members are shaped to accommodate the body and support its weight. They narrow toward the front of the vehicle to permit a shorter turning radius for the wheels and widen under the main part of the body where the body is secured to the frame. Trucks and trailers usually have frames with straight side members to accommodate several designs of bodies and to give the vehicle added strength to withstand heavier loads. Heavy duty trucks and trailers have I-beam frames.

Brackets and hangers which are bolted or riveted to the frame to support the shock absorbers, fenders, running boards, and springs are usually made of case or pressed steel.

www.ingramcontent.com/pod-product-compliance
Lightning Source LLC
Chambersburg PA
CBHW081811300426
44116CB00014B/2313